UN Intervention in Dar Fur

UN Intervention in Dar Fur

Dr. Mohamed H. Fadlalla

iUniverse, Inc.
New York Lincoln Shanghai

UN Intervention in Dar Fur

iUniverse books may be ordered through booksellers or by contacting:

iUniverse
2021 Pine Lake Road, Suite 100
Lincoln, NE 68512
www.iuniverse.com
1-800-Authors (1-800-288-4677)

The views expressed in this work are solely those of the author and do not necessarily reflect the views of the publisher, and the publisher hereby disclaims any responsibility for them.

ISBN-13: 978-0-595-42979-0 (pbk)
ISBN-13: 978-0-595-87319-7 (ebk)
ISBN-10: 0-595-42979-3 (pbk)
ISBN-10: 0-595-87319-7 (ebk)

Printed in the United States of America

List of Abbreviations

AAR	After Action Report
AFS	Avocats sans Frontières
AJIL	American Journal of International Law
AMIS	African Mission in Sudan
ANSP	Academic National des Seguridad Publica
AOR	Area of Responsibility
APC	Armed Personnel Carrier
ASF	Auxiliary Security Force
AWSS	Agreed Weapons Storage Sites
BYIL	British Year Book of International Law
CENTCOM	Central Command
CGDK	Coalition Government of Democratic Kampuchea
CI	Counter Intelligence
CID	Criminal Investigation Division
CNPC	China National Petroleum Corporation
CPA	Comprehensive Peace Agreement
DPA	Dar Fur Peace Agreement
DPKO	Department of Peace-Keeping Operations
ECMM	European Community Monitoring Mission
ECOMOG	ECOWAS Ceasefire Monitoring Group
ECOSOC	Economical and Social Council (UN)
ECOWAS	Economic Community of West African States
EJIL	European Journal of International Law
FCU	Field Co-ordination Unit
FMLN	Frente Farabundo
HRFOs	Human Rights Field Officers
HRPOs	Human Rights Provincial Field Officers
IAEA	International Atomic Energy Agency
ICC	International Criminal Court

ICLQ	International and Comparative Law Quarterly
ICRC	International Committee of Red Cross
ICT	International Criminal Tribunal
ICTY	International Criminal Tribunal for the former Yugoslavia
ICTR	International Criminal Tribunal for Rwanda
IFOR	Implementation Force
IDPs	Internally Displaced Persons
IGAD	Intergovernmental Authority on Development
IPTF	International Police Task Force
JEM	Justice and Equality Movement
MAPE	Multinational Advisory Police Element
MINURSO	UN Mission for the Referendum in Western Sahara
MONUC	UN Mission in the Democratic Republic of the Congo
MPO	Multinational Force and Observer
NATO	North Atlantic Treaty Organisation
NCP	National Congress Party
NRF	National Redemption Force
OAU	Organisation of African Unity
OIC	Officer in Charge
ONUB	United Nations Operation in Burundi
ONUC	United Nations Operation in the Congo
ONGC	India's Oil and Natural Gas Corporation
QRF	Quick Reaction Forces
RDL	Rally for Democracy and Liberty
SOAT	Sudan Organization against Torture
SCAF	Supreme Council of the Armed Forces
SSDF	South Sudan Defence Forces
SPLM	Sudanese People Liberation Movement
SLM	Sudan Liberation Movement
SLA	Sudan Liberation Army
UNITAF	Unified Task Force
UNISOM	United Nations Force in Somalia
UNMIS	United Nations Mission in Sudan
UNDOF	United Nations Disengagement Observer Force
UNDP	United Nations Development Programme
UNDRO	United Nations Disaster Relief Coordinator
UNEF	United Nations Emergency Force
UNHCHR	United Nations Commissioner for Human Rights
UNHCR	United Nations Commissioner for Refugees
UNMIS	United Nations Mission in Sudan

UNMEE	United Nations Mission in Ethiopia and Eritrea
UNOCI	United Nations Operation in Côte d'Ivoire
UNOG	United Nations Observation Group
UNOM	United Nations Observer Mission
UNOSOM	United Nations Operation in Somalia
UNPAs	United Nations Protected Areas
UNPREDEP	United Nations Preventive Deployment Force
UNPROFOR	United Nations Protection Force
UNSG	United Nations Security Guards
UNSF	United Nations Security Force
UNT	United Nations Transitional Administration
UNTEA	United Nations Temporary Executive Authority
UNTSO	United Nations Truce Supervision Organisation

Contents

INTRODUCTION 1

THE ETHNICAL STRUCTURE AND ITS ROLE IN RUNNING
CONFLICTS 15
   The ethnical structure of Sudan 15
      Northern Sudan 16
      East Sudan 20
      Central Sudan 24
      South Sudan 24
      Western Sudan 32

THE ARMED CONFLICTS IN SUDAN AFTER INDEPENDENCE 57
   Is it all about Oil? 85

PEACE ENFORCEMENT THROUGH UN? 90
   The Role of the African Union in Dar Fur 90
      The African Union Troops in Dar Fur 91
   The United Nations Organisation 95
      Enforce sanctions imposed by the Security Council
      (Sanctions Enforcement) 96
      Defend the personnel of Peacekeeping operations (self-defence) 97
      Provide physical protection to civilians in a war situation
      (Protection of Civilians) 97
      Protect activities intended to relieve the suffering of civilians in such
      circumstances (protection of humanitarian activities) 98
      Restore or maintain peace and security in an internal conflict ... 99
      Peace-keeping or peace enforcement..? 99
      The humanitarian intervention right in international public law ... 101
      Intervention and sovereignty 102
      The reasons for humanitarian intervention of the UN 112
   The Exceptions to the principle of (non-use of force) 113
      Self-defence and right of collective self-defence 114
      Peace threat 114

Collective use of force for humanitarian reasons.................................... *115*
Armed attack *115*
Invitation right of Opposition or government *116*
Protection of own citizens *117*
The comparison and experiences with UN mission in Somalia *117*
THE NECESSITY OF INTERNATIONAL CRIMINAL COURT FOR DAR FUR 119
THE US ROLE IN SUDAN'S CONFLICTS 125
UN SECRETARY GENERAL EFFORTS.. 129
POSITION OF SUDANESE GOVERNMENT 130
THE SECURITY COUNCIL'S APPROACH'S CONCERNING DAR FUR 133
The right concept to solve the conflict.. *138*

REFRENCES..141

UN RESOLUTIONS ON DAR FUR 145

INTRODUCTION

Sudan (or The Sudan; officially the Republic of the Sudan or Republic of Sudan, was ruled as Ottoman-Egyptian condominium from 1821 to 1885 and as an Anglo-Egyptian condominium from 1899 until achieving independence as a parliamentary republic on first of January 1956.[1]

Sudan consists of complicated numerous ethnic groups. Besides the north, which is widely Arabic and Muslim there is the south, which consists predominantly of black Nilotic peoples, among the largest of these ethnic groups were the Dinka and the Nuer, followed by the Shuluk. Many of these groups migrated with their herds, seeking areas of rainfall, it was therefore difficult to establish their numbers accurately, and some of whom are members of indigenous faiths and others who are Christians. There is east Sudan, home of Hadandawa, Busharia and Bani Amir tribes, the far north near the Egyptian boarders which is ancient home of Nubia tribes like Al Sakot, Al Mahas and Al Danaglah, the Nuba Mountains home of Nuba tribes and not to forget the west Sudan administrational divided in Kurdofan and Dar Fur regions, the last one which the homeland of the Fur tribes and others immigrated Chadian tribes known as Fallatah.[2]

About 600 ethnic groups speaking around 400 languages were represented in Sudan but Arabic is now the official language with English widely spoken in southern Sudan and till shortly as second official language of the country. The

---

[1] The term (Bilad Al Sudan) which means the land of the blacks has been used by the medieval Arab to describe the lands beyond the Sahara and located between Senegal river to the Red Sea coast above the rain-forest. Sudan is the largest country by area in Africa, situated in Northern Africa. The capital is Khartoum. It is bordered by Egypt to the north, the Red Sea to the northeast, Eritrea and Ethiopia to the east, Kenya and Uganda to the southeast, Democratic Republic of the Congo and the Central African Republic to the southwest, Chad to the west, and Libya to the northwest. It is the tenth largest country in the world

[2] Zaghawa, Masalit, Hawsa, Gorran, Fulani..etc

above mentioned complicated ethnical structure beside the fact that the Sudan is the biggest country Africa's are reasons behind many conflicts which turned to become civil wars after the latest colonial period.[3]

Not only the above mentioned reasons alone are behind turning ethnical conflicts in Sudan into the form they took by the North-South civil war but also the colonial policy which tended to divide the country to deepened the ethnical gap between different tribes of the country. Just like the British policy during the Anglo-Egyptian condominium (1899-1955) which intensified the rift through establishing separate administrations for the two areas and forbade northerners to enter the south. In the 1990s, many southerners continued to fear being ruled by northerners, who lacked familiarity with their beliefs and ethnic traditions and sought to impose northern institutions upon them. Although north Sudanese are less interested in which religion or believe others Sudanese have or not, this fear, to be converted to Islam or even to be dominated by northern Sudanese still existing among southern Sudanese as if being passed through from one generation to the next. Britain largely ignored southern Sudan until after First World War, leaving Western missionary societies to establish schools and medical facilities in the area. After World War I, Sudanese nationalism, which had to choose between either independence or union with Egypt, gathered popular support. Recognizing the inevitable, Britain signed a self-determination agreement with Sudan in 1952, followed by the Anglo-Egyptian accord in 1953 that set up a three-year transition period to self-government. Sudan proclaimed its independence on first of January 1956. During the colonial period, Britain had discouraged industrialization, preferring to keep Sudan as a source of raw materials and a market for goods manufactured in Britain. Following independence, a paucity of development programs as well as better employment opportunities in the Persian Gulf States contributed to a shortage of skilled workers. In the early 1990s, Sudan also had only some bilateral aid from Iran and Libya. Like the World Bank, the United States and the European Community had suspended loans to Sudan but had provided some humanitarian assistance; the value of United States humanitarian aid in 1991 was estimated to exceed US $150 million. Nevertheless, drought, famine, and the massive influx into the north of refugees from the south as a result of the civil war caused the country's already precarious economy to deterio-

---

[3] Nubia are north Sudanese tribes on the Egyptian boarders and believe to be descendents of Pharonen, their main still known tribes are Al Sakot, Al Mahas and Al Danaglah, they have their own tribal languages and culturally strong related with the southern Egyptians known as Saida, not to be exchanged with the Nuba tribes in western Sudan domiciled in the Nuba Mountains. Those are in fact an amalgam of dozens of different tribes with different cultures and languages related to central African tribes.

rate further and complicated the government's ability to rule till mid 1990s where Sudan began Oil exportation which helped economic revival. Also the colonial policy during the Turk-Egyptian before took similar way by providing services to central Sudan ignoring others parts including south of Sudan. The rule was accompanied by the introduction of secular courts and a large bureaucracy. The 1880s saw the rise of the Mahdist revolt which can be seen as the first unification of Sudanese against a foreign enemy, leaded by Muhammad Ahmad ibn as Sayyid Abd Allah came to be known as Al Mahadi, which means the "guided one" and launched a jihad (holy war) against the Ottoman rulers. Britain perceived the Mahdists as a threat to stability in the region and sent first Charles George Gordon and then Herbert Kitchener to Sudan to assert British control. The British conquest led to the establishment of the Anglo-Egyptian condominium and, initially, to military rule of Sudan, followed by civilian administration. After the independence the country had two short-lived civilian coalition governments before a coup in November 1958 established a military regime under Ibrahim Abbud and a collective body known as the Supreme Council of the Armed Forces.[4]

---

[4] Muhammad Ahmad ibn as Sayyid Abd Allah (1844–June 22, 1885) was a Muslim religious leader, a faqir, in the Anglo-Egyptian Sudan. He declared a jihad and raised an army after declaring himself the Mahdi in 1881, and led a successful war of liberation from the Ottoman-Egyptian military occupation. He died soon after his liberation of Khartoum, and the state he founded fell victim to colonial manoeuvrings that doomed it to reconquest in 1899. Muhammad Ahmad was born in 1844 in Dirar Island off Dongola, a member of an Arabized Nubian family from Dongola. They moved to Khartoum for better prospects for his family, and all of Muhammad's brothers entered the boatbuilding business, following their father. Muhammad instead focussed on religious studies like his great-grandfather, a respected sharif. He learned the Qur'an in Khartoum and Kararie, and later he studied fiqh under Sheikh Muhammad Kheir. He was interested mostly in the Sufi teachings. In 1861 he approached Sheikh Muhammad ash Sharif, the leader of Sammaniyya Sect, to join his students and learn more on Sufism. When Sheikh Muhammad realized Muhammad's dedication he appointed him sheikh, and permitted him to give Tariqa and Uhuud to new followers. In 1871 his family moved again to Aba Island in western Sudan where he built a mosque and started to teach the Koran. He soon gained a notable reputation among the local population as an excellent speaker and mystic. The broad thrust of his teaching followed that of other reformers, his Islam was one devoted to the words of the Prophet and based on a return to the virtues of prayer and simplicity as laid down in the Koran. Any deviation from the Koran was therefore heresy. Over the next ten years he travelled widely, to Dongola, Kordofan and Sinnar. During his travels he was struck by the hatred for the Ottoman-Egyptian rulers, and found that as soon as anyone educated and well-spoken appeared, the local populations would declare him Mahdi and hope for his deliverance. He was joined on his travels by Abdallahi ibn Muhammad, a Baqqara from southern Dar Fur, whose organizational capabilities proved

invaluable. On his return to Aba Island in 1881, Muhammad Ahmad proclaimed himself Al Mahdi al Muntazar and started to raise an army. Even after the Mahdi proclaimed a jihad, or holy war, against the Turkiyah, he was dismissed as a religious fanatic. The government paid more attention When his religious zeal turned to denunciation of tax collectors. To avoid arrest, the Mahdi and a party of his followers, the Ansar (known in the west inaccurately as the Dervishes), made a long march to Kordofan. There he gained a large number of recruits, especially from the Baqqara. There he wrote to many Sudanese tribal leaders and gained their support, or at least neutrality, and he was also supported by the slave traders who were looking to return to power. They were also joined by the Hadendowa Beja, who were rallied to the Mahdi by an Ansar captain, Osman Digna. Early in 1882, the Ansar, armed with spears and swords, overwhelmed a 7,000-man Egyptian force not far from Al Obied and seized their rifles and ammunition. The Mahdi followed up this victory by laying siege to Al Ubayyid and starving it into submission after four months. The town remained the headquarters of the Ansar for much of the decade. The Ansar, now 30,000 strong, then defeated an 8,000-man Egyptian relief force at Sheikan, captured Dar Fur, and, in 1883, took Jabal Qadir in to the south. At the same time another rebellion by the Beja (the fuzzy-wuzzies) in the east started. The western half of the Sudan was now largely in Ansar hands, and this state of affairs lasted for several years. An understanding of the British role in these events is important. In 1869 the Suez Canal opened, and to defend the waterway Britain sought a greater role in Egyptian affairs. In 1873 the British government supported a program where an Anglo-French debt commission assumed responsibility for managing Egypt's fiscal affairs. This commission eventually forced Khedive Ismail to abdicate in favor of his son Tawfiq in 1877, leading to a period of political turmoil. Ismail had appointed Charles George Gordon to the post of governor general of Sudan in 1877. Soon after he arrived he started to end the slave trade, which at that point was majority of the economy. Before his arrival some 7 out of 8 negros in the Sudan were enslaved by the tiny minority of Arabs, well Over 80% of the overall population. Gordon's policies were effective, but the effects on the economy were disastrous, and soon the population saw this not a liberation from slavery, but a modern-day European Christian crusade. It was this anger that fed the Ansar's ranks. Upon Ismail's abdication shortly after Gordon's arrival in the Sudan, he found himself with dramatically decreased support. He eventually resigned his post in 1880, exhausted by years of work, and left early the next year. His policies were soon abandoned by the new governors. By September 1882 the situation in the Sudan was poor, and given their lack of interest in the area the British decided to abandon it in December 1883, ordering Gordon to return to Khartoum and organize a withdrawal. Gordon reached Khartoum in February 1884. He found that the routes northward were too dangerous to extricate the garrisons, and so pressed for reinforcements to be sent from Cairo to help with the withdrawal. He also suggested that his old enemy Zubayr, a fine military commander, be given tacit control of the Sudan in order to provide a counter to the Ansar. London rejected both proposals, and so Gordon prepared for a fight. In March 1884 Gordon tried a small offensive to clear the road northward to Egypt, but a number of the officers in the Egyptian force went Over to the enemy and their forces fled the field after firing a single salvo. This convinced him that he could carry out only defensive operations, and he returned to Khartoum to construct defensive works. By April 1884 Gordon had managed to evacuate some 2,500 of the foreign population that were able to make the trek northwards. His mobile force under Colonel Stewart then returned to the city as well, after repeated incidents where the 200 or so Egyptian forces under his command would turn and run at the slightest provocation. That month the Ansar had reached Khartoum, and Gordon was completely cut off. Nevertheless his defensive works, consisting mainly of mines, proved so frightening to the Ansar that they were unable to penetrate into the city. Stewart maintained a number of small skirmishes using gunboats on the Nile once the waters rose, and in August managed to recapture Berber for a short time. However Stewart was killed soon after in another foray from Berber to Dongola. Under increasing pressure from the public to support him, the British sent a "flying column" overland to Khartoum while four gunboats navigated the Nile. The camel forces under Lord Garnet Joseph Wolseley were stopped at Abu Tulayh by the Beja, and the boats arrived on January 28, 1885, to find the town had fallen two days earlier. The Ansar had waited for the Nile spring flood to recede before attacking the poorly defended river approach, overcoming the garrison. Gordon was killed, apparently with a revolver in each hand firing until he ran out of ammunition, and his head was delivered to the Mahdi's tent. Kassala and Sannar fell soon after, and by the end of 1885 the Ansar had begun to move into the southern regions of Sudan. In all Sudan, only Suakin, reinforced by Indian army troops, and Wadi Halfa on the northern frontier remained in Anglo-Egyptian hands. With Sudan now in Sudanese hands, the Mahdi formed a government. The Mahdiyah (Mahdist regime) imposed traditional Islamic laws. Sharia courts enforced Islamic law and the Mahdi's own commands. He also authorized the burning of lists of pedigrees and books of law and theology because of their association with the old regime, and because he believed that they accentuated tribalism at the expense of religious unity. The Mahdi modified Islam's five pillars to support the dogma that loyalty to him was essential to true belief. The Mahdi also added the declaration and Muhammad Ahmad is the Mahdi of God and the representative of His Prophet to the recitation of the shahada. Moreover, service in the jihad replaced the hajj, pilgrimage to Mecca, as a duty incumbent on the faithful. Zakat (almsgiving) became the tax paid to the state. The Mahdi justified these reforms as responses to instructions conveyed to him by God in visions. Six months after the capture of Khartoum, Muhammad Ahmad died of typhus. The Mahdi had planned for this eventuality and chosen three deputies to replace him, in emulation of the Prophet Muhammad. This led to a long period of disarray, due to rivalry among the three, each supported by people of his native region. This continued until 1891, When Abdallahi ibn Muhammad, with the help primarily of the Baqqara Arabs, emerged as unchallenged leader. Abdallahi, referred to as the Khalifa (successor), purged the Mahdiyah of members of the Mahdi's family and many of his early religious disciples.

The Khalifa was committed to the Mahdi's vision of extending the Mahdiyah through jihad, which led to strained relations with practically everyone else. For example, the Khalifa rejected an offer of an alliance against the Europeans by Ethiopias negus (king),

Abbud's government sought to arabise the south and in 1964 expelled all western missionaries. Northern repression of the south led to open civil war in the mid-sixties and the rise of various southern resistance groups, the most powerful of which were the Anya Nya guerrillas, who sought autonomy. Civilian rule returned to Sudan between 1964 and 1969, and political parties reappeared. In the 1965 elections, Muhammad Ahmad Mahjub became prime minister, succeeded in June 1966 by Sadiq al Mahdi, a descendant of the Mahdi. In the 1968 elections, no party had a clear majority, and a coalition government took office under Mahjub as Prime minister. In May 1969, the Free Officers' Movement led by Jaafar an Nimeiri staged a coup and established the Revolutionary Command Council (RCC). In July 1971, a short-lived procommunist military coup occurred, but Nimeiri quickly regained control, was elected to a six-year

---

Yohannes IV. Instead, in 1887 a 60,000-man Ansar army invaded Ethiopia, penetrated as far as Gonder, and captured prisoners and booty. The Khalifa then refused to conclude peace with Ethiopia. In March 1889, an Ethiopian force, commanded personally by the king, marched on Gallabat; however, after Yohannes IV fell in battle, the Ethiopians withdrew. Abd ar Rahman an Nujumi, the Khalifas best general, invaded Egypt in 1889, but British-led Egyptian troops defeated the Ansar at Tushkah, the first battle the Mahdiyah lost. Further attacks into Equatoria were stopped by the Belgians, and in 1893 the Italians repulsed an Ansar attack at Akordat (in Eritrea) and forced the Ansar to withdraw from Ethiopia. By this point British interest in the area was once again growing, due to the interest of the French and Belgians in nearby areas. As each of these forces moved up the Nile, the British felt they required a presence in the Sudan in order to validate their claims to it via Egypt's annexation. In 1892 Field Marshal Herbert Kitchener had been promoted to the post of commander in Egypt, and in 1895 they started plans for the reconquest of the Sudan. Kitchener's forces, the Anglo-Egyptian Nile Expeditionary Force, consisted of 25,800 men, including 8,600 British regulars, and a flotilla of gunboats. They reached and fortified Wadi Halfa in 1895, and started south at a very slow pace the next March. In September Kitchener captured Dongola, and constructed several rail lines to ensure supplies. There were small battles at Abu Hamad and Atbara, both times the Ansar were defeated by the massive English firepower which now included Maxim machine guns. Kitchener then marched on Omdurman. On September 2, 1898, the Battle of Omdurman opened with a frontal assault by the Mahdiyah's 52,000-man army. Over the next five hours some 11,000 of their forces would be killed, against about 40 of the Anglo-Egyptian forces (and about 400 wounded). The Mahdiyah ended at this point and the British once again took control of the Sudan. The Khalifa escaped and reformed an army, but this was defeated in 1899 at the Battle of Umm Diwaykarat and the Khalifa was killed. During their short reign, the Mahdiyah had destroyed the Sudanese economy, and about half of the population died due to famine, disease, persecution, and warfare. Their efforts to wipe out the former tribal differences left few loyalties intact, and internecine warfare was common. In general the country welcomed the fall of the Mahdiyah.

term as president, and abolished the RCC. Meanwhile in the south, Joseph Lagu, a Christian, had united several opposition elements under the Southern Sudan Liberation Movement. In March 1972, the southern resistance movement concluded an agreement with the Nimeiri regime at Addis Ababa, and a ceasefire followed. The Constituent Assembly was created in August 1972 to draft a constitution at a time when the growing opposition to military rule was reflected in strikes and student unrest. Despite this dissent, Nimeiri was re-elected for another six-year term in 1977. During the early stages of his new term, Nimeiri worked toward reconciliation with the south. As the south became stronger, however, he considered it a threat to his regime and in June 1983, after abolishing the Southern Regional Assembly, he re-divided the southern region into its three historic provinces. The Sudanese People's Liberation Movement (SPLM) and the Sudanese People's Liberation Army (SPLA), founded in 1983, opposed this division. They intensified their opposition following the imposition of Muslim sharia law throughout the country. In early 1985, while Nimeiri was returning from a visit to the United States, there was a general strike that the government could not quell, followed by a successful military coup led by Lieutenant General Abd ar Rahman Siwar adh Dhahab. A transitional government was created but proved incapable either of establishing a national political consensus or of dealing with the deteriorating economic situation and famine threatening southern and western Sudan. In March 1986, the government and the SPLM signed the Koka Dam Declaration, which called for a Sudan free of "discrimination and disparity" and for the repeal of the sharia. Sadiq al Mahdi formed what came to be a weak coalition government following the April 1986 elections. An agreement with the SPLM was signed by Sadiq al Mahdi's coalition partners at Addis Ababa in November 1988, the agreement included a ceasefire and an end to the enforcement of the sharia. Al Sadiq al Mahdi's failure to end the civil war in the south or improve the economic and hunger crises led to the overthrow of the government at the end of June 1989 by Colonel Omar Hassan Ahmed al Bashir who later claimed becoming president of Sudan and still governing Sudan till now. Since the military coup of June 30, 1989, the constitution had been suspended, political parties banned, and the legislative assembly dissolved. For practical purposes, in mid-1992, Bashir made political decisions in his capacity as president or head of state, prime minister, commander in chief, and chairman of the legislative body created by the 1989 coup, the Revolutionary Command Council for National Salvation shortly called RCC-NS. [5] Several members had ties to the National Islamic Front (NIF), the

---

[5] The RCC-NS consisted of fifteen members who had carried out the coup along with Bashir

political arm of the Muslim Brotherhood, an Islamist (sometimes seen as funda-
mentalist) activist group. Although political parties were illegal under the Bashir
government, the NIF represented the equivalent of a party. The nature of the
relationship between Bashir and the NIF is unclear. Some considered Bashir to
be a tool of the NIF in spreading its Islamist programs and its strong advocacy
of the imposition of the sharia. Others believed that Bashir was using the NIF
for his own purposes. until March 2004 where Al Bashir marginalised Al Turbai
role as spiritual and political leader of the NIF and put him in jail till 30 of
April 2005 where he later moved to house arrest till June 28, 2005. This move
ended Turabi participation on shaping Sudan's politics but marked on the other
hand the beginning of Al-Turbai's conspiracy to inflame unrest in Sudan by supporting some armed groups like the Justice and Equity Movement group in Dar
Fur and the Eastern Front in eastern Sudan.[6]

---

[6] Al-Turabi was born in the province of Kassala, in eastern Sudan near the border with
Eritrea, in 1932, the fact that makes clear his support for the Eastern Sudan Front. He
was influential as a government figure under several Sudan's governments, Turabi was leader of the National Islamic Front, a powerful which attempts to impose sharia upon the
country firstly during Al-Nimeiri's period in 1983, even though radical Islamists form a
small minority of the population. Turbai Studied Law in University of Khartoum in, post-
graduate master degree After graduating, he returned to Sudan and became a member of
the Islamic Charter Front an offshoot of the Sudanese branch of the Muslim Brotherhood.
Within a five year period, the Islamic Charter Front became a large political group that
identified Al-Turabi as its Secretary general in 1964. Through the Islamic Charter Front,
Al-Turabi worked with two factions of the Sudanese Islamic movement, Ansar and
Khatmiyyah, to draft an Islamic constitution. Members of Ansar define themselves as the
followers of Al Mahdi stemming from nineteenth century Sudan. Al-Turabi remained
with the Islamic Charter Front until 1969, when Gaafar Nimeiri assumed power in a
coup. The members of Islamic Charter Front were arrested, and Turabi spent six years in
custody and three in exile in Libya. The coup and the two factions of the Islamic movement in Sudan attempt to reach a compromise in 1977, part of that compromise is the
release of Al-Turabi and a return from exile. Under the agreement, Al-Turabi is permitted to become a leader of the Sudanese Socialist Union, and is eventually promoted to
Justice Minister in 1979. His frequent close relationships with Sudanese Governments has
resulted in great dislike of Turabi from the Sudanese nation which resulted in the famous
association against him in the 1986 votes where all political parties decided to withdraw
their nominees and keep only one nominee against Turabi which led to the loss of Turabi
being part of the only Democratic government in Sudan during the last four decades. This
has led later on to the careful planning of Turabi and his crew to take over authority by
force in June 1989 forming what was so called the National Salvation Revolution. In 1996
Al-Turabi chose to run in the first general election of the new regime. After winning a seat,
Al-Turabi was selected as Speaker of Parliament, second only to the president, al-Bashir,

Sudan's different governments inherited the colonial administrative problems and mistakes which escalated ethnical problems. As an example the Nimeiri regime had created a pyramidal structure with councils at various levels which fully and suitable to administrate and rule a large country like Sudan with such different ethnic groups with poor communication and transport structure. The councils were theoretically elective, but in practice the only legal party at the time, the Sudan Socialist Union, dominated them. Al-Bashir's government introduced a federal structure in February 1991, creating nine states that resembled the nine provinces of Sudan's colonial and early independence years. The states were subdivided into provinces and local government areas, with officials at all levels appointed by the RCC-NS. Although the governors of the three southern states were southerners, power laid in the hands of the deputy governors who were Muslim members of the NIF and who controlled finance, trade, and co-operatives. Below them, Muslims also held the most important ministerial posts in the southern states, including the posts of ministers of education, culture, youth, guidance, and information. In a further step in mid-February 1992, Al Bashir announced the formation of an appointed 300-member Transitional National Assembly to include all RCC-NS members, federal cabinet ministers, and state governors. Al Bashir also indicated in March that beginning in May, popular conferences based on religious values would be held in the north and in "secure areas" of the south to elect chairmen and members of such conferences.

The election process would create a "general mobilization of all political institutions." Although the agendas for conferences over the succeeding ten-year period would be based on national issues set by the head of state and local issues raised by the governors, the government touted the process as one that would "fulfil the revolution's promise to hand over full power to the people". The proposed conference committees were somewhat reminiscent of the popular committees established by the Popular Defence Act of October 1989. Initially, these popular committees had the function of overseeing rationing, but their mandate was broadened to include powers such as arresting enemies of the state.

The control exerted by the RCC-NS over various parts of the country varied. For example, western Sudan, especially Dar Fur, enjoyed considerable autonomy, which at times approached anarchy, as a result of the various armed ethnic groups and the refugee population that existed within it. The situation was even more

---

of Sudan. Al-Turabi's first instance of holding a political position with some consistency continued until March of 2004, where al-Bashir put him in Jail than under house arrest tilll June of 2005.

confused in the south, where until 1991 the government had controlled the major centres and the SPLM occupied the smaller towns and rural areas. The government launched a military campaign in 1991-92 that succeeded in recapturing many military posts that had served as SPLM and SPLA strongholds. The government's success resulted in part from the acquisition of substantial military equipment financed by Iran, including weapons and aircraft bought from China. Another reason for the successes of the government forces was the split that occurred in August 1991 within the SPLA between Garang's Torit fraction (mainly Dinka from southern Al Istiwaia) and the Nasir group (mainly Nuer and other non-Dinka from northern Al Istiwaia). The two groups launched military attacks against each other, thereby not only destroying their common front against the government but killing numerous civilians. The Nasir group had defected from the main SPLA body and tried unsuccessfully to overthrow John Garang over human rights violations, his authoritarian leadership style, and his favouritism toward his ethnic group, the Dinka. Abortive peace talks with representatives of both groups as well as the government were held in Abuja, Nigeria, in May and early June 1992. In December 1989, former United States president Jimmy Carter had attempted, without success, to mediate peace talks between the government and the SPLA.

The Torit fraction sought a secular state and an end to the sharia; the Nasir group wanted self-determination or independence for southern Sudan. During the talks, both groups agreed to push for self-determination, but when the government rejected this proposal, they decided instead to discuss Nigeria's power-sharing plan. A major basis of southern dissidence was strong opposition to the imposition of the sharia; the SPLA had vowed not to lay down its arms until the sharia was abrogated. The other source of concern was the fear of northern pressures to arabise the educational system. Al Bashir regime had declared Arabic the language of instruction in the south in early 1992, government offices, and society in general. These fears had led to the civil war, which, with a respite between 1972 and 1983, had been ongoing since 1955. The Bashir government's need for assistance in pursuing the war in the south determined Sudan's foreign policy to a large degree in the 1990s. Al Bashir recognized that the measures taken in the south, which outside observers termed human rights abuses, had alienated the West. Historically, the West had been the source of major financial support for Sudan. Furthermore, by siding with Iraq in the 1991 Persian Gulf War, Sudan had antagonized Saudi Arabia and Kuwait, principal donors for Sudan's military and economic needs in the preceding several decades. Bashir therefore turned to Iran, especially for military aid, and, to a lesser extent, to Libya. Iranian president Ali Hashemi Rafsanjani visited Sudan in December 1991, accompanied by several cabinet ministers. The visit led to an Iranian promise of military and economic assistance. Details of the reported aid varied, but in July 1992, in addition to the provision of one million tons of oil annually for military and civil consumption, aid was thought to include the financing of Sudanese weapons and aircraft purchases from China in the amount of at least US $300 million. China has now increased investment and is developing its political relations with Khartoum.

A recent Financial Times article quoted a Sudanese official explaining that China is now important "not only on an economic level but also a political level." According to the article, "China has stepped up sales of arms including fighter aircraft. The manufacture in Sudan of Chinese weapons and ammunition complicates the enforcement of a UN embargo on supplies to militias in Dar Fur. Chinese-designed arms and radios are reported to have been used across the border in Chad—where France keeps a garrison—by rebels alleged to be operating with Sudanese support."

Some accounts alleged that 3000 Iranian soldiers had also arrived in January 1992 to engage in the war in the south and that Iran had been granted use of Port Sudan facilities and permission to establish a communications monitoring station in the area; these reports were not verified as of mid-August 1992, however. The only other country with which Sudan had close relations in the early 1990s was Libya. Following an economic agreement signed between the two countries in July 1990, head-of-state Muammar al Qadhafi paid an official visit to Khartoum in October. Bashir paid a return visit to Libya in November 1991. Libyan officials arrived in Khartoum for talks on unity, primarily economic unity, in January 1992. While the government was cultivating relations with Iran and Libya, the SPLM and SPLA were seeking sources of aid elsewhere in Africa. They had lost their major source of support when the government of Mengistu Haile Mariam in Ethiopia was overthrown in May 1991. The SPLM and SPLA subsequently sought help from Kenya, Uganda, and several other African countries, thereby creating tensions between those nations and the Bashir regime. Furthermore, Sudan's relations with Egypt had soured in 1991 as a result of the Bashir government's failure to support Egypt's position in the Persian Gulf War. One manifestation of the deteriorating relations occurred in April 1992, when Sudan became involved in a border confrontation with Egypt. The disagreement resulted from an oil concession granted by Sudan to a subsidiary of Canada's International Petroleum Corporation for the exploration of a 38,400-square-kilometre area onshore and offshore near Halaib on the Red Sea coast, an area also claimed by Egypt. Although the Bashir regime prominently featured the PDF's participation in the 1991-92 campaign in the south, informed observers believed that its role lacked military significance. In view of the ongoing civil war, internal security was a major concern of the Bashir regime, which reportedly had been the target of attempted coups in 1990, 1991, and 1992. Thus the government faced problems on several fronts. There was dissidence or outright rebellion from several southern ethnic groups. There was also the creation in January 1991 of opposition abroad in the form of a government in exile. This body, called the National Democratic Alliance, was headed by Lieutenant General Fathi Ahmad Ali, former commander of the armed forces under Sadiq al Mahdi. There was also increasing opposition in the north on the part of those who favoured a secular state, including professionals, trade union leaders, and other modernizers. Such persons opposed the application of Islamic Hudud punishments, the growing restrictions on the activities and dress of women, and the increasing authoritarianism of the government as reflected, for example, in the repression of criticism through censorship, imprisonment, and death sentences.[7] On a wider scale, members of the public in the north staged protests in February 1992 against the price increases on staples after price supports were removed. The human rights group Africa Watch has estimated that at least 500,000 civilian deaths occurred between 1986 and the end of 1989 as a result of repressive measures taken by the government and the actions of armed government militias in the south as well as retaliatory measures of the SPLA forces. The overall number of deaths between 1983 and mid-1992 was far greater, an outcome not only of the civil war, but of the famine and drought in the late 1980s and early 1990s.[8] In late 1989, the government, which has never taken famine relief efforts seriously, ended its cooperation with relief efforts from abroad because it feared such measures were strengthening southern resistance. The pressure of world public opinion, however, obliged Sudan to allow relief efforts to resume in 1990. The United Nations (UN) World Food Program had initiated Operation Lifeline Sudan (OLS) in March 1989, which had delivered more than 110,000 tons of food aid to southern Sudan before it was forced by renewed hostilities to close down operations in October 1989. OLS II was launched in late March 1990 by the UN and the International Committee of the Red Cross to fly in food via Kenya and Uganda. In the spring of 1990, WFP indicated it was helping 4.2 million people in Sudan. In addition to these sources of suffering, the government began in the 1980s to undertake campaigns to destroy the Dinka and the Fur and Zaghawa ethnic groups in Dar Fur. Moreover, the government had to deal with the return in 1991 of Sudanese citizens who had been working in Iraq and Kuwait; according to estimates of the International Labour Organisation, such persons numbered at least 150,000. Finally, during late November 1991 and early

---

[7] Hudud (pl.) Had (single.) are fixed crimes with fixed punishments in Islamic Criminal Law "Sharia"

[8] The civil war was extremely costly; according to one Sudanese government estimate, it cost approximately US $1 million each day. Obviously, then, it destroyed the economy.

1992, the government forcibly uprooted more than 400,000 non-Arab southern squatters, who had created shanty towns in the outskirts of Khartoum, and transported them to the desert about fifty kilometres away, creating an international outcry. [9] In August 1992 the Bashir government found itself in a very difficult position. Although the country's economic problems had begun to be addressed, the economic situation remained critical. At peace negotiations in Abuja, slight progress had been made toward ending the civil war in the south, but the central concerns about imposition of the Sharia and barbarisation remained unresolved.

Moreover, the regime appeared to be facing growing dissension, not only in the south but from elements in the north as well. These considerations raised serious questions about the stability of the Bashir government. Khartoum's neglect of southerners is responsible for the war in the south. The level of underdevelopment in the region, the size of Kenya, Uganda, and Rwanda combined, is so acute that there is only a 12-kilometre asphalted road in Juba, the main city in south Sudan under government control. There are no schools and no hospitals except the structures that the church and non-governmental organisations (NGOs) are trying to set up in the region. Finally, a peace agreement between Khartoum and the main rebel group in southern Sudan, SPLM/A, was signed in Nairobi on January 9, 2005, ending more than 20 years of a civil war that erupted in May 1983. The agreement provides for 50/50 oil wealth sharing between the government and SPLM/A. Under the power sharing arrangement, John Garang would become the first vice president of Sudan during the six-year interim period, which was to begin as soon as a government of national unity had been formed in Khartoum. Under the agreement, all the other political parties, both in the north and south, who did not participate in the peace talks, would divide the remaining 20 percent of posts in the proposed government of national unity.

About 10,000 UN peace keeping troops arrived on April, 12, 2005, as part of a peace keeping force decided to be sent by UNSC on March 24, 2005, but some thousands of southern Sudanese are still fleeing across the border into Uganda because of citing ethnic tension, food shortages, and forced recruitment into the former rebel army. Leaders of all southern Sudanese rebel groups, political factions, and religious organisations signed a covenant on April 21, 2005, binding them to back unconditionally the signed peace agreement. Participants also

---

[9] The refugees from neighboring countries is an additional problem faced Sudan's different governments and severed ethnical troubles, 1.8 million refugees in Khartoum, 1.4 million people in rural areas of the south, 600,000 who had sought refuge in southern towns, and 400,000 in the "transition zone" between the north and the south in Dār Fūr and Kurdofan.

resolved to form a 40-member committee to draft a constitution for southern Sudan as stipulated in the January peace agreement, and another committee to monitor the progress of implementing the peace agreement and resolutions.

It can be said that military had played a major role in determining Sudanese foreign and domestic policy since independence. Initially, the military was seen as being free of specific ethnic or religious associations and thus in apposition to accomplish what civilians could not, namely, to resolve economic problems and to bring peace to the south. Such hopes proved futile, however. The growing civil war in the south, from 1955-72 and again from 1983 to January 9, 2005, as well as the increasing ethnical conflicts in west and east Sudan posed tremendous problems for the military and for the internal security forces. [10]

---

[10] where both Sudan Government and SPLMA signed peace agreement

THE ETHNICAL STRUCTURE AND ITS ROLE IN RUNNING CONFLICTS

The ethnical structure of Sudan

One of the remarkable characteristic of Sudan population is that its pyramidal ethnical structure. It consists of numerous tribal ethnical groups with complicated structure. The main tribe consists of many small tribes which build together the mother tribe. [11]

Although Sudanese themselves internally and in daily live pay less attention to ethnically based differences, on the other hand ethnical differences are the major dilemma and after independence growingly in last years, in spite of Sudanese unlimited tolerance, became the main reason for all internal conflicts. [12]

To make clear the ethnical structure of Sudan we have to adopt geographical locations measures from which the major cities Khartoum, Omdurman and Khartoum North building exceptions.[13] Accordingly Sudan can mainly

---

[11] The Arabic definition or description for sub tribes is Botoun (stomachs) of the main tribe, the best examples therefore are the group of Bagarah tribes in western Sudan and Dinka tribes in southern Sudan.

[12] Especially in major cities and towns it doesn't play notably role from which part of Sudan your neighbour is or from which tribe he descends. Such questions of descendant and ethnical backgrounds rise in small villages because of the tribal structure of such villages and in cases of marriages.

[13] Khartoum North (also known as Khartoum Bahri or just Bahri which means riverside. The ethnical structure of the above mentioned three cities build mix of all Sudanese eth-

be divided in following geographical ethnical regions, North, East, Central, Southern and West Sudan.[14]

Northern Sudan

Commonly north Sudan, administrational called north province or *Al Iqleem Al Shamali* and stretches from the boarder with Egypt to the north from Khartoum Province, can be seen as the homeland of two main tribes groups, the Nubian tribes and Arab tribes.[15] From the sixteenth until the nineteenth century the northern

---

nical groups, all Sudan is represented under the population of those three cities where the population of others Sudanese cities and towns consists of ethnical groups and tribes located in the region around them.

[14] The above mention division was also the long lasted administrative one, until the new administrative change. Now Sudan as a federal republic, is administratively divided into 26 states: Upper Nile State its capital Malakal, Red Sea State its capital Port Sudan, Bahr-AL-Jabal State its capital Juba, Lakes State its capital Rumbek, Gezira State its capital Wad Medani, Jungoli State its capital Bor, South Dar Fur State its capital Nyala, South Kordufan its capital Kadugli, Khartoum State its capital Khartoum, Sennar State its capital Sennar, East Equatoria State its capital Kapoita, North Bahr-AL-Gazal State its capital Awil, North Dar Fur State its capital AL-Fashir, North Kordufan State its capital AL-Obied, Northern State its capital Dongula, West Equatoria State its capital Yambio, West Bahr-AL-Gazal State its capital Wau, West Dar Fur State its capital Geneina, West Kordufan State its capital AL-Fula, Gedarif State its capital Gedarif, its capital, Kassala State its capital Kassala, River Nile State its capital AL-Damar, White Nile State its capital Rabak, Blue Nile State its capital AL-Damazin, Warap State its capital Warap, and the Unity State its capital Bantio.

[15] North Sudan (called Shamal Al Sudan or shortly Al Shamal (also Al Shamalia) is also the description for people of Arabic decedent. Arabs are people living in North Africa and the Middle East, from western Morocco to Oman, and from Turkey in the north to Yemen and Sudan in the south. Arabs living in an area of 10 million km with total population of 250 million. This makes them by far the largest population in the region. About 4 million Arabs live in Europe, and 2 million in north and south Americas. The Arabic heartland is Hijaz, now Saudi Arabia and Yemen. Although Arabs descend from the Arab heartland at some time immigrated into all new territories which today have a population defined as Arabs. These territories were already peopled by population far larger than the immigrants. For a number of reasons, however Arab lifestyle, Arab identity and language would come to replace the original lifestyles, identity and languages. Arabs would come to have influence to the race, but in most cases the Arab people living in lands originally non-Arab, represent about the same racial composition as before the arabization .e.g. Egyptians and Berbers are still there but they have simply changed their identifies. Ethnically Arabs are mostly dark haired with brown eyes, and medium light skin. But there are now Arabs

and western provinces of Sudan was dominated by two states. The Funj kingdom of Sinnãr lay in the Nile valley between Egypt and Ethiopia and the swamps of the southern Sudan.[16] The Keira Sultanate of Dãr Fur which covered the region of the-today Dar Fur province, the Nuba Mountains including Jabal Mara which is the heart of Dar Fur till the neighbouring state of Wadai in the west and till the Sahara in the north. Kordofan remained disputed territory between Sinnãr and Dãr Fur states until the decline of Sinnãr the Keira were able to occupy it at the end of the eighteen century. To mention that the northernmost part of the modern Sudan was not included in the Funj Kingdom.

The Nubia or Nubians with their now known subtribes are one of main north tribes groups, their homeland being the Nile River valley in far northern Sudan and southern Egypt. Consisting of many tribes, such as the al Sakot, al Mahas, and Danaqlah, they are mainly referred to as Danaqlah. Historically, Nubia extended from Dongola, in northern Sudan, up the Nile to Aswan in southern Egypt. Today, as mentioned above. Their history goes far before the Arabic invasion of Sudan. The first unification of Nubia in the sixteenth century may be seen as both a Nubian reaction against the invaders, and a positive response to the new economic and social changes that the newcomer hat created [17]

Following the Arabic conquest of Egypt, an informal and occasionally uneasy truce was maintained between Egypt as represented by Cairo and the Nubian states.[18] Till the thirteen century were the Nubian sacked the Egyptian-controlled Red Sea part of Aydhab and attached Aswan. Warfare between Eygpt and Nubia had rarely reached such proportions during the seven centuries, and with the Nubian attack on Aswan they precipitated a series of events that were to bring usurpers,

---

that are black or are quite blond. These differences are regional and a result of the process described above. Moreover the number of ethnically pure Arabs might constitute only a single digit percentage. More than 58% of all Arabs are Sunni, with only 10% Shiit in Yemen, Iraq, Gulf coast while less than 5% are Christians like in Egypt, Lebanon, Syria, Palestine, Jordan, Israel. An estimated number of 55% live in urban areas while 45% live in rural areas.

[16] The Funj were a southern Nubian People whose homeland lay along the White Nile below the great swamps, like their northern neighbours, they were heirs to the ancient cultures of the riverain Sudan. Under the pressure of attachks by the Shilluk in the south and confronted by the advance of the northerners up the Blue Nile, the early sixteenth century Funj leader Amara Dunga crossed the Gezira and challenged the army Abdallah Jamma.

[17] those are Sakot, Mahas, and Danaglah

[18] Cairo has always seen southern Egypt as part of Nubian, southern Egyptians share many relations with Nubian than with north Egyptians.

puppets and Muslims to their throne, which led the country to be plundered and the whole northern Sudan opened to the penetration of nomadic Arabs. Nubian tribes, Sakot, Mahas and Danaglah, share beside same history and culture relatively closely languages.[19] The Mahas are located in Northern Sudan along the banks of the Nile. The regional identity of the Mahas inhabitants appears to be long-established and the Mahas toponym can be traced back to at least the 1580s (CE) when a 'Sanjak of the Mahas' was created by the Ottoman conquerors of Egypt, advancing south along the Nile a local distinction between the Mahas and Sakoot Nubians also appears to have already existed at that time. The Third Cataract may also have marked a much older frontier, the medieval writer al-Aswani recorded that the Cataract marked the border between the heartlands of the Nubian Kingdom of Makuria, and its northern province of el-Maris (comprising Middle and Lower Nubia). This was reported to have been both linguistically and administratively distinct.

---

[19] Nubian language is the common feature that characterizes Nubian of today and it is the centre of their identity. Ethnologically this spoken language is divided into two main groups: Fiadidja-Mahas: Sudan is the country of this language group, although slightly more than 50% of Nubian in Egypt are Fadidja. In Sudan it is the main spoken language group among the majority of Nubian south of Dongola and up to the borders with Egypt. While in Egypt it is spoken by all Nubian to the Kunuz areas in the north. Fadidja and Mahas are two variants of this group, but there is only a slight difference in accent between them. Kenuzi Dongola: This is talked by people of Dongola of Sudan and Kunuz of Egypt Both language group bear a lot of lexical similarities and a good number of people of Dongola and Kunuz understand the Fadidja-Mahas which is the tongue of the majority of Nubians. While old Nubia had had systems for archiving and documentation prior to the Christian Nubia era, most if not all of the ancient texts date back to this era. The context of these manuscripts are of Christian Nature and the most known of all is the 'MS or The Old Nubian Miracle of Saint Menas' from Qasr. During the Christian Nubian era the Old Nubian alphabets had resemblance to Old Greek and Coptic alphabets. Both Coptic (31 or 32 letters) and Old Nubian (26) had more letters than old Greek (24), either to add special letters with no equivalent in old Greek (the Old Coptic) or to represent special sounds (the Old Nubian). The structure and formation of the Old Nubian language is characterized by its reliance on produced tones that is known as intonation or chanting. In this respect the general structure of this language is not a group of words linked by a common syntax to form a sentence. The speaker tackles this formation by putting parts together integrally with intonation and chanting. This takes place without interruption to conform with grammar thus most parts of a sentence are composed by adding a suffix or prefix to the word stem.

The distinction between Nubian areas north and south of the Cataract seems likely to reflect the early frontiers of the embryo Nubian kingdoms of Nobatia and Makuria which were emerging in the fifth century CE, following the disintegration of the Meroitic state which had controlled this region for many centuries. On current evidence, it also seems likely that during this early period we may see the first development of the 'typical' northern Nubian way of life. Based on irrigated agriculture using the waterwheel (Arabic 'saqia'/Nobiin 'eskalee'-waterwheel), a ribbon of small farming villages along the palm-fringed Nile, lie at the heart of the traditional Nubian world.

The Nubians today are the second most significant Muslim group in Sudan; Nubians are concentrated in three cities: Kom Ombo in southern Egypt, and Wadi Halfa and Khashm el-Girba in Sudan. Nubians have a proud and rich heritage. They existed long before the pharaohs and were once a Christian people. In 580 AD, Christianity became the official religion of Nubia. Almost all Nile Nubians speak Arabic as a second language; some, near Dunqulah, have been largely arabised. In the mid-1960s, in anticipation of the flooding of their lands after the construction of the Aswan High Dam, 35,000 to 50,000 Nile Nubians resettled at Khashm al Qirbah on the Atbarah River in what was then Kassala Province. It is not clear how many Nubians remained in the Nile Valley. Even before this resettlement, many had left the valley for varying lengths of time to work in the towns, although most sought to maintain a link with their traditional homeland. In the 1955-56 censuses, more Nile Nubians were counted in Al Khartum Province than in the Nubian country to the north. A similar system of working in towns was apparently followed by those resettled at Khashm al Qirbah. Many Nubians there retained their tenancies, having kin to oversee the land and hiring non-Nubians to work it. The Nubians, often with their families, worked in Khartoum, the town of Kassala, and Port Sudan, at jobs ranging from domestic service and semi-skilled labour to teaching and civil service, which required literacy. Despite their knowledge of Arabic and their devotion to Islam, Nubians retained a considerable level of self-identity and tended to maintain tightly-knit communities of their own in the towns.

The second group of north tribes are the Arabs. The Sudanese Arabs find their heritage in the Bedouin who roamed the deserts of Saudi Arabia centuries ago. They comprise the largest tribal group in Sudan. They are now a diverse group of 16 million people who find their commonality in the Arabic language and the religion of Islam. Their first arrival into Sudan predates the appearance of Islam in the region. Contacts between Nubians and Arabs long predated the coming of Islam, but the Arabisation of the Nile Valley was a gradual process that occurred over a period of nearly 1000 years. Arabian nomads continually wandered into the region in search of fresh pasturage, and Arab seafarers and merchants traded in Red Sea ports for spices and slaves. Intermarriage and assimilation also facilitated Arabisation. Sudanese Arab tribes are mainly divided into two groups, the northern and the southern Arab tribes. The northern Arab tribal groups (also known in Sudan as al Jaalyien tribes) consist, among others, of al Jaaliyin, al Jumuia, al Jemi, and al Jawama Ja'alein, Arakeien, Shigia, Rubatab, Shokrya, Manasir. Al Manasir are settled in the region of the Fourth Cataract, the most impassable of all rapids of the Nile. It is the homeland of the Arab tribe of the Manasir and from them gets its name. Still today the water rapids cannot be crossed by any large boats making the region accessible only via a sandy and rocky desert track.[20]

At the height of the Island of Muqrat (N 19°30') the Nile river is blocked from its northward course taking a sharp turn SSW for 280 kilometres before continuing to flow north. In the middle of this S-shape between the Bayudah Desert to the south and the Nubian Desert to the north, the Nile is forced by the topography to split up into a multitude of tributaries forming a fertile river oasis of small rocky islands. Next to al-Manasir is the Rubatab tribe in the area of Abu Hamed and the downstream Shaiqiyah tribe past the village of Birti
The southern Arabs, called Juhyina they descended from southern part of Arabic peninsula which today Yemen is. They also which consist of many sub-tribes, the largest group of which is called the Bagharah tribes, including al Shukria, al Habania, Rizigat and al Miseria.

East Sudan

East Sudan, administrational called East Province or *Al Iqleem Al Sharqi*, shares its boarders with the north province, central province, Ethiopia, Eritrea and read sea. There are many groups of eastern Sudanese tribes settled in Eastern Sudan area. Like the Bisharin, the Amarar, the Hadendowa, the Bani Amir, and the Beja. The largest group is the Hadendowa, but the Bisharin have the most territory, with settled

---

[20] Similar to other Arab tribes, the people trace their origins back to one usually legendary apical ancestor. According to the current oral tradition of many Manasir this person is called Mansur and belongs to the line of descendents of al-'Abbas, the uncle of the Prophet Mohammed. According to their self presentation in a recent publication by a committee of Manasir responsible for relocation issues resulting from the Hamdab High Dam, which is going to effect all villages of Dar al-Manasir, multiple explanations of their Origin are offered (LAGNAH 2005:2): Since a tribe called Manasir is well known in the Gulf States and plays a prominent role in today's Arab Emirates, it is proposed that they originate from this region and migrated via Egypt to Sudan. One group of the Manasir settled further south in Central Kurdufan among the Humur tribe.

tribes living on the Atbarah River in the far south of the Beja range and nomads living in the north. A good number of the Hadendowa are also settled and engage in agriculture, particularly in the coastal region near Tawkar, but many have remained nomadic. The Amarar, living in the central part of the Beja range, seem to be largely nomadic, as is the second largest group, the Bani Amir, who live along the border to northern Ethiopia. The precise proportion of nomads in the Beja population in the early 1990s is not known, but it was far greater than the nomadic component of the Arab population. The Beja are characterized as conservative, proud, aloof even toward other Beja, and very reticent in relations with strangers. They have long been reluctant to accept the authority of central governments. The Beja, a nomadic people group with one and a half million members, live in the north-eastern portion of Sudan. Eastern Sudan has been the homeland of the Beja since the days of the pharaohs 4,000 years ago. Despite contact with the Egyptians, along with Greeks and Romans, it was the Muslims who have finally had a real and lasting influence on the Beja. Although the Beja had partially accepted Christianity in 500 A.D., their conversion was only superficial and, beginning in 640 A.D. when Arabs first invaded Sudan, the Beja gradually began to adopt the Islamic faith. The Arabs did not conquer Sudan, and although many Beja tribes still do not speak Arabic, Islam has left a lasting impact on their lifestyle, customs, and religious practices. In general, the Beja have always rejected authority and they greatly value their nomadic freedom. For the most part they have not changed their lifestyle or practices in the last 1,500 years. Most Beja are nomadic herders of camels and goats, although some have adopted sedentary lifestyles in the towns and cities of eastern Sudan. They are divided into five distinct clans, and under these clans are smaller groups of one to ten extended families. The sparse distribution of grazing due to low rainfall further isolates the families from one another. With no settled homes, the Beja live in tents made from woven palm matting and exist mainly on a diet of milk and grain, supplemented occasionally by meat and sugar. Their crown of fuzzy hair (tiffa) has characterized the Beja for centuries. Long greased ringlets hang down from the head, which has a fluffed crown of looser hair on top. The Beja like to sing and play musical instruments, particularly the rababa, which is similar to a guitar. As the Beja are renowned camel herders, camels are the most popular subject matter for songs, but many songs also describe the beauty of women or speak about a longing for a special place, such as a village, mountain, or good grazing lands. Coffee, or jabana, is very important to the Beja. Drinking coffee involves relaxing with friends and talking. As noted by one historian, "A Hadendowa would rather starve than go without coffee." The Beja often marry cousins. Polygamy is unusual, but sometimes practiced by wealthy men. In this society, the birth of a baby boy is greeted with a trill of exaltation or with chanting, while a newborn girl is greeted with silence. Sharia, or Muslim religious law, is of some importance for settled Beja but matters little to the nomads. Salif, customary Beja law, is more important than either sharia or modern Sudanese code. Salif emphasizes the mandate of hospitality and provides for rates and modes of compensation for all manner of physical injury, ranging from one blow to murder. Throughout their history, the Beja have practiced a number of different religions, including idolatry, ancestor and demon worship, devotion to Egyptian gods, Jacobite Christianity, and now Islam. Although they are Muslims, Islam is neither deeply rooted nor well understood by the Beja. They still associate with traditional belief and do not adhere to Islamic prayer rituals. The Beja continue to be highly afraid of jinn, or bad spirits, which they believe exist everywhere and cause sickness and accidents and disturb the peace between individuals. A subgroup of the Beja is the Ababda who is a nomad tribe of African Bedouins; some still speak the Cushitic Beja language, while others speak Arabic. They extend from the Nile at Aswan to the Red Sea, and reach northward to the Kena-Kosseir road, thus occupying the southern border of Egypt east of the Nile. They call themselves "sons of the Jinns." With some of the clans of the Bisharin and possibly the Hadendoa they represent the Blemmyes of classic geographers, and their location today is almost identical with that assigned them in Roman times.

They were constantly at war with the Romans, who eventually conquered them. In the middle ages they were known as Beja, and convoyed pilgrims from the Nile valley to Aidhab, the port of embarkation for Jedda. From time immemorial they have acted as guides to caravans through the Nubian Desert and up the Nile valley as far as Sinnar. They intermarried with the Nuba, and settled in small colonies at Shendi and elsewhere up to Mehmet Ali's conquest of the region in the early 19th century. They are still great trade carriers, and visit very distant districts. As of 1911, the Ababda of Egypt numbered some 30,000, and were governed by a hereditary "chief". Although nominally a vassal of the Khedive, he paid no tribute. Indeed he was paid a subsidy, a portion of the road-dues, in return for his safeguarding travellers from Bedouin robbers. The sub-sheikhs were directly responsible to him. The Ababda of Nubia, according to Joseph von Russegger who visited the country in 1836, number some 40,000, but have since diminished, probably amalgamated with the Bisharin, their hereditary enemies. The Ababda generally speak Arabic (mingled with Barabra Nubian words), the result of their long-continued contact with Egypt; but the southern and south-eastern portion of the tribe in many cases still retain their Beja language, To Bedawie. Those of Kosseir would not speak this before strangers in 1911, as they believed that to reveal the mysterious dialect would bring ruin on them.

The Beja also took their part in the unrest spreading through Sudan's different regions, on 20th of May 2005, the Eastern Front, which includes the Beja Congress and the Free Lions, have captured 20 government troops in a major military offensive launched near the Red Sea in coordination with JEM a rebel group also active in Dar Fur. Its forces were advancing on the town of Tokar, south of the harbour city of Port Sudan also the capital of the Red Sea state. The attack led to the seizure of a significant amount of weaponry during the rebel push towards the town of Tokar, which lies half-way between the border with Eritrea and Port Sudan. Several hundred thousand Eritrean refugees live in Sudan and relations between the two governments have been very volatile in recent years. The Eastern Front was formed in February by the Beja Congress, its main component, and the Free Lions, with the support of assorted other factions. The Beja Congress and Free Lions are officially members of the NDA but they pulled out of the reconciliation talks in Cairo. Last April 2005 the newly-formed Eastern Front vowed to carry on the fight against Khartoum at a meeting with others in rebel-held territory in eastern Sudan near the Eritrean border. The Beja Congress first took up arms against Khartoum in 1994 and now controls the region north of the town of Kassala near the Eritrean border. Since 1994, fighting has been sporadic in the region. On June 21, 2005 government troops have quelled the rebels uprising who attempted to seize Tokar; heavy casualties were reported on both sides. Another tribe although domiciled in the region of eastern Sudan neighbouring the above eastern Sudanese tribes groups but never related to them, is the Rashaida. The Rashaida are closely related to the Saudi Arabia Bedouin, who migrated to Sudan from the Arabian Peninsula about 150 years ago. Many Rashaida also live in the neighbouring country of Eritrea; in fact, they make up five percent of the population of Eritrea (3.75 million people). In Sudan, their number around 68,000 and mainly live in the northeast part of the country on the outskirts of the city of Kassala, one of the most frequently visited spots in Sudan. The Rashaida are a nomadic people who live in tents made of goatskins. They are herdsmen, primarily breeding goats and sheep. Since they are largely illiterate, they memorize in great detail the pedigree of their animals, keeping mental records of their herds over seven or eight generations of the flock, although they usually only emphasize the female lines. Besides herding, the Rashaida also earn income by making jewellery. It is the veiled Rashaida women who craft much of the silver jewellery sold in the Kassala souq, or market, which is said to be one of the best in Sudan. Along with the jewellery, the Kassala souq is reputed to market some of the best and juiciest fruits Sudan has to offer. Kassala, with a population of 150,000, is a popular spot for tourists and Sudanese honeymooners, for it offers cooler temperatures than the rest of Sudan, along with beautiful mountains and tens of thousands of trees. The Rashaida are primarily Muslim, and very few Christians are known to exist among the group.

Central Sudan

Central Sudan, central Province or *Al Iqleem Al Awsat*, consists mainly of the three cities of Khartoum, Omdurman and Khartoum Nord and suburban.

The population of those three cities is mix of all Sudanese and representing a difficult to identify ethnical structure with exception to some tribes historically located near the later became three-cities-triangle Khartoum, Omdurman and Khartoum North, along the White Nile river, like al Hassania and Jumuia and dominated the majority of three cities population.

South Sudan

South of Sudan, Southern Province or *Al Iqleem Al Janube*, traditionally consists of Equatorial, Upper Nile and Bahr Al Gazal states. Now Southern Sudan is devided in ten states, formerly composing the provinces of Equatoria (Central Equatoria, East Equatoria, and West Equatoria), Bahr el Ghazal (North Bahr al Ghazal, West Bahr al Ghazal, Lakes, and Warab), and Upper Nile (Junqali, Wahdah, and Upper Nile). Southern Sudan has been described as a large basin gently sloping northward (Roth 2003),through which flow the Bahr el Jebel River, the (White Nile), the Bahr el Ghazal (Nam) River and its tributaries, and the Sobat, all merging into a vast barrier swamp Vast Sudanese oil areas to the south and east are part of the flood plain, a basin in the southern Sudan into which the rivers of Congo, Uganda, Kenya, and Ethiopia drain off from an ironstone plateau that belts the regions of Bahr El Ghazal and Upper Nile. The terrain can be divided into four land classes: Highlands higher than the surrounding plains by only a few centimeters; are the sites for "permanent settlements.Vegetation consists of open thorn woodland and/ or open mixed woodland with grasses Intermediate Lands lie slightly below the highlands, commonly subject to flooding from heavy rainfall in the Ethiopian and East/Central African highlands; Vegetation is mostly open perennial grassland with some acacia woodland and other sparsely distributed trees Toic land seasonally inundated or saturated by the main rivers and inland water-courses, retaining enough moisture throughout the dry season to support cattle grazing *Suddud* permanent swampland below the level of the toic; covers a substantial part of the floodplain in which the Dinka reside; provides good fishing but is not available for livestock; historically it has been a physical barrier to outsiders' penetration. Ecology of large basin is unique; until recently, wild animals and birds flourished, hunted rarely by the agro-pastoralists.

The Southern region has a population of around 9 million and a predominantly rural, subsistence economy. This region has been negatively affected by the First and Second Sudanese Civil Wars for all but 10 years since independence in 1956, resulting in serious neglect, lack of infrastructure development, and major destruction and displacement. More than 2 million people have died, and more than 4 million are internally displaced or have become refugees as a result of the civil war and war-related impacts.

Southern Sudanese tribes are mainly domiciled in the area south of Kosti in Bahr al Ghazal, al Istiwa'iyah, and A'ali an Nil. They consist of many groups, the most important of which are the Dinka, Nuer, Azande, and Shilluk. Most southern communities are small, except for the large conglomerate of Nilotes, Dinka, and Nuer, who dominate the Bahr al Ghazal and the Aali an Nil provinces, and the Azande people of Al Istiwai. Southern Sudanese profess many diverse faiths, predominately indigenous animistic religions, but including Christianity, some Muslims, and also many atheists. These tribes suffered most from the enduring civil war.
The largest group of Sudan's southern tribes is Dinka. The Dinka are a tall, thin, and very dark-skinned people who are mainly found in southern Sudan along the White Nile River and the surrounding countryside, generally to the west. The Dinka are widely distributed over the northern portion of the southern region, particularly in Aali an Nil and Bahr al Ghazal. There are five distinctive groups of Dinka. They are the largest group in the south and make up roughly two-thirds of the general category, 40 percent or more of the population of the region, and more than 10 percent of Sudan's total population. Despite this fact, however, they are disdained by many other Sudanese, particularly those with lighter skin. They inhabit the swamplands of the Bahr el Ghazal region of the Nile basin. They are chiefly a pastoral people, relying on cattle herding at riverside camps in the dry season to growing millet in fixed settlements during the rainy season. They number around 1-2 million people, constituting about 12% of the population of the entire country, making them the largest Ethnic tribe in Sudan. They are a black African people, differing markedly from the Arab tribes inhabiting northern Sudan; they are noted for their height, often reaching as much as seven feet. Many are Catholic and have mixed Christianity with traditional African religions, while some still follow animistic practices. The Dinka are traditionally cattle herders and value their livestock highly. For example, they give their cows names, and sometimes a herder will take the name of his favourite cow and prefer to be called by that name. The Dinka have no centralised political authority or social structure, instead comprising of many independent but interlinked clans. Certain of those clans traditionally provide ritual chiefs, known as the "masters of the fishing spear", who provide leadership for the entire people. Their language—also called Dinka or "thuong jang" is one of the Nilotic family of languages, belonging to the Chari-Nile branch of the Nilo-Saharan family. The name means "people" in the

Dinka language. It is written using the Latin alphabet with a few additions. they refer to themselves, Moinjaang, are one of the branches of the River Lake Nilotes mainly pastoral peoples of E. Africa who speak Nilotic languages, including the Nuer and Masai. The Dinka's migrations are determined by the local climate, their agro-pastoral lifestyle responding to the periodic flooding and dryness of the area in which they live. They begin moving around May-June at the onset of the rainy season to their "permanent settlements of mud and thatch housing above flood level, where they plant their crops of millet and other grain products.

These rainy season settlements usually contain other permanent structures such as cattle byres (luaak) and granaries. During dry season (beginning about December-January), everyone except the aged, ill, and nursing mothers migrate to semi-permanent dwellings in the toic for cattle grazing. The cultivation of sorghum, millet, and other crops begins in the highlands in the early rainy season and the harvest of crops begins when the rains are heavy in June-August. Cattle are driven to the toic in September and November when the rainfall drops off; allowed to graze on harvested stalks of the crops.

The Dinka's pastoral lifestyle is also reflected in their religious beliefs and practices (which are animist in character). They have one God, Nhialic, who speaks through spirits which take temporary possession of individuals in order to speak through them. The sacrificing of oxen by the "masters of the fishing spear" is a central component of the Dinka. Age is an important factor in Dinka culture, with young men being inducted into adulthood through an initiation ordeal which includes marking the forehead with a sharp object.

The Dinka have no centralised political authority, instead comprising of many independent but interlinked clans. Certain of those clans traditionally provide ritual chiefs, known as the "masters of the fishing spear", who provide leadership for the entire people. The region has been struck by occasional famine. A 1998 famine killed hundreds of thousands, while a food emergency was declared in mid-2005.

In recent years, a significant amount of foreign-based oil drilling has begun in Southern Sudan, raising the land's geopolitical profile abroad. The largest overseas consortium is controlled by; the People's Republic of China, with a 40% stake, Malaysia, with 30%, and India, with 25%. Canadian-based oil company Talisman withdrew operations in Sudan in 2003, due largely to external lobbying and pressure over political and human rights issues.

The Dinka are also rejected by other Sudanese people because of their leadership in the civil war that has ravaged the country for over a decade. The Dinka make up a majority of the rebel army and in fact John Garang, the rebel leader, is a Dinka. The civil war in Sudan has been hard on the Dinka.[21] The Sudan People's Liberation Army, led by late Dr. John Garang De Mabior, a Dinka, took up arms against the government in 1983. During the subsequent 21-year civil war, many thousands of Dinka, along with fellow non-Dinka southerners, were killed in the civil war. The Dinka have also engaged in a separate civil war with the Nuer. Among the points agreed to in the reconcoilation that pending elections, seats in both the Southern Sudan Assembly and the Government of the Southern Sudan are to be divided in a fixed proportion between the SPLM (70%), the NCP (the former NIF) (15%), and "other Southern political forces" (15%). Before his death on 30 July 2005, longtime rebel leader John Garang was the President of Southern Sudan. Garang was succeeded by Salva Kiir Mayardit who was sworn in as first vice president of Sudan on 11 August 2005.

The Nuer is a confederation of tribes located in Southern Sudan and some regions of East Africa. Collectively, the Nuer form one of the largest ethnic groups in East Africa. They are a pastoral people that rely on cows for almost every aspect of their daily lives. They are one of the very few African groups that successfully fended off colonial powers in the early 1900s. The Nuer warriors were noted as some of the most skilled in East Africa, with weapons made of fine crafted iron. Since the Nuer were so successful at fending off European powers, they spent much of their time interacting with bordering groups like those of the Dinka and Anuaks. The Nuer, being very well organized, were often able to conduct cattle raids against the Dinka, a tribe larger in population. Their traditional political organization, presented to the outside world through the ethnographic work by Evans-Pritchard, has become a classic example of an indigenous anarchist political structure without a single leader or leader group.

The nature of relations among these various southern tribes was greatly affected in the nineteenth century by the intrusion of Ottomans, Arabs, and eventually the British. Some ethnic groups made their accommodation with the intruders and others did not, in effect pitting one southern ethnic group against another in the context of foreign rule. For example, some sections of the Dinka were more accommodating to British rule than were the Nuer. The Dinka treated the resisting Nuer as hostile, and hostility developed between the two groups as a result of their differing relationships to the British.

---

[21] Among well-known Dinka are supermodel AlekWek former NBA player Manute Bol, one of the two tallest players in the league's history current NBA player Luol Deng, Daniel Den, the founder and CEO of the Daniel Deng Nonprofit Consulting and Development Corporation (Fiscal Sponsorships and Financial Management).

Culture Cattle have historically been of the highest symbolic, religious and economic value among the Nuer. Cattle are particularly important in their role as bridewealth, where they are given by a husband's lineage to his wife's lineage. It is this exchange of cattle which ensures that the children will be considered to belong to the husband's lineage and to his line of descent. The classical Nuer institution of ghost marriage, in which a man can "father" children after his death, is based on this ability of cattle exchanges to define relations of kinship and descent. In their turn, cattle given over to the wife's patrilineage enable the male children of that patrilineage to marry, and thereby ensure the continuity of her patrilineage. The Nuer receives facial markings (called gaar) as part of their initiation into adulthood. The pattern of Nuer scarification varies within specific subgroups. One common initiation pattern consists of six parallel horizontal lines across the forehead, with dip in the lines above the nose. Dotted patterns are also common (especially among the Bul Nuer). Typical foods eaten by the Nuer tribe include beef, sourdough corn ball pasta (called Kop), Injera bread (large, sour dough pancake), milk, and mangos.

Because of the civil wars in Southern Sudan over the past 50 years, many Nuer have emigrated to Kenya and elsewhere. Approximately 25,000 Nuer were resettled in the United States as refugees since the early 1990s, with many Nuer people now residing in Nebraska, Iowa, South Dakota, Tennessee, Georgia, and many other states. The Nuer are the next largest group found in south Sudan, numbering approximately one million and thus only one fourth to one-third the size of the Dinka. Traditionally, they are cattle herders whose total way of life revolves around their livestock. Cattle are used for payment of fines and debts and as bride prices in marriage. Children mould figures of cows out of clay, ash, wood, or any other available material. Young boys have a favourite ox which they name and treat as a pet. Unfortunately, Sudan's civil war, which has lasted more than a decade, has devastated this traditional way of life and displaced many Nuer to the safety of the neighbouring country of Ethiopia or to places in northern Sudan, such as the capital city of Khartoum. Many Nuer serve with the Sudanese rebel army, although some are at odds with the rebel leader, a member of the Dinka tribe.

In the past, war and tribal fighting have broken out between Nuer and their Dinka neighbours. Although Nuer are predominantly cattle herders, some Nuer also engage in agriculture. They determine their calendar based on current activity and weather conditions. The fishing season begins in December and lasts until the rain season begins in spring. The planting season follows in summer, followed by the windy season. The Nuer are careful astronomers and have their own names for various stars and constellations. The evening star, for example, is called "Lipai chiing"; to the Nuer, it looks like a girl in a village waiting for the moon to rise, and the name means "waiting in the village for the moon". Nuer society is patri-lineal; all rights, privileges, obligations, and relationships are regulated through kinsmen.

Marriage is one of the most important Nuer traditions and is arranged by the families of the bride and groom. The Nuer believe in monogamy, but divorce is not unheard of and is usually grounded by a lack of children. If a woman does not produce children, a man may demand the return of the cattle he paid for the mar-riage and may return woman to her own village. Many Nuer have remained ani-mists or are nominal Christians. In the south, many claim to be a Christian so as not to be identified as a Muslim northerner. It is very common to find a Nuer who worships a tree or some kind of animal, such as a frog. The third largest group, the Shilluk, has only about one-fourth as many people as the Nuer, and the remain-ing Nilotic groups are much smaller. The larger and more dispersed the group, the more internally varied it has become. The Dinka and Nuer, for example, did not develop a centralized government encompassing all or any large part of their groups. The Dinka are considered to have as many as twenty-five tribal groups. The Nuer have nine or ten separately named groups.

Armed conflict between and within ethnic groups continued well into the twen-tieth century. Sections of the Dinka fought sections of the Nuer and each other. A number of small, sometimes fragmented groups live in western Al Istiwai and Bahr al Ghazal. The largest of these groups is the Azande, who comprise 7 to 8 percent of the population of southern Sudan and are the dominant group in western Al Istiwai. Originally Azande are people of north central Africa, the word Azande means the people who possess much land, and refers to their his-tory as conquering warriors. Their number is estimated by various sources at between 1 and 4 million. They live primarily in the northern part of Democratic Republic of the Congo, in south-western Sudan, and in the south-eastern Central African Republic. The Congolese Azande live in the province of Upper Zaire; the Sudanese Azande live along the shores of the Uele River, and the Central African Azande live in the districts of Rafaï, Zémio, and Obo. They speak an Adamawa-Ubangi language, and most practice a traditional animist religion. Their beliefs revolve mostly around magic, oracles and witchcraft. Witchcraft is believed to be an inherited substance in the belly which lives a fairly autonomous life perform-ing bad magic on the person's enemies. A witch can sometimes be unaware of his/her powers and can accidentally strike people to whom the witch wishes no evil. Because it's always present there are several rituals connected to protection and cancelling of witchcraft, performed almost daily.

The Azande emerged in the eighteenth and nineteenth centuries when groups of hunters, divided into aristocrats and commoners, entered the north-eastern part of present-day Zaire (and later south-western Sudan) and conquered the peoples already there. Although the aristocrats provided ruling kings and nobles, they did not establish an inclusive, centralized state. The means of succession to kingship, however, encouraged Azande expansion. A man succeeded to his father's throne only when he had vanquished those of his brothers who chose to compete for it. Thus, Azande became a heterogeneous people. Their earlier military and political successes notwithstanding, the twentieth century Azande were poor, largely dependent on cultivation (hunting was no longer a feasible source of food), and afflicted by sleeping sickness. The British colonial authorities instituted a project, known as the Azande Scheme, involving cotton farming and resettlement in an effort to deal with these problems. The program failed, however, for a variety of reasons, including colonial planners' inadequate understanding of Azande society, economy, and values. Azande society deteriorated still further, the deterioration being reflected in a declining birth rate. Azande support of the Anya Nya guerrilla groups, as well as conflicts with the Dinka, also served to worsen the Azande's situation. In the early 1980s, there was talk of resurrecting a revised Azande project but the resumption of the civil war in 1983 prevented progress.

The Shilluk (self-named Collo), were not dispersed like the Dinka and the Nuer, but settled mainly in a limited, uninterrupted area along the west bank of the Bahr al Jabal, just north of the point where it becomes the White Nile proper. A few live on the eastern bank. With easy access to fairly good land along the Nile, they rely much more heavily on cultivation and fishing than the Dinka and the Nuer, and have fewer cattle. The Shilluk have truly permanent settlements and do not move regularly between cultivations and cattle camps. Unlike the larger groups, the Shilluk, in the Upper Nile, have traditionally been ruled by a single politico-religious head (reth), believed to become at the time of his investiture as king the representative, if not the reincarnation, of the mythical hero Nyiking, putative founder of the Shilluk. The administrative and political powers of the reth have been the subject of some debate, but his ritual status is clear enough: his health is believed to be closely related to the material and spiritual welfare of the Shilluk. It is likely that the territorial unity of the Shilluk and the permanence of their settlements have contributed to the centralization of their political and ritual structures. In the late 1980s, the activities against the SPLA by the armed militias supported by the government seriously alienated the Shilluk in Malakal. Nilote is a collective name for many of the peoples living on or near the Bahr al Jabal and its tributaries. The term refers to people speaking languages of one section of the Nilotic sub-branch of the eastern Sudanese branch of Nilo-Saharans and sharing a myth of common origin. They are marked by physical similarity and many common cultural features. Many have a long tradition of cattle-keeping, including some for whom cattle were no longer of practical significance.

Because of their adaptation to different climates and their encounters, peaceful and otherwise, with other peoples, there is also some diversity among the Nilotes. Despite civil war and famine, the Nilotes still constitute more than three-fifths of the population of southern Sudan.

Besides the above mentioned southern Sudanese tribes there are also the Acholi (also Acoli) who are the people of the districts of Gulu, Kitgum Pader (known as Acholiland) in northern Uganda, and Magwe County in southern Sudan. The 1991 Ugandan census counted 746,796 Acholi; a further 45,000 Acholi live outside of Uganda. They are said to have come to northern Uganda from the area now known as Bahr el Ghazal in southern Sudan. Starting in the late seventeenth century, a new socio-political order developed among the Luo of northern Uganda, mainly characterized by the formation of chiefdoms headed by Rwodi. By the mid-nineteenth century, about 60 small chiefdoms existed in eastern Acholiland. During the second half of the nineteenth century Arabic-speaking traders from the north started to call them Shooli, a term which transformed into 'Acholi'. The Acholi language is a Western Nilotic language, classified as Luo, and is mutually intelligible with Lango and other Luo languages. Their traditional dwelling-places were circular huts with a high peak, furnished with a mud sleeping-platform, jars of grain and a sunk fireplace, with the walls daubed with mud and decorated with geometrical or conventional designs in red, white or grey. They were skilled hunters, using nets and spears, and kept goats, sheep and cattle. In war they used spears and long, narrow shields of giraffe or ox hide. During Uganda's colonial period, the British encouraged political and economic development in the south of the country, in particular among the Baganda. In contrast, the Acholi and other northern ethnic groups supplied much of the national manual labor and came to comprise a majority of the military, creating what some have called a "military ethnocracy." This reached its height with the coup d'état of Acholi General Tito Okello, and came to a crashing end with the defeat of Okello and the Acholi-dominated army by the National Resistance Army led by now-President Yoweri Museveni.

The Acholi are known to the outside world mainly because of the insurgency of the Lord's Resistance Army (LRA) led by Joseph Kony, an Acholi from Gulu. LRA's activities have been concentrated within Acholiland, and populous Acholi remain internally displaced persons

The southern Sudanese practice mainly indigenous traditional beliefs, although some follow Christianity. The south also contains many tribal groups and many more languages are used than in the north. The Dinka, whose population is estimated at more than 1 million, is the largest of the many black African tribes of the Sudan. Other Nilotic tribes are the Shilluk and the Nuer. The Azande, and Jo Luo

are 'Sudanic' tribes in the west, and the Acholi and Lotuhu live in the extreme
south, extending into Uganda.

The distinctive Juba Arabic language is a widely used lingua franca in Southern
Sudan, although the language of education and government business is English.
Two widely-used tribal languages are Thuongjang and Nuer. Thuongjang is offi-
cially and culturally active in the state of North Barh al Ghazal, West Barh al
Ghazal, Lakes, Warab, Jonglei, and autonomus independent Abiey. Nuer is active
in Unity State and Upper Nile state.

Following the Naivasha Agreement which granted autonomy to Southern Sudan,
the Interim Constitution of Southern Sudan was adopted in December 2005,
leading to the creation of the Government of Southern Sudan.

The relationship between autonomous Southern Sudan and the neighbouring
areas of Blue Nile State, Nuba Mountains/Southern Kordofan, and Abyei has yet
to be definitively determined, although for the time being these are effectively
part of the North.

Western Sudan

Western Sudan, the western province or *Al Iqleem Al Gharbe* consists of the largest
provinces of Sudan those are Dar Fur and Kordofan.[22]

The region of western Sudan historically comprises the Kordofan and Dar Fur
regions. Kordofan is a former province of central Sudan. In 1994 it was divided
into three new federal states: North Kordofan, South Kordofan, and West Kordofan
Kordofan covers an area of some 146,932 km² (56,730 miles²); with an estimated
population in 1983 of around 3 million people. It is largely undulating plain, with
the Nuba Mountains (Jebel Nuba) in the south east quarter. During the rainy season
from June to September the area is fertile, but in the dry season it is virtually desert.
The region's chief town is El Obeid. Traditionally the area is known for production
of gum Arabic. Other crops include groundnuts, cotton, and millet. The main ethnic groups are the Nuba, Shilluk, and Dinka. Large grazing areas used by Arabic-
speaking, semi-nomadic Baggara and camel-raising Kababish. The Kordofanian
languages are spoken by a small minority in southern Kordofan and are unique
to the region, as are the Kadu languages. The Mahdi captured El Obeid in 1883.
The Egyptian government despatched a force from Cairo under the British General
William Hicks, which was ambushed and annihilated at Sheikan to the south of El
Obeid. Following British reoccupation in 1898, Kordofan was added to the number

---

[22] Have been written in many different ways, also Darfur, but the right way is Dar Fur
because they are two separated words Dar which means home (house, land) and Fur which
refers to the indigenous tribes of this region. Kordofan, also known as Kurdufan.

of provinces of the Sudan. Kordofanis, with exception to Nuba Mountains Area, are predominantly Arabs. In addition to Rizeigat, Taisha, Habbaniya, Misseiria, Humur, Hammer, Hawazma, and Gawama, the largest group of Arabic tribes is called Baggara.

The Baggara or Baqqarah are nomadic cattle herders of western Sudan and eastern Chad. They are settled in the area of Dār Fur region in western Sudan and Chad. They are cattle-herders, migrating seasonally between grazing lands in the wet season and river areas in the dry season. They are mostly Arabic speaking Muslims, thought to be the descendants of Arab tribes who settled the region during the middle Ages. Their name is a term widely used in western Sudan for Arab pastoralists, meaning literally "cattle herder." They are Muslims since the 13th century; they practice a unique mix of Sunni and folk Islam. Numbering over one million, the Baggara are the second largest tribal group in western Sudan. They are primarily nomadic cattle herders and their journeys are dependent upon the seasons of the year. Other Baggara family groups, being the minority of the two, have settled in larger villages or cities. Baggara is actually a collective name applied to the separate cattle-herding tribes of Sudan and eastern Chad. The Baggara peoples identify more with their tribal names than with the generic term "baggara". There are at least seven principal tribes which include the Humr/Messiria, Rizaygat, Shuwia, Hawazma, Ta'isha, and Habbaniya. These nomads originated from the Guhayna group, a clan of Bedouin Arabs who poured across the Senai Peninsula from Saudi Arabia and eventually successfully invaded the Nile region of Upper Egypt and surged into Sudan in 1504. After a time, the Baggara branched off from the large Guhayna clan and took their name because of their newfound opportunity to herd cattle in the savannah region of the Sahara Desert. (The Arabic word for cow is baqqara.) After staking their claim on the land, they intermarried with the Africans who originally inhabited these regions, thus giving them their dark skin. Although their practices most closely resemble those of the Sunnis, most of the villagers would be more accurately classified as having folkIslamic faith. Many tribes of the Baggara believe strongly in the evil eye and wish to protect their cattle from jealous onlookers, even within their own villages. The presence of witch doctors is the second piece of evidence that ties the beliefs of the Baggara to that of folkIslam. Children who are ill will often have either a bracelet or necklace tied to a small leather pouch which contains Quranic verses.

This is a classic example of how Islam has been combined with traditional African religions. The Baggara pray toward Mecca five times a day and the children who attend school learn both reading and writing from the Quran. The women wear tobes(a loose-fitting cover draped about the body and over the head) each day but do not veil their faces. During wedding celebrations and other festivals, younger women dress in costumes which reveal their figures and their heads remain uncovered in order to display their ornate hairstyles and feathered headbands.

They dance with the men and their movements are clearly of African origin.

The amount of gold worn by a man's wife during these festivals and the number of cattle within his herd are the determining factors of his prestige within the community. The men wear pristinely white jallaybiyas (a dress-like cotton robe that reaches mid-calf) and pants underneath. The turbans for their heads are worn thicker in the villages than in the cities for better protection against the Sahara sun. The Baggara tribes live in tents made from sticks, grass, and mats roped together. During travel, the tent materials serve a second purpose. The bark and grass are used for padding for a more comfortable journey and to protect the cattle from back sores. The ropes are used for attaching the loads to the animals and to the carts and the mats are used for resting during the day and are placed over the pitched tents at night. The migration period is usually completed in one month's time, depending on the tribe, its location, and the average rainfall in the area. If the intention of a family group is to settle for a time longer than six weeks, they will begin constructing more permanent tents, which are made from similar materials but are sturdier. The women and children bring water each morning from either wells or small lakes, which are filled by rain water and are used throughout the dry seasons. Baggara women are given a number of responsibilities within their communities. These include assisting with building tents and shelters, selling milk and meat in the markets, producing baskets to sell and mats fashioned from goat hair to be used as tent decoration, and lastly, handling most of the financial matters. In addition to these, they occupy the traditional women's role as mothers, cooks, and hostesses. The men care for the cattle and sometimes go ahead of the women into migration, taking the herds before the mosquito and tsetse fly season begins. The men also build and repair the fences that are necessarily placed around their water sources and assist in the construction of houses and shelters. Men and women do not eat together unless they are married. The women prepare the meals and take the food to the men's "racuba (place for shelter and resting) three times each day. Spending time together is a vital component of an Arab community and it is highly disapproved to deny friends or family of this time. There are few extramarital relationships between men and women, even on a friendship level. Both male and female children are circumcised between the ages of 5 and 7 years. A festival ensues for each candidate and the child is encouraged to not cry because a crybabywill forever be labelled as such.

The women have extreme difficulty in childbirth because of the circumcision. Nevertheless, an uncircumcised woman is considered unclean and unmarriageable. Men are allowed up to four wives by the Quran but most cannot afford to support this number. Relations at this point are said to have improved; in most cases, however, the damage is irreparable. Because the Baggara as a whole are an uneducated people, few are involved in the political arena in the capital city of Khartoum. They have strong political opinions; however, these views are biased to their nomadic lifestyle.

The Kababish are known as the camel herders of Sudan. Kababish is a loosely defined name that describes a group of people who are both Arabian and African.
These nomadic people herd their camels across the Sahara Desert in search of food and water. They are traditionally Muslim but do not strictly follow the rules of Islam due to their harsh desert lifestyle. The Kababish territory (Northern Kordofan) is located in north-western Sudan at the edge of the Libyan Desert. Like other nomadic African-Arab tribes, the Kababish live in tents and herd their camels in search of vegetation and water. They have a complex system of migration, in which different parts of the family move to different places during certain times of the year. Some of the Kababish have become semi-nomadic and live most of the time in villages located to the west of Khartoum. Most of their ancestors came from Arabia and intermarried with Beja, Moors, and various other North African tribes. They flourished in Sudan by crossing huge expanses of land to support their large camel herds. Today, the confederation of the tribes that form the Kababish is vague. Affiliations are loose, administrative control is difficult to enforce because the territory is so broad, and there is no infrastructure in the area. Ever since the drought in the mid-80s, life for the Kababish has been hard. The camel herds have decreased dramatically and many clans have moved out of the desert and closer to the cities. The Kababish have darker complexions than traditional Arabs but are lighter than the very dark-skinned tribes of the south. Other Sudanese tribes will say that the Kababish are white-skinned Arabs; compared to most other tribes, this description is true.

The Baggaras' pastoral lifestyle has led to conflict with the sedentary African farmers of the region concerning access to water and grazing land. This has been the source of ethnic tensions for many years, culminating in the bloody Dār Fur conflict which began in 2003. The Baggara include several tribes, such as the Rizeigat, Habbaniya, Beni Halba and Ta'isha in Dar Fur and Misseiria and the Humur and Hawazma in Kordofan. The Misseiria of Jebel Mun speak a Nilo-Saharan language, Tama (also called Miisiirii.) They are also known as Shuwa Arabs. They are cattle-herders, migrating seasonally between grazing lands in the wet season and river areas in the dry season. They are mostly speakers of the Shuwa dialect of Arabic, and thought to be partly descendants of Arab tribes who settled the region primarily from the fourteenth to the eighteenth century, descendants of the Juhayna group of Arabs that trace their ancestry to Libya. Those Juhayna who moved south where rainfall was more plentiful, such as south of the Marrah Mountains, took up the herding of cattle and became known as the Baggara, literally "those of the cow" or "cattle people". Their kinspeople who stayed north remained Abbala, "camel-men".

The Baggara of Dar Fur and Kordofan were the backbone of the Mahdist revolt against Turko-Egyptian rule in Sudan in the 1880s. The Mahdi's second-in-command, the Khalifa Abdallahi ibn Muhammad, was himself a Baggara of the Ta'aisha tribe. During the Mahdist period (1883-98) tens of thousands of Baggara migrated to Omdurman and central Sudan where they provided many of the troops for the Mahdist armies. After their defeat at the Battle of Karari in 1898, the remnants returned home to Dar Fur and Kordofan. Under the British system of indirect rule, each of the major Baggara tribes was ruled by its own paramount chief, known as Nazir. Most of them were loyal members of the Umma Party, headed since the 1960s by Sadiq el Mahdi.

The main Baggara tribes of Dar Fur were awarded "hawakir" (land grants) by the Fur Sultans in the 1750s. As a result, the four largest Baggara tribes of Dar Fur— the Rizeigat, Habbaniya, Beni Halba and Ta'isha—have been only marginally involved in the Dar Fur conflict. However, the Baggara have been deeply involved in other conflicts in both Sudan and Chad. Starting in 1985, the Government of Sudan armed the Rizeigat of south Dar Fur and the Missiriya and Hawazma of neighboring Kordofan as militia to fight against the Sudan People's Liberation Army in South Sudan and the Nuba Mountains. Known as "Murahaliin", these militia were complicit in many human rights abuses including the abduction and forced labor of women and children. However, by the mid-1990s they had mostly negotiated local truces with the SPLA forces. In Dar Fur, a Benni Halba militia known as "Fursan" (horsemen) fought against the SPLA in 1990-91. In Chad, Salamat Baggara were also involved in the 1980s Janjaweed activities.

Among Kordofan's non-Arabic tribes are also the Nuba. The word Nuba is a collective term used for the peoples located in the Nuba Mountains, in Kordofan province of Sudan. Although the term is used to describe them as if they were a single tribe, in fact the Nuba are quite diverse, and are made up of different ethnic and linguistic groups. Estimates of the number of Nuba vary widely; the Sudanese government estimated that they numbered 1.1 million in 1993. The Nuba people reside in one of the most remote and inaccessible places in all of Sudan, the foothills of the Nuba Mountains in central Sudan. The Nuba Mountains are located in Southern Kordofan, covering about 30,000 square miles, about the size of Scotland at the geographical center of the Sudan. Perhaps a third of the area consists of the mountains or hills themselves, with most of the rest being fertile, clay-heavy plains with great stretches of the "black-cotton" soil that makes walking exceedingly difficult when wet. The hills jut up from the flatlands in rocky beauty, some to almost 1,500 meters. Well-watered and quite green in the rainy season, the territory contains few significant roads or towns. With Kadugli the principal reference-point, the area stretches to Dilling in the north, below Talodi and Buram in the south, Lagowa to the west, and past Heiban in the east. The Nuba people are not, in the recent cultural sense, related to the Nubians farther north near Egypt. They represent a "bewildering complexity" of cultures and more than 50 languages, with some of the latter apparently related to tongues of peoples as distant as the Shona and Ndebele.4 The numbers of Nuba are unclear. Some Nuba sources suggest there are up to two million, but the numbers of migrants, displaced people, and refugees cloud the issue. In 1993, the Government asserted there were 1.1 million Nuba. In August 1995, Yusuf Kuwwa estimated the total at 1.2 million, with perhaps 350,000 in SPLA-controlled areas, a percentage that roughly comports with a 1992 SPLM census figure for areas under its control.

The 1955/6 census was the only systematic attempt to enumerate Sudan's different ethnic groups, and found 572,935 Nuba, 61% of the population of South Kordofan. But by that stage there was already large-scale labour migration, so at least another 5% must be added to the figure. On the basis of subsequent censuses and population growth statistics, it can be estimated that by the time the war intensified in 1989, the Nuba population was more than 1.5 million, plus migrants. Since then, the number in the Nuba Mountains has probably decreased, due to deaths, fewer births, and mass out-migration to Khartoum. There has also been massive population movement within the Nuba Mountains, with hundreds of thousands forcibly displaced to government towns and "peace camps", and a large number living as internal refugees in the areas secured by the SPLA. Currently, the best estimate for the population under the administration of the SPLA is between 350,000-400,000 people; those under government control number about one million.

Most of the people in the Nuba Mountains belong to the myriad Nuba tribes. But the presence of other groups indigenous to the area must not be overlooked. Perhaps one quarter of the inhabitants of the region are Arabs, mainly pastoralists, traders and civil servants. There are also non-Arab groups, principally the Daju (an offshoot of a Dar Fur tribe, living south of Lagowa) and Fellata communities spread throughout the area. The Fellata are descendants of West African immigrants to Sudan, and are farmers, herders and traders.

The Nuba people, despite their historical attempts to participate in the greater Sudan, have largely been a disenfranchised population in Sudanese society. Confronted by the government's pursuit of an Arabized society, the diverse Nuba developed an identity out of their persistent adversity. Faced with economic encroachment and little viable access to justice in government actions, in a context where powerful elites manipulated local hostilities in pursuit of control of Nuba lands and the substantial resources they represent, the Nuba have largely been the losers. Their tolerant religious diversity bought them no respite. Politically isolated and culturally an obstacle to the government's persistent larger design for Sudanese society, the Nuba identity emerged. Thus, African Rights contends, "The central theme of Nuba history is the tension between political Incorporation into the state of Sudan and the maintenance of local identity," a theme that also characterizes the war in the South and elsewhere in the Sudan.

At one time the area was considered a place of refuge, bringing together people of many different tongues and backgrounds who were fleeing oppressive governments and slave traders. As a result, over 100 hundred languages are spoken in the area and are considered Nuba languages, although many of the Nuba also speak Sudanese Arabic, the official language of Sudan.

The Nuba, living in the Nuba Mountains of southern Kordofan are perhaps three dozen small groups collectively called the Nuba but varying considerably in their culture and social organisation. For example, some are patrilineally organized whereas others adhere to matrilineal patterns, and a very few the south-eastern Nuba have both patrilineal and matrilineal groupings within the same community. The Kordofanian languages of these peoples are generally mutually intelligible except for those of some adjacent communities. Despite the Arabisation of the people around them, only small numbers of Nuba have adopted Arabic as a home language, and even fewer have been converted to Islam. Some have, however, served in the armed forces and police. Most have remained cultivators; animal husbandry plays only a small part in their economy.

The Nuba Mountains mark the southern border of the desert sands and the northern limit of fertile soils washed down by the Nile. Many Nubas, however, have migrated to the Sudanese capital of Khartoum to escape persecution and the effects of Sudan's civil war. Most of the rest of the 1,000,000 Nuba people live in villages of between 1,000 and 50,000 inhabitants in areas in and surrounding the Nuba Mountains. Nuba villages are often built where valleys run from the hillsout on to the surrounding plains, because water is easier to find at such points and wells can be used throughout the year. There is no political unity among the various Nuba groups who live on the hills. Often the villages do not have chiefs but are instead organized into clans or extended family groups with village authority left in the hands of clan elders. The Nuba people are primarily farmers as well as herders who keep cattle, goats, chickens, and other domestic animals.

They often maintain three different farms: a garden near their house where vegetables needing constant attention, such as onions, peppers, and beans, are grown;

fields further up the hills where quick-growing crops such as red millet can be cultivated without irrigation; and farms farther away, where white millet and other crops are planted. A distinctive characteristic of the Nubas is their passion for athletic competition, particularly traditional wrestling. The strongest young Sudan's Religions and Ethnic Groups 17 men of a community compete with athletes from other villages for the chance to promote their personal and their village's pride and strength. In some villages, older men participate in club-or spear-fighting contests. The Nubas' passion for physical excellence is also displayed in the young men's vanity—they often spend hours painting their bodies with complex patterns and decorations. This vanity reflects the basic Nuba belief in the power and importance of strength and beauty. The majority of the Nuba, those living in the eastern, western, and northern parts of the mountains, are Muslims, while those living to the south are either Christians or practice traditional animistic religions. In those areas of the Nuba Mountains where Islam has not deeply penetrated, ritual specialists and priests wield as much control as the clan elders, for it is they who are responsible for controlling the rain, keeping the peace, and performing rituals to insure successful crops. Many are guardians of the shrines where items are kept to insure positive outcomes of the rituals (such as rain stones for rain magic), and some also undergo spiritual possession. Because of their unique culture and overall resistance to conformity, both the Muslim and Christian Nuba face the fiercest persecution. During the British rule in Sudan (1896–1956) the Nuba Mountains was a separate province with its own administration and its capital at Talodi until it was amalgamated in 1929 into the larger Kordofan. It then remained a 'closed district' until shortly before independence in 1956.

The Nuba share South Kordofan with Sudanese Arabs, cattle herders and these are Misiriya Zurug and Hawazma Baggara. Some Nuba groups historically developed close relations with the Baggara while others were isolated from them, but the relationship was always one of underlying suspicion. The advent of the Baggara was one main factor in driving the Nuba to the mountains.

A second category of Arabs includes Jellaba traders from Khartoum and the Northern Nile valley, and Arab soldiers and administrators. These urban Arabs represent the power of the Sudanese state, and the basic reason for their presence in the Nuba Mountains was—and is—to bring the area and its peoples under the writ of the Central Government.

The central theme of Nuba history is the tension between political incorporation into the state of Sudan and the maintenance of local identity. There is an irony here. Local, tribal identities are strong. But, until recently, many Nuba villagers had no conception of the wider community of the Nuba as a whole. They had little reason to travel to other Nuba areas. The geography of the region is central to its history. The Nuba hills themselves rise sharply from the plains, sometimes

in long ranges, sometimes as isolated massifs or single crags. They rise some 500-
1000 metres from the surrounding plains. The mountains are rocky, with cultiva-
ble hill slopes and valleys. Though they dominate the landscape, the area covered
by the hills themselves is less than a third of the total area of the Nuba Mountains;
the remainder of the land is extensive clay plains, some forested, some farmed.
It is some of the most fertile land in Sudan, a fact that is both a blessing and
a curse to the Nuba. While drought-induced famine is almost unknown in the
Nuba Mountains, the fertile soils have also attracted the attention of outsiders.
The common elements in traditional Nuba culture essentially reflect the way in
which dissimilar groups have adjusted to living in similar conditions. One of these
common elements is the farming system. The Nuba are largely farmers, cultivating fields in the hills, at the foot of the hills, and in the plains. The hill farms
(sometimes called "near farms") can be elaborately terraced, or gardens divided
into small plots by lines of stones, and sometimes they are irrigated. Farms in
the clay plains (sometimes called "far farms") are generally larger and more productive. The main crops are sorghum, beans and sesame, grown during a single
rainy season that lasts from May-June until September. The harvest is gathered
during November-January. All small-holders cultivation is by hand. Dependence
on the rain has contributed to many rituals around rainfall in many Nuba tribes,
with ceremonies to encourage the rain. These ceremonies are usually conducted
by rainmakers known as "kujur" whose power in some Nuba tribes is equal to that
of the chief of the tribe.

The famous linguist of the Nuba, Roland Stevenson, 1984, classified more than
fifty Nuba languages and dialect clusters into ten separate groups. There is thus
more linguistic diversity within the Nuba Mountains than the entire rest of
Sudan, and indeed as much diversity as the whole of Africa south of the Equator.
To give one illustration: the Katla language is linguistically closer to Shona and
Ndebele than it is to the Nyima language, whose speakers live on the next range
of hills. (Nyima belongs to the Nilo-Saharan language group, along with Dinka,
Acholi and others, whereas Katla, like the majority of Nuba languages, is in the
Niger-Kordofanian group, which includes Bantu languages.) Cultural diversity is
equally marked. Several Kordofanian languages are spoken in the Nuba hills of
Kordofan, in Sudan. They are usually grouped together with the Niger-Congo
languages, forming the Niger-Kordofanian languages. The "Tumtum" or Kadu
languages were formerly considered Kordofanian, but are now normally excluded
(since Schadeberg 1981c), and widely seen as Nilo-Saharan. They are divided into

four subgroups.[23] The Nilo-Saharan languages are a group of African languages spoken mainly in the upper parts of the Chari and Nile rivers, including Nubia. Roughly 11 million people spoke Nilo-Saharan languages as of 1987, according to Merritt Ruhlen's estimate. The family is internally extremely diverse—far more so than Indo-European, or even Niger-Congo—and is rather controversial; few historical linguists have attempted work on the family as a whole, and several have denied its validity. Particularly controversial is the inclusion of Songhay.

The actual war in Nuba began in July 1985 After the NIF coup, a virtual cordon sanitaire was imposed on the area. Few outsiders were able to visit, and no one could do so freely. NGO personnel and others such as those of the UN's Operation Lifeline Sudan (OLS) were authorized at times to conduct relief operations to fulfill government policy objectives (e.g. to assist "peace camps" in government-controlled areas); they have never been authorised to observe the conflict or assist civilians in SPLA-controlled sectors as is grudgingly allowed in parts of the South.

Between 1973 and 1994, the Sudanese government introduced programs to promote large-scale, privately owned agriculture to many regions including the Nuba Mountains. The efforts were redoubled as a result of IMF structural adjustment programs instituted in 1978. Large-scale mechanized farms were introduced, which pushed small peasants into marginal land between semi-arid and lusher savanna areas. Sudanese governments during the period misperceived the Nuba as a unified ally of the Sudan People's Liberation Army (SPLA), which furthered the oppressive measures against the tribes. These measures were indiscriminately applied, even to groups having no connection to the SPLA, such as the numerous Nuba Muslims. An example of these measures is the refusal to grant leases for undeveloped land that had been marked for future large-scale agricultural uses to peasants who were starving during the drought between 1983 and 1985. By 1999, over 100,000 people had been forcibly displaced by the agriculture programs, many of whom moved to urban areas, and are forced to face the difficulties associated with that type of transition.

In the 1986 elections, the Umma Party lost several seats to the Nuba Mountains General Union and to the Sudan National Party, due to the reduced level of support from the Nuba Mountains region. There is reason to believe that attacks by the government-supported militia, the Popular Defense Force (PDF), on several

---

[23] 1. Heiban languages (also called Koalib, Koalib-Moro)
   2. Talodi languages (also called Talodi-Masakin, Lafofa)
   3. Rashad languages (Tegali-Tagoi)
   4. Katla languages

Nuba villages were meant to be in retaliation for this drop in support, which was seen as signalling increased support of the SPLA. The PDF attacks were particularly violent in nature, and have been cited as examples of crimes against humanity that took place during the Second Sudanese Civil War.

The Fur, who number more than 700,000, live in western Sudan, primarily on the plains and foothills surrounding the volcanic mountain Jebel Marra in the Region (province) calledafter their tribes name. In 1994, Dar Fur was divided into three federal states within Sudan: Northern (*Shamal*), Southern (*Janub*), and Western (*Gharb*) Dar Fur. Northern Dar Fur's capital is Al Fashir; Southern Dar Fur's is Nyala; and Wester Dar Fur's is Geneina. The division was the idea of Ali al Haj, Minister of Federal Affairs, who hoped that by dividing the Fur so they did not form a majority in any state that it would allow Islamist candidates to be elected. Dar Fur was ruled until 1916 by an independent sultanate. The Fur are politically and culturally oriented to peoples in Chad, they are sedentary, cultivating people long settled in and around the Jabal Marrah. Some have migrated to cities and towns in order to find jobs, but most are farmers, cultivating both food for their families and cash crops that will enable them to buy items such as cloth, shoes, tea, and sugar.The recorded history of Dar Fur begins in the 14th century with the establishment of a Tunjur sultanate. Independent Dar Fur reached a height as the Keira dynasty began in the seventeenth century. In 1875, the Anglo-Egyptian Condominium in Khartoum ended the dynasty. The British allowed Dar Fur a measure of autonomy until formal annexation in 1916. However, the region remained underdeveloped through the period of colonization and into independence in 1956. The majority of national resources were directed toward the riverine Arabs clustered along the Nile near Khartoum. This pattern of structural inequality and underdevelopment resulted in increasing restiveness among Dar Furis. The influence of regional geopolitics and war by proxy, coupled with economic hardship and environmental degradation, from soon after independence led to sporadic armed resistance from the mid-1980s. The continued violence culminated in an armed resistance movement around 2003.

Developments in the Dar Fur region are dependent on the terrain and climate, Dar Fur being composed mostly of semi-arid plains that cannot support a dense population. The one exception is the area in and around the Jebal Marra Mountain. It was from bases in these mountains that a series of groups expanded to control the region.

The Daju, inhabitants of Jebel Marra, appear to have been the dominant group in Dar Fur in the earliest period recorded. How long they ruled is uncertain, little being known of them save a list of kings. According to tradition the Daju dynasty was displaced, and Islam introduced, about the 14th century, by the Tunjur, who reached Dar Fur by way of Bornu and Wadai. The first Tunjur king is said to have been Ahmed el-Makur, who married the daughter of the last Daju monarch. Ahmed reduced many chiefs to submission, and under him the country prospered.

His great-grandson, the sultan Dali, a celebrated figure in Dar Fur histories, was on his mother's side a Fur, and thus brought the dynasty closer to the people it ruled. Dali divided the country into provinces, and established a penal code, which, under the title of Kitab Dali or Dali's Book, is still preserved, and differs in some respects from Quranic law. His grandson Soleiman (usually distinguished by the Fur epithet Solon, the Arab or the Red) reigned from c.1596 to c.1637, and was a great warrior and a devoted Muslim; he is considered as the founder of the Keira dynasty.

Soleiman's grandson, Ahmed Bukr (c.1682-c.1722), made Islam the religion of the state, and increased the prosperity of the country by encouraging immigration from Bornu and Bagirmi. His rule extended east of the Nile as far as the banks of the Atbara. The death of Bukr initiated a long running conflict over the succession. On his death bed Bukr stated that each of his many sons should rule in turn. Once on the throne each of his sons instead hoped to make their own son heir, leading to an intermittent civil war that lasted until 1785/6 (AH 1200) Due to these internal divisions Dar Fur declined in importance and engaged in wars with Sennar and Wadai.

One of the most capable of the monarchs during this period was Sultan Mohammed Terab, one of Ahmad Bukr's sons. He led a number of successful campaigns. In 1785/6 (AH 1200) he led an army against the Funj, but got no further than Omdurman. Here he was stopped by the Nile, and found no means of getting his army across the river. Unwilling to give up his project, Terab remained at Omdurman for months and the army began to grow disaffected. According to some stories Tayrab was poisoned by his wife at the instigation of disaffected chiefs, and the army returned to Dar Fur. While he tried to have his son succeed him, the throne instead went to his brother Abd al-Rahman.

Abdel-Rahman, surnamed el-Rashid or the Just. It was during his reign that Napoleon Bonaparte was campaigning in Egypt; and in 1799 Abd-er-Rahman wrote to congratulate the French general on his defeat of the Mamluks. To this Bonaparte replied by asking the sultan to send him by the next caravan 2000 black slaves upwards of sixteen years old, strong and vigorous. Abd-er-Rahman also established a new capital at Al Fashir, the royal township, which he established as capital in 1791, the capital had formerly been at a place called Kobb.

Mohammed-el-Fadhl, his son, was for some time under the control of an energetic eunuch, Mohammed Kurra, but he ultimately made himself independent, and his reign lasted till 1838, when he died of leprosy. He devoted himself largely to the subjection of the semi-independent Arab tribes who lived in the country, notably the Rizeigat, thousands of whom he slew. In 1821 he lost the province of Kordofan, which in that year was conquered by the Egyptians ordered to conquer the Sudan by Mehemet Ali. The Keira dispatched an army but it was routed by the Egyptians near Bara on August 19, 1821. The Egyptians had been intending to conquer the entirety of Dar Fur, but their difficulties consolidating their hold on the Nile region forced them to abandon these plans.

Al-Fadl died in 1838 and of his forty sons, the third, Mohammed Hassan, was appointed his successor. Hassan is described as a religious but avaricious man. In 1856 he went blind and for the rest of his reign his sister Zamzam, the iiry bassi, was the de facto ruler of the sultanate.

Beginning in 1856 a Khartoum businessman al-Zubayr Rahma began to set up operations in the land south of Dar Fur. He set up a network of trading posts defended by well-armed forces and soon had a sprawling state under his rule. This area known as the Bahr el Ghazal had long been the source of the goods that Dar Fur would trade to Egypt and North Africa, especially slaves and ivory. The natives of Bahr el Ghazal paid tribute to Dar Fur, and these were the chief articles of merchandise sold by the Dar Furians to the Egyptian traders along the road to Asyut. Al-Zubayr redirected this flow of goods to Khartoum and the Nile.

Hassan died in 1873 and the succession passed to his youngest son Ibrahim, who soon found himself engaged in a conflict with al-Zubayr. Al-Zubayr, after earlier conflicts with the Egyptians, had become their ally and in cooperation with them agreed to conquer Dar Fur. The war resulted in the destruction of the kingdom. Ibrahim was slain in battle in the autumn of 1874, and his uncle Hassab Alla, who sought to maintain the independence of his country, was captured in 1875 by the troops of the khedive, and removed to Cairo with his family.

The Dar Furians were restive under Egyptian rule (under colonization by the British Empire). Various revolts were suppressed, but in 1879 the British General Gordon (then governor-general of the Sudan) suggested the reinstatement of the ancient royal family. This was not done, and in 1881 Slatin Bey (Sir Rudolf von Slatin) was made governor of the province. Slatin defended the province against the forces of the self-proclaimed Mahdi Muhammad Ahmad, who were led by a Rizeigat sheik named Madibbo, but was obliged to surrender (December 1883), and Dar Fur was incorporated in the Mahdi's dominions. The Dar Furians found his rule as irksome as that of the Egyptians had been, and a state of almost constant warfare ended in the gradual retirement of the Mahdi's forces from Dar Fur. Ahmad's successor, Abdallahi ibn Muhammad, was a Dar Furi of the minor Ta'isha tribe of cattle-herders. Abdallahi forced warriors of the Western tribes to move to the capital Omdurman and fight for him, sparking rebellions by the Rizeigat and Kababish nomads. Following the overthrow of Abdallahi at Omdurman in 1898, the new (Anglo-Egyptian) Sudan government recognized (1899) Ali Dinar, a grandson of Mohammed-el-Fadhl, as sultan of Dar Fur, on the payment by that chief of an annual tribute of 500 British Pounds. Under Ali Dinar, who during the Mahdi's era had been kept a prisoner in Omdurman, Dar Fur enjoyed a period of peace and a de facto return to independence.

However, the British allowed Dar Fur *de jure* autonomy until they convinced themselves during World War I that the sultanate was falling under the influence of Turkey, invaded, and incorporated the region into Sudan in 1916.

During Anglo-Egyptian period, the bulk of resources were devoted toward Khartoum and Blue Nile Province, leaving the rest of the country relatively undeveloped. The inhabitants of the riverine states, referred to themselves as the *awlad al-beled* ("children of the country") in pride over their primary role and referred to the Westerners as *awlad al-gharb* ("children of the west"), an implicit slur. Meanwhile, the "Africans" were pejoratively known as *zurga* ("Blacks"). Over the course of the Condominium, 56% of all investment occurred in Khartoum, Kassala and Northern Province versus 17% for both Kordofanand Dar Fur, resulting in about 5-6% in Dar Fur as Kordofanreceived the bulk of funds in the West. This was despite the provinces in the Nile Valley having a population of 2.3 million versus 3 million people in the West. Dar Fur, like the rest of Sudan outside the Nile Valley, remained an undeveloped backwater even as independence was achieved in 1956.

After independence, it became a major power base for the Umma Party, led by Sadiq al-Mahdi. By the 1960s, some Dar Furis were beginning to question the neglect of the region by the Umma, despite their consistent political support. Disillusionment with the religious sect based parties, Khatmiyya Sufi/Democratic Unionist Party in the East and Ansar/Umma in the West, led to a temporary rise of regionally-based parties, including the Dar Fur Development Front (DDF). During the discussions of the proposed Islamic constitution proposed by Hassan al-Turabi, Muslims from Dar Fur, the Nuba Mountains and the Red Sea Hills joined the Southerners in opposition, perceiving the constitution as a ploy by the center to consolidate their dominance of the marginalized regions. The fracturing of the Umma led to the first political demagoguery attempting to split the "Africans" from the "Arabs" in the 1968 elections, a difficult task as they were substantially intermarried and could not be distinguished by skin tone. Sadiq al-Mahdi, calculating that the Fur and other "African" tribes formed a majority of the electorate, allied with the DDF in blaming "the Arabs" for Dar Fur's neglect. This left Sadiq's opponent, his uncle Iman al-Hadi, courting Baggara using the rhetoric of "Arabism" to offer hope of somehow being a part of the wealthy center.

To this underdevelopment and domestic political tension was added cross-border instability with Chad. Premiere al-Mahdi allowed FROLINAT, the guerilla movement trying to overthrow Chadian President François Tombalbaye, to establish rear bases in Dar Fur in 1969. However, FROLINAT factional infighting killed dozens within Dar Fur in 1971, leading Sudanese President Gaafar Nimeiry to expel the group. This was further complicated by the interest of new Libyan President Muammar al-Gaddafi in the Chadian conflict. Obsessed with the vision of creating a band of Sahelian nations that were both Muslim and culturally Arab, Gaddafi made an offer to Nimeiry to merge their two countries in 1971. However, Gaddafi was disillusioned with Nimeiry's Arab credentials after the Sudanese president signed the 1972 Addis Ababa Agreement, ending the First Sudanese Civil War with the South. Libya claimed the Aozou Strip, began supporting the FROLINAT against the black Christian Tombalbaye, and supporting racist and Arab supremacist militants to achieve his goals by force, including the Arab Union in Dar Fur, which claimed the province to have an "Arab" nature. Nimeiry, concerned by the warm welcome Gaddafi had given to al-Mahdi, his exiled opposition, began to encourage the fragile administration of Félix Malloum, the new Chadian president after Tombalbaye's 1975 assassination. In retaliation, Gaddafi sent a 1200-man force across the desert to assault Khartoum directly. The Libyan force was barely defeated after three days of house to house fighting and Nimeiry chose to support the most anti-Libyan of the various Chadian leaders, Hissène Habré, giving his Armed Forces of the North sanctuary in Dar Fur. All of these external events buffeted the traditional structure of Dar Furi society. Tribes that had seen themselves in local terms were asked to declare if they were "progressive, revolutionary Arabs" or "reactionary, anti-Arab Africans". The Khartoum government, rather than trying to calm these new ethnic tensions, instead exacerbated them when it seemed useful in the Sudan-Libya-Chad struggle.

In 1979, Nimeiry appointed to Dar Fur the only provincial governor who was not of the local population. The appointment of a Nile Valley *walad al-beled*, chosen to oversee the support to Habré, sparked riots by Dar Furi across Sudan in which three students were killed. Nimeiry relented due to fears that his anti-Libyan bases were being jeopardized.

In a longer term cycle, the gradual reduction in annual precipation, coupled with a growing population, had begun a cycle in which increased use of arable land along the southern edge of the Sahara increased the rate of desertification, which in turn increased the use of the remaining arable land. Drought from the mid-1970s to early 1980s led to massive immigration from northern Dar Fur and Chad into the central farming belt. In 1983 and 1984, the rains failed. When the Khartoum government refused to heed warnings of critical crop failure because they feared it would affect the administrations image abroad the Governor of the Fur-dominated administration in Dar Fur resigned in protest. The region was plunged into a horrific famine. When 60-80,000 Dar Furis walked across the country to Khartoum seeking food, the government declared them be Chadian refugees and trucked them to Kordofanin "Operation Glorious Return", only to see them walk back to Khartoum as there was no food in Kordofan. The famine killed an estimated 95,000 Dar Furis out of a population of 3.1 million and it was clear that the deaths had been entirely preventable. The incompetence of the regime, combined with the start of the Second Sudanese Civil War in 1983, proved unbearable for the country and Nimeiry was overthrown on 5 April 1985. Sadiq al-Mahdi came out of exile, making a deal with Gaddafi, which he had no intention of honoring, that he would turn over Dar Fur to Libya if he was supplied with the funds to win the upcoming elections.

Nimeiry had been heavily supported by the United States and the military junta that had taken power moved quickly to discontinue pro-American policies. Beginning in August 1985, Libya began sending military/humanitarian convoys from Benghazi, including an 800-strong military force that set up base in Al-Fashir and began arming the local Baggara tribes, whom Gaddafi considered to be his local Arab allies. By the time that Libyan relations with the United States had worsened so that American planes bombed Tripoli in April 1986, Libya was providing key logistical and air support to Sudanese offensives against the Sudan People's Liberation Army in the rebel South. Meanwhile, the famine had severely upset the structure of Dar Furi society. The farmers had claimed every available bit of land to farm or forage for food, closing off the traditional routes used by the herders. The herders, faced with watching their animals die of starvation in the desiccated landscape, tried to force the routes south open, attacking farmers who tried to block their path and shedding blood. Dar Fur was awash in small arms from the various neighbouring conflicts and stories spread of herders raiding farming villages for all of their animals or villagers who had armed themselves in self defense. To Dar Furis facing starvation, the dichotomous ideology of African versus Arab began to have explanatory power. Amongst some stationary Africans, the ideas that uncaring Arabs in Khartoum had let the famine happen and then Dar Furi Arabs armed by their Libyan allies had attacked African farmers began to gain credence. Similarly, semi-nomadic Dar Furi Arabs began to seriously consider that Africans had vindictively tried to punish them for the famine by trying to keep them from pastureland and that perhaps the difference between *awlad al-beled* and *awlad al-gharb* was not as great as between Arab and *zurga*.

In December 1991, a Sudan People's Liberation Army force that included Dar Furi Daud Bolad entered Dar Fur in the hopes of spreading the southern rebellion to the West. Before Bolad's force could reach the Marrah Mountains they were attacked by a combined force of regular army and Beni Halba militia mounted on horses. Dozens of Fur villages that had not resisted the SPLA force were burned in reprisal.

The primary crop is millet (dukhn), which is made into a thick porridge-like paste called *Asida*. The paste is eaten with a hot sauce normally made of vegetables, although meat may be added on special occasions. Beer brewed from dukhn (called *Araqi or Marisa*) is also an important part of the diet, and is used as payment for help with fieldwork, the work continues until the beer gives out. Livestock has played a small part in the subsistence of most Fur. Those who acquired a substantial herd of cattle could maintain it only by living like the neighbouring Baqqara Arabs, and those who persisted in this pattern eventually came to be thought of as Baqqara. Fur society is unique in that husband and wife remain separate units even after marriage. Each owns and looks after his or her own fields and storage units, and each disposes of his or her respective produce separately. A wife may cook and brew beer for her husband, but she does so out of his food storage, not hers, while she cooks for herself and her children out of her own supplies. In return, a husband may help his wife with work such as the terracing of fields (which is often done to prevent erosion) or the hauling of manure, but each spouse remains a separate economic unit. Villages vary in size from four or five households to 60 or more. People from the smaller villages travel to weekly markets in order to purchase supplies, but larger villages have their own market. Political power within the villages is usually determined by hereditary position. The village sheik, or religious leader, usually serves for life and is elected by villagers to represent them in relation to higher government appointed officials. Centuries ago, the old Fur sultans (political rulers) used to derive power from direct and indirect control of the trade of ebony, ivory, spices, rich cloth, slaves, and other goods from Dar Fur to Egypt over the so-called Forty Days Road (Darb al-Arba'een). Remarkably, the Fur maintained their independence until 1916, when the ruling sultan was defeated by the British and the province was politically integrated into Sudan. It is thought that Islam was introduced and accepted into Fur society because of the old sultanates, who granted privileges to Muslim immigrants, built mosques, and established Islamic education for boys. (Today, every boy goes to Koran school at the age of 8-10 to study Islam's holy book unless he is already in the government's formal school system.)

Although the ruling dynasty and the peoples of the area have long been Muslims, they have largely not been arabised. It is the Fur language that distinguishes this group from surrounding tribes. With the passage of time, however, many Fur are becoming increasingly arabised, especially those who move to the cities and regularly speak Sudanese Arabic, the language of politics, trade, and commerce.

Although they still practice traditional rituals, Islam has penetrated to the extent that the name of Allah is in addition to the names of tradional deities. Despite this Arabisation and Islamisation, though, the Fur continued to maintain cultural and political consciousness, and their traditions are still very much alive. Today, the

Fur are politically associated with Sudan yet still maintain their tribal solidarity and are committed Muslims who pride themselves on the fact that they brought Islam to the western part of Sudan.

Living on the plateau north of the Fur are a semi-nomadic people who call themselves Beri and are known to the Arabs as Zaghawa. The Zaghawa is an African ethnic group, mainly living in eastern Chad and western Sudan, including the Dar Fur province of Sudan. They are semi nomadic and obtain much of their livelihood through herding cattle, camels and sheep, and harvesting wild grains. Several centuries ago, they converted to Islam though they still maintain some of their religious traditions. They have their own language, which is also called Zaghawa, and the breed of sheep that they herd is also called Zaghawa. They, however, refer to themselves as the Beri, while the name Zaghawa was given to them by the nearby Arab peoples, and became more well-known. While they are not very powerful in Sudan, they politically dominate Chad. The current president, Idriss Déby and several former prime ministers of Chad are Zaghawa, as well as many other members of the government. The presidential's private army is also formed from Zaghawa. Several of the leaders of the Dar Fur armed movements, including Minni Arkoy Minawi (Sudan Liberation Army) and Khalil Ibrahim (Justice and Equality Movement) are Zaghawa. Large numbers of this group live in Chad. Herders of cattle, camels, sheep, and goats, the Zaghawa also make a substantial part of their livelihood by gathering wild grains and other products. Cultivation has become increasingly important but remains risky, and the people revert to gathering in times of drought. Converted to Islam, the Zaghawa nevertheless retain much of their traditional religious orientation. Another large group of African tribes scattered between Kordofanand Dar Fur came to be known as Fallata tribes. These tribes originally migrated from Chad to Sudan and include the Zaghawa, Masalit, Haussa, Fulani, and Berti. The most important peoples living in Dar Fur speaking Nilo-Saharan languages and at least nominally Muslim are the Masalit, Daju, and Berti. All are primarily cultivators living in permanent villages, but they also practice animal husbandry to varying degrees. The Masalit, living on the Sudan-Chad border, are the largest group. Historically under a minor sultanate, they are positioned between the two dominant sultanates of the area, Dar Fur (in Sudan) and Wadai (in Chad). A part of the territory they occupy had formerly been controlled by the Fur, but the Masalit gradually encroached upon it in the first half of the twentieth century in a series of local skirmishes carried out by villages on both sides, rather than the sultanates.

In 1990-91, much of Dar Fur was in a state of anarchy, with many villages being attacked. There were many instances in which Masalit militias attacked Fur and other villages. The Berti consists of two groups. One lives northeast of Al Fashir; the other migrated to eastern Dar Fur and western Kordofan provinces in the nineteenth century. The two Berti groups do not seem toshare a sense of common identity and interest. Members of the western group, in addition to cultivating subsistence crops and practicing animal husbandry, gather gum Arabic for sale in local markets. The Berti tongue has largely given way to Arabic as native language. The term Daju is a linguistic designation that is applied to a number of groups scattered from western Kordofan and south-western Dar Fur to eastern Chad. These groups call themselves by different names and exhibit no sense of common identity.

An estimated number of 1, 5 million people of West African origin are living in Sudan. Together, West Africans who have become Sudanese nationals and resident non-nationals from West Africa made up 6.5 percent of the Sudanese population in the mid-1970s; West Africans had been estimated at more than 10 percent of the population of the Northern provinces. Some are descendants of peoples who had arrived five or more generations earlier; others are recent immigrants. Some had come in self-imposed exile, unable to adjust to the colonial power in their homeland. Others had been pilgrims to Mecca, settling either en route or on their return. Many arrived over decades in the course of the great dispersion of the nomadic Fulani; others arrived, particularly after World War 11, as rural and urban labourers or to take up land as peasant cultivators. Nearly 60 percent of the people included in the West African category are said to be of Nigerian origin (locally called Borno after the Nigerian emirate that was their homeland). Given Hausa dominance in northern Nigeria and the widespread use of their language there and elsewhere, some non-Hausa might also be called Hausa and describe themselves as such. The Hausa themselves, however, particularly those long in Sudan, prefer to be called Takari. The Fulani, even more widely dispersed throughout West Africa, may have originated in countries other than Nigeria. Typically, the term applied to the Fulani in Sudan is Fallata, but Sudanese also use that term for other West Africans. The Fulani nomads are found in many parts of central Sudan, from Dar Fur to the Blue Nile, and they occasionally compete with indigenous populations for pasturage. In Dar Fur, groups of Fulani origin have adapted in various ways to the presence of the Baggara tribes. Some have retained all aspects of their culture and language. A few have become much like the Baqqara in language and in other respects, although they have tended to retain their own breeds of cattle and ways of handling them.

Some of the Fulani groups in the eastern states are sedentary, descendants of sedentary Fulani of the ruling group in northern Nigeria.

According to Human Rights Watch, hostilities broke out in West Dar Fur in 1998. The 1998 clashes were relatively minor, but more than 5000 Masalit were displaced. Clashes resumed in 1999 when nomadic herdsmen again moved south earlier than usual.

The 1999 clashes were bloodier, with many hundreds killed, including a number of Arab tribal chiefs. The government brought in military forces in an attempt to quell the violence and took direct control of security. A reconciliation conference held in 1999 agreed on compensation. Many Masalit intellectuals and notables were arrested, imprisoned, and tortured in the towns as government-supported Arab militias began to attack Masalit villages; a number of Arab chiefs and civilians were also killed in these clashes.

In 2000, an unknown group published the *Black Book*, a dissident manuscript detailing that domination of the north and the impoverishment the other regions. It was widely discussed, despite attempts to censor it, and many of the writers went on to help found the rebel Justice and Equality Movement.

The region became the scene of a rebellion in 2003 against the Sudanese government, with two local rebel groups—the Justice and Equality Movement (JEM) and the Sudanese Liberation Army (SLA)—accusing the government of oppressing non-Arabs in favor of Arabs. The government was also accused of neglecting the Dar Fur region of Sudan. In response, the government mounted a campaign of aerial bombardment supporting ground attacks by an Arab militia, the Janjaweed. The Janjaweed were accused of committing major human rights violations, including mass killing, looting, and systematic rape of the non-Arab population of Dar Fur. They have frequently burned down whole villages, driving the surviving inhabitants to flee to refugee camps, mainly in Dar Fur and Chad; many of the camps in Dar Fur are surrounded by Janjaweed forces. By the summer of 2004, 50,000 to 80,000 people had been killed and at least a million had been driven from their homes, causing a major humanitarian crisis in the region.

On September 18, 2004, the UN Security Council passed Resolution 1564, which called for a Commission of Inquiry on Dar Fur to assess the Sudanese conflict. On January 31, 2005, the UN released a 176-Page report saying that while there were mass murders and rapes, they could not label it as genocide because "genocidal intent appears to be missing".

In May 2006 the main rebel group, the Sudanese Liberation Movement, agreed to a draft peace agreement with the Sudanese government. On May 5th, the agreement, drafted in Abuja, Nigeria, was signed by both sides.

The on May, 5, 2006 signed agreement between the Sudanese government and Sudan Liberation Army, the main African rebel group in Dar Fur, in Abuja, Nigeria to end the ethnic fighting there is "nearly dead. Since its signing, the Dar Fur peace agreement has been violated day after day, week after week," UN special envoy for Sudan Jan Pronk told an open meeting of the UN Security Council. Rape has become "a tool of terror," used frequently by attackers who show no mercy towards women and children. He said villages were bombed at night and government helicopters were flown to support the Sudanese Armed

Forces. Despite the signing of a peace agreement, violence has escalated. While the government and rebels have clashed and attacks on civilians have continued in certain areas of Dar Fur, fighting between different branches of the rebellion has increased, plunging Dar Fur into deeper insecurity.

As a consequence, over 2 million people in Dar Fur remain trapped in camps for Internally Displaced Persons, civilians "too scared to return to their homes and continue to live in camps that amount to open-air jails." And the camps themselves are increasingly dangerous, with a growing prevalence of weapons, the presence of rebels soldiers, and deadly incursions into the camps by Khartoum's Janjaweed militia proxy.

At the same time, the Dar Fur Peace Agreement of May 5, 2006 has collapsed completely, even as Khartoum has made clear that it has no intention of re-starting or re-energizing the peace process. From the Sudan Tribune:

Nafie Ali Nafie who is assistant to the Sudanese President and Deputy Chairman of the ruling National Congress Party (the renamed National Islamic Front), pointed out that the file of negotiation on Dar Fur was closed finally, and will never be opened again whatever the reasons are.

And although the fatuous Jan Pronk, Kofi Annan's special representative to Sudan, declared that "Sudan has left a 'tiny' window open for negotiation on accepting UN troops in its violent Dar Fur region, this claim has no meaningful basis. Pronk could only point to an expedient statement made by Khartoum's Foreign Minister, Lam Akol at the Brussels donors meeting for the African Union force in Dar Fur:

The minister of foreign affairs declared in Brussels that the decision on deployment of a UN force has not yet been taken. Sudanese government stressed that Nafie Ali Nafie and Omar el-Bashir speak much more authoritatively for the National Islamic Front regime than Lam Akol, the lapdog "Foreign Minister from the southern SPLM and that Pronk would attempt to use statements by the powerless Lam Akol as a sign of encouragement for the possibility of UN deployment.

Although Khartoum's culpability in this renewed act of war is patent here, the chaotic nature of the fighting and the factionalizing of the combatants needs some clarification, particularly as this factionalized fighting on the part of the Dar Furi insurgency movements is now a primary source of insecurity throughout Dar Fur.

The main fighting elements of the National Redemption Force (NRF) in North Dar Fur are those of the Sudan Liberation Army faction know as SLA-United, or SLA-G19 after the 19 SLA commanders who split from Abdel Wahid el-Nur. Abdel Wahid is the SLA leader who did not sign the Abuja agreement and who shows signs of both political and military weakness and increasing isolation Because he is a Fur, however, the largest ethnic group in Dar Fur, he retains considerable significance in any peace or reconciliation effort. Abdel Wahid's primary military base is in the rugged Jebel Marra area in central Dar Fur.

SLA-United/SLA-G19 enjoys considerable popular support and has gained military control over virtually all territory north of el-Fasher in North Dar Fur, having defeated the forces of yet another SLA faction, that of Minni Minawi, who did sign the Abjua accord and is widely reviled by Dar Furis, even those in his own Zaghawa tribe. It is Minawi who has been receiving military support directly from Khartoum in his attacks on civilians in North Dar Fur in a desperate bid to regain his previous control of the area. Minawi is slated to become the fourth-ranking member of the National Islamic Front Government of National Unity, with the title of Presidential Assistant. Minni Minawi does not control North Dar Fur; the group SLA/United-SLA/G19 that does control the northern part of North Dar Fur is accusing the African Union (AU) of supporting the Government of Sudan and Minni Minawi. In an attempt to open a dialogue between the AU and those who control the territory (in order to facilitate access for nongovernmental humanitarian organizations), SLA-United/SLA-G19 agreed to meet with political figures from the AU in their own territory. But while the meeting was convening, the Government of Sudan sent 10 vehicles with armor and heavy weaponry in the direction of the meeting. This intelligence came even as one rebel commander was criticizing the AU for cooperating with the Government of Sudan.

The obvious implication is that the AU tipped off Khartoum's forces as to the location of the meeting. Minni Minawi's forces in the south of Dar Fur are in disarray, entering IDP camps, threatening them, beating them, and looting their property. In el-Fasher Minawi's forces are roaming the town drunken and spending their time with prostitutes. In Khartoum Minawi is fully controlled by the National Congress Party and those who object to this are expelled from Minawi's SLA faction. Cooperation between Minawi and the Government of Sudan in the most recent fighting in North Dar Fur is very clear: Government of Sudan trucks were captured, supply orders were found, and Government of Sudan soldiers are being held as prisoners of war, and have been shown to the International Committee of the Red Cross. Some Government of Sudan soldiers were from Southern Sudan and they were brought by Khartoum to train Minawi soldiers on new heavy artillery made and supplied by the Government of Sudan.

The US is banking on a loser in Minni Minawi, and by the time he returns from the US where he recently met with President Bush and Secretary of State Condoleezza Rice, he will be at a total loss, without forces, political support, or land under his control.

Violence is getting worse, as are banditry and Janjaweed activities. Minni Minawi has nothing north of el-Fasher and his official story is that he lost the area because of Chadian supporting mercenaries the same sort of excuses the NIF is using to explain its military actions in the area.

The remaining troops loyal to Minawi are out of control. They are entering Internally Displaced Persons camps in their vicinity, and armed. Last week they entered ZamZam camp, 17 kilometers south of el-Fasher and arrested 15 civilians claiming that they were soldiers with them who escaped military service. They entered a girls' school, and harassed the girls inside classes; when the teacher complained she was beaten and they told her that they can do anything they wish to her.

All the people in Dar Fur view Minni Minawi as a criminal, and no one knows why the United States wants to have anything to do with him. It is another disaster for US policy. Refugees International does much to confirm the irresponsible nature of violence on the part of the US government's new "partner for peace in Dar Fur. From their recent report:

Leaders from within Minawi's own tribe have separated from him, leading to intra-Zaghawa fighting as well. While Minawi and his soldiers deny responsibility for the violence in Tawilla, west of el-Fasher in North Dar Fur, and other towns in the region, a group of sheikhs said that they knew that Minawi's troops were involved because they recognized the attackers as their neighbors. Another sheikh reported that when his town was being attacked, his people were told that the soldiers would kill half of those who were against Minni Minawi in order to urge the other half to follow. Other victims from the region have said that the attackers announced they had arrived to enforce the peace.

A spokesperson for the SLA-Minawi faction told Refugees International, that they want peace and to punish the people who don't want peace. One woman in the Tawilla camp described the nature of these punishments. She said that hundreds of Minawi's soldiers entered her village and started shooting. They went inside the houses one by one shooting the men, including her husband, and beating or raping the women and girls. The soldiers took whatever they could find clothing, shoes, money, livestock. Her story is remarkably consistent with thousands of others in the region that detail targeted executions of men and violent, forced displacement.

The camp residents, an overwhelming number of whom are women, agree that the situation has deteriorated since the signing of the Dar Fur Peace Agreement. One sheikh said, 'There is no peace in Dar Fur. Our situation is worse now than ever and this is why no one supports the Dar Fur Peace Agreement. A woman pointed out that at least the Janjaweed would leave after attacking and looting a village, but Minawi's SLA faction has stayed to control the area and terrorize the population. The women are afraid to walk the few hundred meters into the town market during the day for fear that they will be attacked. An elderly grandmother was beaten just a few days ago, allegedly by Minawi's troops, when she tried to return to her farm to begin planting. The soldiers told her that this was an example of what would happen to the residents who tried to farm.

Dar Fur rebel groups that have not signed the peace agreement have splintered and realigned, creating alliances and divisions that have made the conflict more complex and dangerous. Elements of a faction of the Sudan Liberation Army and the Justice and Equality Movement, an Islamist group, have formed the National Redemption Front.

The US, in its inexcusable haste to ram through a peace agreement in Dar Fur, did not care that in the end the only signatories were Khartoum's genocidaires and the murderous Minni Minawi. The picture of President Bush and the soon-to-be Presidential Assistant Minni Minawi of the National Islamic Front makes a mockery of the Bush administration genocide determination for Dar Fur, and the President's consistently glib invocation of the word.

UN and humanitarian workers were harassed and their movement curtailed, he said. A total of 12 workers were killed in the last two months. A leading humanitarian agency called for warring parties to respect the provision of medical care to people in western Sudan's Dar Fur region. Increased insecurity has forced Medecins Sans Frontieres on August 04, 2006, an independent international medical relief organization, to suspend its medical assistance activities, leaving thousands of patients untreated each day.

MSF field workers have been attacked on at least four separate occasions since July 14. Vehicles, including ambulances, have been shot at and staff were beaten and robbed. Such incidents have led to the evacuation of a number of MSF teams operating in the region, interrupting mobile clinics and hampering the transferal of emergency patients. MSF teams have worked in Dar Fur since 2003, providing medical consultations, surgery, emergency referrals and nutritional programs. The United Nations and African Union condemned the Sudanese army and Janjaweed militias for attacking rebels in Dar Fur's Jebel Moon area. This marked the first time since the latest peace deal that the Sudanese army has been confirmed as fighting there. On August 21, 2006 Two African Union peacekeepers were killed and three wounded when their convoy was ambushed in Sudan's Dar Fur region. A group of unidentified armed men attacked an AU fuel convoy traveling to the African Union's headquarters of El Fasher in North Dar Fur. The increased fighting and the attacks against aid workers means it is harder for those who remain to direct humanitarian assistance to those in need. As many as 1.6 million people were now inaccessible. The UN World Food Programme (WFP) said that funding shortages could force cuts to the rations now going to 6 million people in Dar Fur and warned that this would lead to nutritional degradation.

The African Union peacekeeping force that is supposed to monitor the peace agreement is running out of money and unable to protect itself, much less civilians. Two Rwandan soldiers were killed when a convoy of fuel tankers they were escorting came under attack. Attacks on aid workers have put hundreds of thousands of people beyond the reach of food, medicine and clean water supplies, according to the United Nations. Last month nine aid workers were killed in Dar Fur, more than in the entire conflict before then. An international aid group said sexual assaults have risen dramatically at a large camp for displaced persons in Sudan's troubled Dar Fur region. The New York-based International Rescue Committee said more than 200 women have been sexually assaulted at the Kalma refugee camp. The committee said it is used to hearing about just two to four incidents of sexual assaults at the camp per month.

A committee spokesman said the figures are a sign of deteriorating security in the war-ravaged region. A civil war that began in 2003 has degenerated into chaotic violence that has killed an estimated 200,000 people and displaced two million others. Sudanese children in Dar Fur and southern Sudan continue to face threats to their safety including recruitment into armed forces and sexual abuse. Rebel groups, including the Sudanese Liberation Army (SLA) and Chadian opposition forces, along with janjaweed militia in Sudan's embattled western Dar Fur region are widely reported to be recruiting boys under the age of 18 to serve in their ranks. It is estimated that thousands of children are still associated with armed forces and groups in Dar Fur and were actively involved in conflict between May and July 2006.

THE ARMED CONFLICTS IN SUDAN AFTER INDEPENDENCE

The after independence years have seen many unrest periods and rash changes of governments in Sudan.[24] Although most military coups came to power through armed force but they weren't ethnically motivated and consequently don't fall under the category ethnical but they are somehow armed conflicts. Military coups in Sudan began with Ibrahim Abbud's coup on November 1958.[25] The ethnical outcome of such coups was to be seen later. As Abbud's government sought to arabise the south and in 1964 expelled all western missionaries. This led to open civil war in the mid-1960s and the rise of various southern resistance groups, the most powerful of which were the Anya Nya guerrillas, who sought autonomy marking the beginning of a long running north-south civil war.

The resulting conflict was known as the civil war and lasted from 1955 to 1972. In 1972, the Addis Ababa Agreement led to a cessation of the north-south civil war and a degree of self-rule. This led to a ten-year hiatus in the civil war. Under the Addis Ababa Agreement Southern Sudan was given considerable autonomy.

In 1983 the civil war was reignited following President Gaafar Nimeiry's decision to circumvent the Addis Ababa Agreement. President Gaafar Nimeiry attempted to create a Federated Sudan including states in Southern Sudan, which violated the Addis Ababa Agreement which had granted the South considerable autonomy. The Sudan People's Liberation Army formed in May 1983 as a result. Finally, in June 1983, the Sudanese Government under President Gaafar Nimeiry abrogated the

---

[24] Sudan has experienced after its independence on 1956 and till now, more than 9 different civil and military governments with different live periods.

[25] Lit. General Ibrahim Ahmed Abbud and a collective body known as the Supreme Council of the Armed Forces made an end for Sudan's first civil government.

Addis Ababa Peace Agreement. The situation was exacerbated after President Gaafar Nimeiry went on to implement Sharia Law in September of the same year.

The civil war went for more than 20 years, resulting in the deaths of 2.2 million Christians and Animists, and displacing roughly 4.5 million people within Sudan and into neighbouring countries. It damaged Sudan's economy and led to food shortages, resulting in starvation and malnutrition. The lack of investment during this time, particularly in the south, meant a generation lost access to basic health services, education, and jobs.

The negotiations between Sudanes governmnet and SPLAM/A started already on 20 July 2002 in Nairobi-Kenya where the delegation of the Government of the Sudan successfully concluded on 20 July 2002 the prescribed peace negotiations with "Sudan People's Liberation Movement Army SPLM/A under the supervisor of the IGAD which has been closed by issuing the Machakos protocol. The two parties have achieved substantial progress by reaching to agreement on the previously outstanding contentions issues. They agreed to proceed with the positive outcome and framework and to resume negotiations on next August 2002. Machakos protocol included following points:

1. The Government of Sudan (GoS), the Sudan People's Liberation Movement/ Army (SPLM/A) thereafter referred to as the parties met in Mechakos, Kenya, from 18th June to 20th July, 2002, under the auspices of the IGAD peace process.

The meeting was chaired by Lt. Gen. Lazaro Sumbeiyua, the special envoy of the IGAD peace process in Sudan with assistance of the IGAD sub-committee's envoys, namely H.E Mohamed Omaro of Eritrea, H.E. Murad Musa of Ethiopia, H.E. Francis Butagaria of Uganda, and observors from Italy, the United Kingdom, Norway and the United States of America.

2. The parties agreed to conduct discussions in accordance with an agenda based on the framework of the IGAD Declaration of Principles (DOP) and with a view to resolving the long-standing conflict that has afflicted the Sudan.

3. The parties agreed that a peaceful and just resolution based on the unity of the Sudan is their common objective, and that a military solution is neither viable nor desirable. They agreed to discuss the outstanding issues of state and religion, self-determination for the people of south Sudan, power sharing, wealth sharing and human rights.

4. After lengthy discussion, the parties agreed to a single negotiating framework document, which states the principles to which the parties have already agreed, the transitional phase of the peace process and the political structures to be implemented through a constitutional framework.

5. The parties made substantial progress and specifically reached agreement on the two most contentious issues, namely:-the right to self-determination for the

people of south Sudan, and the state and religion. The parties also agreed on the preamble, principles and the transition process from the framework mentioned above, all of which will be incorporated into a final comprehensive peace agreement. They also signed a protocol and initialed the specific texts on these issues.

6. The parties agreed to continue negotiations on the other outstanding issues of power sharing, wealth sharing, human rights and cease-fire when negotiations resume in mid August 2002.

Peace talks between the southern rebels and the government made substantial progress in 2003 and early 2004. The peace was consolidated with the official signing by both sides of the Naivasha treaty on 9 January 2005, granting Southern Sudan autonomy for six years, to be followed by a referendum about independence. It created a co-vice president position and allowed the north and south to split oil equally, but also left both the North's and South's armies in place. John Garang, the south's elected co-vice president died in a helicopter crash on August 1, 2005, three weeks after being sworn in. This resulted in riots, but the peace was eventually able to continue.

The United Nations Mission in Sudan (UNMIS) was established under UN Security Council Resolution 1590 of March 24, 2005. Its mandate is to support implementation of the Comprehensive Peace Agreement, and to perform functions relating to humanitarian assistance, and protection and promotion of human rights.[26]

---

[26] "MACHAKOS PROTOCOL" 20TH JULY 2002

Whereas the Government of the Republic of the Sudan and the Sudan People's Liberation Movement/Sudan People's Liberation Army (the parties) having met in Machakos, Kenya, from 18 June 2002 through 20 July 2002 under the auspices of the IGAD Peace Process; and

Whereas the parties reiterated their commitment to a negotiated, peaceful comprehensive resolution to the Sudan conflict within the unity of Sudan; and

Whereas the parties discussed at length and agreed on a broad framework which sets forth the principles of governance, the general procedures to be followed during the transitional process and the structures of government to be created under legal and constitutional arrangements to be established; and

Now record that the parties have agreed to negotiate and elaborate in greater detail the specific terms of this framework, including aspects not covered in this phase of the negotiations, as part of the overall Peace Agreement; and

Further record that within the above context, the parties have reached specific agreement on the right to self-determination for the people of South Sudan, State and Religion, as well as the preamble, principles, and the transition process from the draft framework, the

The UN Security Council extended on Sept 22, 2006 the mandate of the UN force deployed in southern Sudan for two weeks, to allow more time for continued world pressure on Khartoum to accept a UN takeover of peacekeeping in Dar Fur. The 15-member council unanimously adopted a resolution extending the mandate of the 12,273-strong force known as UNMIS, which was due to expire on Sept. 24, 2006 Sunday, with the intention to renew it for further periods. US Ambassador to the UN John Bolton said ahead of the vote that the purpose of the two-week extension was to gain more time to build up momentum for pressure on the government in Khartoum to accept to accept the inevitability of a UN peacekeeping force" in its strife-torn western Dar Fur region. The Security Council plans to replace the African Union force (AMIS) through the better equipped UNMIS.

Before the signing of the peace accord in January, political analysts had been warned of a possible attempt to undermine the agreement if the estimated 36 armed and political groups operating in the south were excluded from the negotiations.
However, both the government and SPLM/A had ignored appeals to include the militias in the talks, mediated by the Inter-governmental Authority on Development (IGAD). IGAD comprises Kenya, Uganda, Ethiopia, Eritrea, Djibouti, Sudan, Eritrea, and Somalia.

At the conference held on April 21, 2005, however, officials gave conflicting reasons why pro-government militias did not attend the four-day meeting aimed at persuading other southern Sudan groups to honour the Jan. 9 peace agreement between the main rebel force, the Sudan People's Liberation Movement, and the government. Officials from the government and the Sudan People's Liberation Movement said that pro-government militias were invited to attend but gave con-

---

initialed texts of which are annexed hereto, and all of which will be subsequently incorporated into the final agreement; and
It is agreed and confirmed that the parties shall resume negotiations in August, 2002 with the aim of resolving outstanding issues and realizing comprehensive peace in the Sudan.
(Signed) (Signed)
Dr. Ghazi Salahuddin Atabani
For: the Government of Sudan
Cdr.Salva Kiir
For:Sudan People's Liberation Movement/Army
WITNESSED BY: (Signed)
Lt. Gen. Lazaro K. Sumbeiywo
Special Envoy
IGAD Sudan Peace Process and on behalf of the IGAD Envoys"

flicting reasons. Gabriel Tanginya and Paulino Matib, who are also senior officers in the Sudanese army and control much of Upper Nile, the oil-rich state on the border with northern Sudan, failed to join the conference. Both men are known for their hatred of the rebel Sudan People's Liberation Movement/Army (SPLM/A) which signed a peace deal with the Islamic regime in Khartoum in January. While John Garang accused the government of Sudan of preventing the militia leaders from attending the conference, the Sudanese government denied Garang's claims. It said no instructions had been given to the militias not to attend the April 18-21 meeting.

Now a new conflict is threatening to start another war in Sudan. This time, it is as much about oil as it is ethnicity. Unequal distribution of oil revenues, bungled oil contracts, and differences in ethnic power sharing are creating new fault lines in an already divided country. The South Sudan Defense Front (SSDF), a former ally of the Khartoum government in its battle against the rebel Sudanese People's Liberation Army (SPLA), has threatened to attack SPLA positions once again. The group, formed by Riek Marchar, now vice president of the Government of South Sudan, complained that its people are not benefiting from oil revenues.

The Comprehensive Peace Agreement (CPA), signed in January 2005, requires Khartoum to channel 50 percent of oil revenues to the GOSS. The southern government must then commit 2 percent of the revenue to communities within the oil fields. But the SSDF says that is not happening.

Most of the oil fields fall within areas formerly controlled by the SSDF and inhabited by the Nuer. The peace agreement may be part of the problem. When the CPA was being negotiated, the SPLA was recognized as a sole representative of the interests of southern Sudan despite the presence of other armed groups in the region, including the SSDF.

According to Sudanese-based intelligence sources, the SSDF's attempted to join the CPA negotiations were thwarted when SPLA and U.S. delegates insisted that the rebel group was "part of Khartoum." It was understood that, once the CPA was signed, the SPLA-led administration would work to incorporate other armed and political groups into the government.

That process was disrupted in August, when John Garang, SPLA leader and GOSS president, died in a plane crash while returning from Uganda. The region's new leader, President Silva Kirr, continued the talks and, in January, got the SPLA and SSDF to sign the Juba Declaration.

The declaration was meant to fulfill the CPA provision for taking care of "Other Armed Groups," and requires both parties to protect the peace by continuing to integrate their armed forces and political parties into the government. Some SSDF officials, however, are not happy with the results of the negotiations. When senior

SSDF military commander Paulino Matip joined the SPLA, the SSDF viewed it as a defection and blamed President Kirr.

According to the SSDF external liaison office, that defection raised fears that dialogue would take a back seat in the new southern Sudan. The SSDF-SPLA relationship is further complicated by the reality that each of the groups predominantly represents the interests of a single ethnic group.

The SPLA (and, by extension, the GOSS) is dominated by members of the Dinka tribem while the SSDF is dominated by members of the Nuer tribe. Some smaller tribes have also joined the SSDF. Dinka-Nuer ethnic conflict is not new and continued even as Khartoum was exterminating the black population in the south. According to Human Rights Watch, a 1999 peace agreement ending eight years of Dinka-Nuer cross-border raids has failed to end the animosity.

These raids involved thousands of civilian casualties, large-scale theft of cattle, abduction of women and children, and destruction of hundreds of villages. In addition, says the human rights monitoring agency, the government in Khartoum only made this conflict worse by arming whichever faction or militia would fight the SPLA.

The peace agreement stipulates that 70 percent of the representatives of the southern government should come from the SPLA, 15 percent from the northern ruling National Democratic Party of President Umar al-Bashir, and 15 percent from other southern parties. In the eyes of some, this gives the oil-rich SSDF short shrift.

What's more, the failure by the southern government to dedicate 2 percent of oil revenues to surrounding communities is seen as discrimination against the Nuer people. David Chand, the deputy leader of the SSDF's political wing, said in an interview that while most of the oil fields are located in the Nuer land, the Dinka-dominated government is taking all the revenue. This is the bottom line. Groups like Global Witness have noted this in profiling the main actors of wars in Liberia, Sierra Leone, and Angola. In Sudan, that presence is Jarch Management Group, a firm based in the British Virgin Islands and Hong Kong.

For Jarch, however, it is not about resource plundering, but rather the recognition of a legitimate oil exploration contract signed by southern Sudan leaders. Those leaders have disowned the contract. Phil Heilberg, an American investor and the chairman of Jarch, says Paulino Matip Nhial, a former SSDF and current SPLA leader signed numerous agreements with Jarch for oil and gas exploration on March 1 and 7, 2004.

He said that several ministers, in addition to John Garang, were present. Further, according to Heilberg, the agreements included a provision stating that they "shall remain in force and survive if the SSDF joins forces with other groups in southern Sudan to form the GOSS." Heilberg notes that "Mr. Paulino and the GOSS have not enforced this clause, contrary to assurances from Mr. Paulino that he would, with the current president of the GOSS, Mr. Salva Kiir. Both the SPLA and the SSDF signed the agreements under the "right of self-determination" clause of the CPA and 1997's Khartoum Peace Agreement. Heilberg believes that, because of this, Jarch's contracts are valid. According to the documents held by Heilberg, in February 2003 the SPLA signed a contract with Jarch Management Group and its partners to allow exploration in an area called Block B.

In addition, this contract gave Jarch exclusive rights to all commodity contracts until 2009. Further, the SPLA was required to contact Jarch prior to any commodity deals. "Eighteen months after the signing of our agreement," lamented Hielberg, "the SPLM/A signed a contract with a public company called White Nile Ltd." "Jarch Capital," he continued, "considers the signing of this new deal a violation of the representations and warranties given by the SPLM/A, and a violation of the agreement as a whole."

He estimates that damages could exceed $10 billion. The Block B area in southern Sudan is also claimed in whole or part by Total, Petronas, White Nile, Moldova's Ascom Group, and Edge Petroleum. Jarch's expanding relationships with regional rebel groups is a factor to watch as reports emerge of armed clashes between the SPLA and the SSDF.

The company has strong relations with an Ethiopian rebel group known as the Ethiopian Unity Patriots' Army (EUPA) which operates from Sudan's eastern border with Ethiopia. Thowath Pal Chay, the EUPA's commander, sits on the newly constituted board of Jarch Management Group. Also on the board is David Chand, leader of the SSDF's political wing and professor at the University of Nebraska.

The SPLA has dismissed Jarch's claims, but is now retreating. According to media reports, the SPLA has asked Heilberg to bring his documents to the National Petroleum Commission so they may examine them to determine their validity. Internal GOSS Conflict In addition to oil, representation, and ethnic disputes, internal conflicts within the GOSS are resurfacing and threatening to erode what stability there has been.

Paulino Matip, who joined the government from the SSDF, has threatened to remove his 3000 fighters from the government if they are not given eight months of back pay before the end of the month. The SSDF's political office also claims that both Matip and current vice president Riek Marchar are negotiating a defection to the SSDF.

Analysts say such a move would weaken the GOSS. SSDF has asked Khartoum to stop oil revenue transfers to the GOSS and the international community to suspend $4.5 billion in pledged aid until further negotiations can take place.

The group, which has threatened to attack oil companies, says such moves are needed to avoid war in southern Sudan. For now, however, the SSDF is only waging propaganda war, printing t-shirts, and caps calling on oil companies to vacate their land.

The Sudanese government agreed to give autonomy to the region in the Comprehensive Peace Agreement signed on January 9, 2005 in Naivasha, Kenya with the SPLA/M, tentatively bringing an end to the Second Sudanese Civil War. Southern Sudan borders Ethiopia on the east, Kenya, Uganda, and the Democratic Republic of the Congo to the south, and the Central African Republic to the west. To the north lies the predominantly Arab and Muslim region directly under the control of the central government.[27]

The South-South Dialogue with southern political opposition groups launched in Nairobi in April was a positive step, but the late June negotiations with the SSDF fell short of an agreement. The recently concluded National Constitutional Review Commission failed to bring in most of the main northern opposition parties; they boycotted it as rigged in favour of the NCP and the SPLM, as well as the armed groups from the east and west. Recent deals signed by the SPLM to develop oil concessions in the South violate the CPA, have generated considerable criticism both from the government and within the SPLM itself, Khartoum's approach to oil has long been even more problematic, the IGAD has recommended to create the National Petroleum Commission called for in the CPA's Wealth Sharing Agreement so it can review all contracts signed in the past year. [28]

The CPA has no mechanism, however, for rapidly resolving disputes that have arisen over North-South boundaries in the oil areas and that promise at least to

---

[27] known as the Naivasha Agreement

[28] The January 2005 Comprehensive Peace Agreement (CPA) formally ended war between the Khartoum government and the insurgent Sudan People's Liberation Movement/Army (SPLM/A), Africa's longest civil conflict. Yet as SPLM Chairman John Garang was sworn in as 1st Vice-President on 9 July, implementation lags badly. The main obstacles are the old regime's lack of will to embrace genuine power sharing and elections, and ultimately allow a southern self-determination referendum after the six-year interim period and lack of capacity in the South to establish and empower basic structures of governance. To keep the accords on track, the international community must focus on broadening participation and transparency, particularly handling of oil revenues, promote SPLM dialogue with the government-allied militias and quickly deploy the UN peace support mission, whose monitoring operations will be key to breaking the links between Khartoum and those southern proxies.

delay disbursement of oil revenue the Government of Southern Sudan vitally needs to meet its CPA commitments.[29]

---

[29] The Recommendations of the IGAD as to effectively preceding the Peace Agreement can be summarized in the following points:

On The Delays in Implementation

To the Government of Sudan and the SPLM:

1. Request the IGAD Secretariat to work with the Joint National Transition Team as a focal point for implementation of the peace accords.

On The Other Armed Groups In The South

To the Government of Sudan:

2. End all support to South Sudan Defence Forces (SSDF) members who have not been integrated into the Sudan Armed Forces and stop directing misinformation to the SSDF regarding the peace accords.

3. Allow SSDF members to participate in the dialogue process with the SPLM.

To the Sudan People's Liberation Movement/Army (SPLM/A):

4. Seek internal agreement on the structures of the new SPLA army and speed up its reorganization, in order to facilitate a transparent, participatory dialogue with the SSDF without pre-conditions.

To the UN, U.S., UK, Norway, Italy, Other Donor Countries and IGAD Member States:

5. Press the government to cease all efforts to recruit and arm new factions in the South and immediately stop inciting clashes there.

6. Give more technical expertise to assist the SPLA transition from a guerrilla force to a professional army.

7. Advance stability in the South by pushing for a reopened SPLM-SSDF dialogue, providing technical expertise and high-level diplomatic support to the efforts of the Moi African Institute to facilitate a swift agreement, and working with churches, women's organisations and other civil society groups to begin an SPLM-SSDF reconciliation process.

8. Establish a mechanism to hold all parties accountable for the actions of former SSDF officers integrated into their respective forces.

To the UN Mission in Sudan:

9. Deploy rapidly throughout the South to monitor and interdict supply lines and especially arms shipments from government garrisons to non-integrated SSDF.

10. Ensure that the peacekeeping force in the South has sufficient rapid response capacity to protect civilians and respond to outbreaks of violence, particularly offensive actions by rogue militias.

To Address SPLM Constraints

To the SPLM:

11. Broaden internal participation in decision-making processes and empower institutions of governance in order to help build the Government of Southern Sudan.

12. Prioritise a 2nd SPLM National Convention as the body to endorse the process of transition to government and support internal democratization.

Dr. John Garang, the leader of the former SPLM/A, arrived in Khartoum in July, 2005, and was sworn in as vice president of a national unity government; Garang

---

13. Address transparency and accountability in the new Government of Southern Sudan by establishing an anti-corruption commission and formalising in the constitution for southern Sudan an auditor general position, a code of conduct for officials, and a requirement for ministers to declare assets, as in the Interim National Constitution.

To Address Problems In The Oil Sector

To the SPLM:

14. Deregister the deal granting White Nile Ltd. an oil concession in Block Ba, sign no new deals until the National Petroleum Commission is established, and clarify the legal status of Nile Petroleum Corp. with respect to the Government of Southern Sudan.

To the Government of Sudan:

15. Cease new activities in the oil sector—including contracts and operations—until the National Petroleum Commission is established.

To the Government of Sudan and the SPLM:

16. Establish the National Petroleum Commission quickly and use it to review contracts signed since conclusion of the Wealth Sharing Agreement and otherwise provide transparency and civilian oversight of the sector.

To the SPLM, the Government of Sudan, the UN Mission, the IGAD Secretariat, and Other Capable Parties:

17. Establish a border commission, similar to the Abyei Boundary Commission, to determine the North-South borders in the oil producing areas..

To the U.S., UK, Norway, Italy, Other Donor Countries and IGAD Member States:

18. Urge the SPLM to cancel the deal granting an oil concession to White Nile Ltd.

On The Need for Broader Political Participation

To the Government of Sudan and the SPLM:

19. Take steps either to empower the inclusive Constitutional Review Process called for in the Machakos Protocol to function as a genuine national dialogue or re-constitute the National Constitutional Review Commission after the 2009 elections, with each party represented as determined by election results and provisions in place to protect key terms of the peace accords.

20. Include women in all positions, including as ministers and members of commissions and as administrators and employees in the civil service of the government of Sudan and the Government of Southern Sudan.

The Security Council, by its resolution 1590 of 24 March 2005, decided to establish the United Nations Mission in the Sudan (UNMIS) to support implementation of the Comprehensive Peace Agreement signed by the Government of Sudan and the Sudan People's Liberation Movement/Army on 9 January 2005; and to perform certain functions relating to humanitarian assistance, and protection and promotion of human rights. On 31 August 2006, the Council, by its resolution 1706, expanded the mandate of UNMIS to include its deployment to Dar Fur to support the early and effective implementation of the Dar Fur Peace Agreement.

became the head of the autonomous government in the south of the country until the self-determination referendum planned for 2011 is held.

To start his new political duties, John Garang, during a meeting with U.S. Secretary of State Condoleezza Rice on June 7, 2005, urged the United States to provide more economic aid to the troubled region in southern Sudan. Rice agreed to consider the request beyond the billions of dollars the United States has already pledged for relief in southern Sudan and in a separate conflict in the country's Dar Fur region. On 30 July 2005, First Vice President of The Sudan and SPLM/A Chairman Dr. John Garang died in a helicopter crash, the accident which couldn't have come at a worse time. Then Salva Kiir Mayardit, the second man in the SPLM became southern Sudan's leader, replacing John Garang

Khartoum also signed a reconciliation agreement on June 19, 2005, with Sudan's largest opposition group, NDA Cairo, seeking to end a 16-year conflict with an agreement those officials hope will also help resolve the bloody fighting in Dar Fur, since the SPLA is a member of this group, the National Democratic Alliance, the largest rebel group in Dar Fur. The conference was attended by Sudanese President Omar el-Bashir and Egyptian President Hosni Mubarak. The alliance includes 13 mainly northern political parties, which have been trying to loosen el-Bashir's lock on power since he came to power in a 1989 military coup.

The armed wings of the various NDA factions clashed with government troops in eastern Sudan and waged a campaign of sabotage in the 1990s, but there has been no violence in recent years.Under the reconciliation agreement, the NDA will be incorporated into a power sharing government formed under the government's peace deal with the main southern rebel army, the Sudan People's Liberation Army. The peace deal poses a real threat to many groups associated with the National Congress Party (NCP) regime, which signed the CPA under some duress both to deflect international pressure over Dar Fur and to strengthen its domestic power base by securing a partnership with the SPLM. Most members recognise the free and fair elections required in 2009 would likely remove them from power. Many also fear the self-determination referendum will produce an independent South, thus costing Khartoum much of its oil and other mineral wealth. There are signs the NCP seeks to undercut implementation through its use of the militias (the South Sudan Defence Forces, SSDF), bribery, and through the tactics of divide and rule. It actively encourages hostility between southern groups, with the hope that intra-south fighting will prove sufficiently destabilising that the referendum can be postponed indefinitely without its being blamed. These tactics will likely intensify if pressure over Dar Fur diminishes.

The series of unrest in Sudan expanded to Eastern Sudan Region. The Beja and others Eastern Sudanese Tribes took their part in the unrest spreading through Sudan's different regions, on 20th of May 2005, the Eastern Front, which includes the Beja Congress and the Free Lions, have captured 20 government troops in a major military offensive launched near the Red Sea in coordination with JEM a rebel group also active in Dar Fur.[30] Its forces were advancing on the town of Tokar, south of the harbour city of Port Sudan also the capital of the Red Sea state. The attack led to the seizure of a significant amount of weaponry during the rebel push towards the town of Tokar, which lies half-way between the border with Eritrea and Port Sudan. Several hundred thousand Eritrean refugees live in Sudan and relations between the two governments have been very volatile in recent years. The Eastern Front was formed in February by the Beja Congress, its main component, and the Free Lions, with the support of assorted other factions. The Beja Congress and Free Lions are officially members of the NDA but they pulled out of the reconciliation talks in Cairo. last April 2005 the newly-formed Eastern Front vowed to carry on the fight against Khartoum at a meeting with others in rebel-held territory in eastern Sudan near the Eritrean border. The Beja Congress first took up arms against Khartoum in 1994 and now controls the region north of the town of Kassala near the Eritrean border. Since 1994, fighting has been sporadic in the region. On June 21, 2005 government troops have quelled the rebels uprising who attempted to seize Tokar; heavy casualties were reported on both sides. The Eastern Front had threatened to block the flow of crude oil, which travels from the oil fields of the south-central regions to outside markets through Port Sudan. A government plan to build a second oil refinery near Port Sudan was also threatened. The government was reported to have three times as many soldiers in the east to suppress the rebellion and protect vital infrastructure as in the more widely reported Dar Fur region. There were also rumors that the government is considering unleashing militias, similar to the Janjaweed of the Dar Fur conflict, against the Rashaida and Beja.[31]

---

[30] The Eastern Front is a coalition of rebel groups mainly consists of Rashida's Free Lions and the Beja Congress militias operating in eastern Sudan along the border with Eritrea, particularly the states of Red Sea and Kassala. They has been active in the remote region near the Eritrean border. The front said it had taken up arms against the Sudanese government in a bid to end the marginalisation of the region and to demand greater autonomy.

[31] The low-intensity conflict between the government and the Eastern Front risks becoming a major new war with disastrous humanitarian consequences if the Sudan People's Liberation Movement (SPLM) proceeds with its scheduled withdrawal from eastern Sudan this month. Competition to fill the security vacuum could spark urban unrest, reprisals and worse. Yet, there is also a peace opportunity. As a partner in the new Government

of National Unity and with troops in the East, the SPLM is in a position to broker a deal. Like Dar Fur and the South, the East suffers from marginalisation and underdevelopment: legitimate claims for more power and wealth sharing in a federal arrangement should be addressed within the framework of the Comprehensive Peace Agreement (CPA) the government and SPLM signed in 2005. But the SPLM needs to push for a provisional ceasefire and use its influence in Khartoum to get serious negotiations. International partners, under UN leadership, should facilitate the process.

The CPA has brought no peace dividend to either eastern Sudan or the Dar Fur region of western Sudan. It dealt with the political and economic marginalisation of the South but ignored the similar structural imbalance in the rest of the country. The ruling National Congress Party (NCP) and the international community are now bearing the consequences of excluding other participants from the long negotiations that were conducted at Naivasha in Kenya. After hundreds of thousands of deaths and the displacement of millions in Dar Fur, the international community is trying to salvage a peace in negotiations conducted under African Union sponsorship at Abuja. At the same time, however, it may be in the process of repeating its mistake by largely ignoring another powder keg.

Under the terms of the CPA, the SPLM is obliged to withdraw from eastern Sudan by 9 January 2006, though fortuitously it is months behind schedule. Its former partner, the Eastern Front, will seek to take over but the NCP is unlikely to permit it to exercise uncontested control. Its efforts to recover territory along the Eritrean border will be all the more dangerous because Eritrea and Ethiopia are on the verge of renewing hostilities. Asmara wants to ensure at least Sudanese neutrality and could be willing to trade away its support for the Eastern Front. If fighting does break out again between the two large neighbours, eastern Sudan, whose humanitarian situation is in some ways worse than Dar Fur's, would face a disastrous flood of refugees.

Credible negotiations are needed immediately to address the simmering conflict in eastern Sudan but these are being delayed because the Government of National Unity, with its SPLM contingent, and the international community are concentrating almost exclusively on Dar Fur. The urgent requirement is to put an end to the piecemeal approach to peacemaking. The East needs to be incorporated into a national process that builds on the CPA and includes Dar Fur. One forum may not be practical to resolve Sudan's regional wars but a common framework is needed to give continuity and consistency to disparate negotiations which have been strung out over the last four years.

The CPA provides the conceptual and substantive framework to solve Sudan's regional wars, in the East as well as Dar Fur. It is based on the premise that the South's long marginalisation by the centre (Khartoum) and its underdevelopment led to the civil war that lasted 21 years. To rectify those underlying causes, the NCP and the SPLM agreed to power sharing commensurate with the South's population as well as significant wealth sharing between the central government and the government of South Sudan. Since Khartoum and the Eastern Front alike say they recognise that the same underlying causes have contributed to conflict in the East (as well as Dar Fur and elsewhere in the North), the same elements of a solution should be applied.

The UN, the U.S., the European Union and its member states have all failed to apply themselves sufficiently to generate a serious peace process for the East. Also a Libyan mediation initiative collapsed in late December 2005. The international Crises Group recommended that to prevent war in the East, the international community needs to work with the key regional actors, particularly Eritrea, to underwrite comprehensive negotiations between the Government of National Unity and the Eastern Front that can produce a sustainable peace based on the CPA framework. Western governments should make it clear that they also want to take a major part in those negotiations, not unlike what they did with the CPA and what they are now attempting with Dar Fur at Abuja.

If Sudan's vicious cycle of violence is not to spread again, a major effort is needed now to construct a forum for credible negotiations that can defuse the situation.[32]

If this is to happen, the SPLM will need to use its leverage as a member of the Government of National Unity and play a robust role. Though this means diverting some time and energy from its major preoccupations in the South, its new responsibilities in Khartoum make it uniquely competent to advance the policy. It has fought side by side with the people in the East and knows the similarities of their situation with that of the South. Moreover, it has a duty to ensure that its withdrawal from eastern Sudan does not create a security vacuum that could invite escalation. It must insist on having strong and senior representation on the government delegation and then press for an early start to credible negotiations with the Eastern Front.

[32] To Avert Conflict in the East:

1. Sudan's Government of National Unity should be prepared to send a high-level delegation, with joint National Congress Party (NCP) and Sudan People's Liberation Movement (SPLM) participation, before the end of January 2006 to begin internationally-backed and facilitated negotiations with the Eastern Front on a solution to the conflict in and problems of eastern Sudan.

2. To give negotiations a chance to succeed, the Government of National Unity and the Eastern Front should:

(a) accept a provisional cessation of hostilities as soon as possible to prevent the withdrawal of the SPLM from leading to violent confrontation for control of Hameshkoreb and other opposition-held areas;

(b) agree that, until a comprehensive ceasefire can be reached, the SPLM should maintain a small force in the region to serve as a buffer and prevent hostilities over Hameshkoreb; and

(c) work out a permanent and comprehensive ceasefire as part of the security arrangements to be discussed during the broader negotiations.

To Create a Credible Negotiation Process:

3. An eastern Sudan negotiating forum should be established that includes:

The Eritrean government in mid-2006 dramatically changed its position on the conflict. From being the main supporter of the Eastern Front they decided that bringing the Sudanese government around the negotiating table for a possible agreement with the rebels would be in their best interests. Some believe this is because they want to avoid any conflict on their Sudanese border in case of war with Ethiopia. The Eastern Front's Chairman is Musa Mohamed Ahmed. While the

---

(a) a special envoy, appointed by the UN Secretary-General and accepted by the parties, who serves as the lead mediator and liaises with the UN Mission in Sudan;

(b) a secretariat, provided by the UN or another capable body, to give the mediation technical capacity; and

(c) international observers from the U.S., UK, Canada, Italy, Norway and the European Union, and regional observers from Eritrea, Libya and the African Union.

4. The CPA should be accepted as the framework for negotiations, in particular its formulae for power and wealth sharing between the central government and a region.

5. The NCP and the SPLM, as the two key partners in the Government of National Unity, must develop a consensus on handling the conflict in eastern Sudan, including accepting participation within the Eastern Front delegation of representatives of the Beja Congress and Rashaida Free Lions from Khartoum and government-controlled areas of the East.

6. A plan of action is needed for the negotiations, including consensus that:

(a) the talks should open and a provisional ceasefire should be in place in January 2006, or at least prior to the completion of the SPLM withdrawal; and

(b) the substantive agenda will cover power sharing, wealth sharing and security, including control over Hameshkoreb and other opposition-held areas.

7. The international observers should be present at the negotiations to facilitate the peace talks and should provide guarantees to ensure its implementation.

8. Other relevant Sudanese parties should participate as observers, such as tribal and religious leaders, civil society representatives including women, and other stakeholders from the East.

9. Consideration should be given to the creation of Joint Integrated Units for the East which, like those provided for in the CPA, would include government troops (the Sudan Armed Forces) and the SPLM's military wing (the SPLA) but also the Eastern Front, and would be deployed after conclusion of a peace agreement between the Government of National Unity and the Eastern Front.

10. Issues of development in the East should be dealt with through a post-conflict needs assessment with the involvement of interested donors, particularly the governments that have taken part in the negotiation process as observers.

To Address the Humanitarian Crisis in the East:

11. Significant donor attention and resources should be directed urgently to reversing a situation in which crude mortality rates and malnutrition levels are significantly higher even than in Dar Fur.

Sudan People's Liberation Army (SPLA) was the primary member of the Eastern Front, the SPLA was obliged to leave by the January 2005 agreement that ended the Second Sudanese Civil War. Their place was taken in February 2004 after the merger of the larger Beja Congress with the smaller Rashaida Free Lions, two tribal based groups of the Beja and Rashaida people, respectively. The Justice and Equality Movement (JEM), a rebel group from Dar Fur in the west, then joined.

Both the Free Lions and the Beja Congress stated that government inequity in the distribution of oil profits was the cause of their rebellion. They demanded to have a greater say in the composition of the national government, which has been seen as a destabilizing influence on the agreement ending the conflict in Southern Sudan. The Eastern Front was strengthened after 17 Beja rioters were killed by police in Port Sudan in late January 2005 and angry young Beja men began to join rebel camps in Eritrea. The Eritrean government in Asmara supported the Eastern Front apparently in retaliation for Sudanese support to the Eritrean Islamist factions. Meanwhile, the JEM has formed an alliance with the Eastern Front and moved troops into the region apparently in an attempt to position itself as a national movement, rather than one limited to its Dar Fur homeland. The Sudanese government and East Sudan Front signed on 03 July 2006 a document on action program regarding the signing of security and military agreements on June 27. This move was in continuation of the Agreement on Declaration of Principles that was reached between the Sudanese government and the East Sudan Front on June 19 in Asmara under the care of the Eritrean government, in a bid to implement the cessation of hostilities. Representatives of both sides and the Eritrean government were present at the signing ceremony.

They were successful in their attempts and on the 19 June 2006, the two sides signed an agreement on declaration of principles. This was the start of four months of Eritrean-mediated negotiations for a comprehensive peace agreement between the Sudanese government and the Eastern Front, which culminated in signing of a peace agreement on 14 October 2006, in Asmara. The agreement covers security issues, power sharing at a federal and regional level, and wealth sharing in regards to the three Eastern states Kassala, Red Sea and The new agreement on cessation of hostilities obliges the two sides to desist from any movement from the places they had occupied prior to June 19, designate army officers who would implement the agreement drawn from both of them and representatives of the Eritrean government in five stations that separates the two parties. This is to say the area around the Red Sea, Setit river, Barka river, Kerayit and Lafa towards facilitating the implementation of the peace process and stability of Sudan.

On the Eritrean side, the Head of Organizational Affairs at the PFDJ, Mr. Abdalla Jabir, and the Commander of Operation Zone 1, Brig. General Tekle Kiflai, and on the Sudanese government side, General Hassan Mohammed Al-Amin and Mr.

Mussa Osman Issa from the East Sudan Front signed the agreement. Meanwhile, the East Sudan Front is holding a three-day congress starting July 2 in Tessenei town on the implementation of the Agreement on Declaration of Principles and cessation of hostilities

The agreement, signed on Sunday in the Eritrean capital, Asmara, follows several months of talks between Sudanese officials and representatives of the Eastern Front. It provides for power- and resource-sharing between Sudan's Government of National Unity and the three eastern Sudan states of Kassala, Red Sea and Gaderaf. The Eastern Front saw the signing of the Comprehensive Peace Agreement (CPA) between the government and the southern Sudan People's Liberation Movement/ Army (SPLM/A) in January 2005, to end civil war in southern Sudan, as a model political arrangement for its own region.

Under the power-sharing part of the deal, the Eastern Front will get the post of one assistant to the president, a presidential adviser and one state minister's post. The front will also be given eight parliamentary seats in Khartoum, the nation's capital, and 10 parliamentary seats in each of the three eastern states.

Many members of the Beja community live in shantytowns on the outskirts of Port Sudan, having moved there to work as labourers after famine killed their cattle and mechanised farming took over their lands in the 1980s.

Eastern Sudan is strategically important for the country. Significant installations in the area include Port Sudan—the country's economic lifeline since most trade passes through it—the oil pipeline, many irrigated and semi-mechanised agricultural schemes, and a long border with Eritrea, with whom Sudan has had rocky relations for the past 12 years. Due in part to the region's economic and strategic significance, as well as the military activities since the mid-1990s, the government has a heavy security presence there, involving, according to the International Crisis Group, three times as many forces as in the war-ravaged western region of Dar Fur, where insecurity has escalated since May.

The SPLA, which was allied to some of the rebel forces in the east before the signing of the CPA, withdrew its forces from the east in June, following which more Sudanese armed forces were deployed in the area.

Just as the decades long North-South civil war was reaching a resolution, a new rebellion in the western region of Dar Fur began in early 2003.

The conflict broke out in West Dar Fur in 1998. The 1998 clashes were relatively minor, but more than 5000 Masalit were displaced. Clashes resumed in 1999 when nomadic herdsmen again moved south earlier than usual. The 1999 clashes were bloodier, with many hundreds killed, including a number of Arab tribal chiefs. The government brought in military forces in an attempt to quell the violence and took direct control of security. A reconciliation conference held in 1999 agreed on compensation. Many Masalit intellectuals and notables were arrested, imprisoned, and tortured in the towns as government-supported Arab militias began to attack Masalit villages; a number of Arab chiefs and civilians were also killed in these clashes.

In 2003 the situation escalted taking rebillion form against the Sudanese government, with two local rebel groups—the Justice and Equality Movement (JEM) and the Sudanese Liberation Army (SLA)—accusing the government of oppressing non-Arabs in favor of Arabs. The government was also accused of neglecting the Dar Fur region of Sudan. In response, the government mounted a campaign of aerial bombardment supporting ground attacks by an Arab militia, the Janjaweed. The Janjaweed were accused of committing major human rights violations, including mass killing, looting, and systematic rape of the non-Arab population of Dar Fur. They have frequently burned down whole villages, driving the surviving inhabitants to flee to refugee camps, mainly in Dar Fur and Chad; many of the camps in Dar Fur are surrounded by Janjaweed forces. By the summer of 2004, 50,000 to 80,000 people had been killed and at least a million had been driven from their homes, causing a major humanitarian crisis in the region.

A report of Human Rights Watch issued on May 07, 2004 accused the Sudanese government and Arab militia of massive abuses in western Dar Fur region. Dar Fur refugees are systematically being starved. Human Rights Watch says black Africans are deliberately being driven off the land. The UN Commissioner for Human Rights described a "reign of terror" in the region.
It said a UN team found "appalling" conditions when it visited the town of Kailek on April 2004. Militias prevented food deliveries and stopped anyone leaving. Sudanese Foreign Minister Mustafa Ismail has acknowledged there might have been human rights violations, but denies a campaign of ethnic cleansing is going on. An aid worker in Kailek described what happened there as the "politics of starvation". Eight or nine children were reported to have been dying from malnutrition every day. The report said women and girls were raped and described inhumane sanitary conditions and a lack of medical treatment.
Members of the UN team were said to be "visibly shaken" by circumstances in the town. Refugees first sought shelter in Kailek, the biggest settlement in the area, after Arab militias started attacking nearby villages.
The horseback militia known as the Janjaweed surrounded the village, effectively holding 1,700 people hostage. The UN report says that as food began to run out, residents were forced to start paying the militia to leave the village to look for supplies. The refugees were later moved to a nearby town, Kass, in advance of a

visit by another UN team. The survivors in Kass have been camping in a disused secondary school.

One three-year-old girl lying on open ground was little more than a skeleton. There was no medicine to treat her and very little food, our correspondent adds.

The local authorities in Kass deny that they colluded in the siege, but survivors tell a different story. The tactics involved include mass rape, summary execution and the systematic burning of villages and crops. Meanwhile, the foreign ministry in Chad has summoned Sudan's ambassador to protest against cross-border incursions by militia from Dar Fur. The Chadian government has urged Sudan to assert control over the militia, following the latest clash.

Later on August 2006, Chad and Sudan agreed two weeks ago to restore diplomatic relations and reopen their border region, which has been plagued by violence linked to the conflict in Dar Fur.

On August, 23, 2006 Chad's Foreign Minister Ahmat Allam-mi declared that Chad had detained seven leaders of a Dar Fur rebel group, leaders of the Justice and Equality Movement (JEM) and would expelled them as part of its efforts to improve relations with neighbouring Sudan. The two governments had long accused each other of backing rebel groups operating on either side of the border but agreed at a summit in Tripoli in February 2006 to stop insurgents setting up bases on their territories. These detentions come in the light of the Abuja peace deal and in the light of our obligations from the Tripoli accord,"

Allam-mi said. JEM leader Khalil Ibrahim said the detained leaders had donenothing wrong and called on Chad's President Idriss Deby to

On July, 31, 2006 Violent clashes between Sudanese Government forces, allied militias and rebel groups continued, the United Nations Mission in Sudan (UNMIS) reported, while a UN humanitarian convoy has also been ambushed.

UNMIS reported that the security situation in Dar Fur's north and west is particularly volatile, with ongoing clashes. In the area around Kulkul in North Dar Fur, Sudanese Government forces fought members of the rebel group known as the National Redemption Front, prompting internally displaced persons (IDPs) in the area to flee towards the provincial capital, El Fasher.

In West Dar Fur, a convoy of 29 trucks belonging to the UN World Food Programme (WFP) was ambushed by six armed men on Saturday as it was returning to its base in the provincial capital, Geneina, after distributing food in the district around Habila. The spokesperson said no injuries were reported.

Scores of thousands of people have been killed in Dar Fur and more than two million others have been displaced since 2003 because of fighting between Government forces, Janjaweed militias and rebels that has led to claims of civilian massacres, rapes and other atrocities.

The rebels accused the central government of neglecting the Dar Fur region, although there is uncertainty regarding the objectives of the rebels and whether they merely seek an improved position for Dar Fur within Sudan or outright secession. Both the government and the rebels have been accused of atrocities in this war, although most of the blame has fallen on Arab militias Janjaweed allied with the government. The rebels have alleged that these militias have been engaging in ethnic cleansing in Dar Fur, and the fighting has displaced hundreds of thousands of people, many of them seeking refuge in neighbouring Chad. The government claimed victory over the rebels after capturing Tine, a town on the border with Chad, in early 2004 the violence continued. But as of 2006, the War in Dar Fur continues with the situation getting worse.

There has been signed a Dar Fur Peace Agreement between some of the parties in Dar Fur. This agreement is supervised by African Union Mission in Sudan (AMIS).

The chairman and commander-in-chief of the rebel Sudan Liberation Movement/Army (SLM/A) in Dar Fur, Minni Minnawi is the leader of the largest of three main rebel groups in Dar Fur and the only one that signed the 5 May Dar Fur Peace Agreement (DPA) with the Sudanese government, brokered by the African Union (AU) in Abuja, the Nigerian capital. He arrived in Khartoum on August, 5, 2006 to be sworn in as assistant to President Umar al-Bashir. His new post in the Sudanese presidency was one of the key political demands of the rebel group in the peace negotiations. Speaking at a press conference following his swearing-in, Minnawi appeared to take a softer line of the hotly-debated issue of the deployment of international peacekeepers in war-torn Dar Fur. He said that his position is clear and will remain clear; his movement has repeatedly demanded that UN forces replace an embattled African Union contingent which has failed to restore stability in the western Sudanese region, if security is maintained in Dar Fur, there will be no need for international forces. While clashes between Minnawi's faction and government forces have stopped since the Abuja deal, violence involving holdout rebel factions has continued to claim lives and hamper the humanitarian effort.

Abdelwahid Mohamed al-Nur, the leader of another faction of the SLM/A with a predominantly Fur following, and Khalil Ibrahim, leader of the Justice and Equality Movement (JEM), refused to sign the DPA, claiming it was unacceptable as it did not fulfil their key demands including more compensation, stronger political representation and more involvement in security arrangements.

Senegal's President Abdoulaye Wade, who is mediating on behalf of the African Union (AU has appealed to rebels in Sudan's who did not sign the Abuja peace accord to join in efforts to resolve the conflict, the official Senegalese news agency said Monday. He said"To the two movements that did not sign the Abuja agreement, I make an appeal. I am ready to meet them wherever they want," Wade said during a weekend visit to Sudan.

"I am ready to do all that I can to meet them to understand why they did not sign the agreement and try to convince them to work towards peace.

The DPA has had little popular support among civilians in Dar Fur, many of whom continue to live in camps for internally displaced persons and refuse to return to their villages for fear of renewed attacks. Since the signing of the DPA, violence has been widespread across Dar Fur due to the fragmentation of various rebel groups and escalating fighting between the signatories and non-signatories of the DPA.

Minnawi's rebel faction has been accused of committing atrocities against other rebel groups that refused to sign the DPA as well as their civilian supporters. As a result, some Dar Furians have dubbed his rebel faction "Janjawid 2", after the government-aligned Janjawid militia notorious for conducting a scorched-earth campaign in Dar Fur.

Earlier this week, Amnesty International issued a statement accusing Minnawi's rebel faction of killing and raping civilians in July in Korma town in North Dar Fur.

In a separate statement, Ambassador Baba Gana Kingibe, the special representative of the chairperson of the AU Commission in Sudan, said his attention had been drawn to allegations of torture by the forces of Minnawi's SLM/A. The AU also accused the SLM/A of beating an unidentified person on two successive days in their quarters in the North Dar Fur capital El Fasher and preventing the African military monitors from intervening.

This incident lends credence to the previous incessant allegations, Kingibe observed. The SLM/A has denied the accusations.

After his arrival on Saturday, Minnawi was expected to address a pro-DPA rally at Khartoum's Green Square. The SLM/A held a political rally at Hajj Yousif, on the outskirts of Khartoum, where many war-displaced Sudanese live. The purpose was to enlighten the people on the culture of peace and to introduce the SLM/A ideology, and its political mission, cultural, social and economic plans for the wellbeing of the New Sudan,

Some Fur citizens who support Abdelwahid Mohamed al-Nur's Dar Fur rebel faction reportedly disrupted the rally, however, by throwing stones and chairs into the crowd, but Hussein dismissed the violence.

The Conflict in Dar Fur is more complex than any peace efforts. The Arab population of the region is about a quarter or nearly one million of the population. Not all of them are janjaweed.

The the majority Arab population of Dar Fur are no less traumatic than their non-Arabs counterparts. They are equally harmed by rebels' attacks, which see them as the extrapolation of the Khartoum regime. But the truth is that they have shared land for years with their black African compatriots, even though then were alleged to behave as if their fair skin which they share with the Arab elite that runs the show from Khartoum put them miles ahead of their African darker skin counterparts. Africa's essential dilemma in Dar Fur is that its 7000 peace keeping force cannot hold out on its own.

The Chad-Sudan conflict officially started on December 23, 2005, when the government of Chad declared a state of war with Sudan and called for the citizens of Chad to mobilize themselves against the "common enemy," which the Chadian government sees as the Rally for Democracy and Liberty (RDL) militants, Chadian rebels backed by the Sudanese government, and Sudanese militiamen. Militants have attacked villages and towns in eastern Chad, stealing cattle, murdering citizens, and burning houses. Over 200,000 refugees from the Dar Fur region of north western Sudan currently claim asylum in eastern Chad. Chadian president Idriss Déby accuses Sudanese President Omar Hassan Ahmed al-Bashir of trying to destabilise Chad, to drive people into misery, to create disorder and export the war from Dar Fur to Chad.

The incident prompting the declaration of war was an attack on the Chadian town of Adré near the Sudanese border that led to the deaths of either one hundred rebels (as most news sources reported) or three hundred rebels. The Sudanese government was blamed for the attack, which was the second in the region in three days, but Sudanese foreign ministry spokesman Jamal Mohammed Ibrahim denied any Sudanese involvement, he said that Sudanese government is not for any escalation with Chad and denied involvement in Chadian internal affairs. The Adre attack led to the declaration of war by Chad and the alleged deployment of the Chadian airforce into Sudanese airspace, which the Chadian government denies. The relationship between the two countries has, however, been tense for months with each accusing the other of supporting anti-government movements. Chad severed diplomatic ties with neighbouring Sudan after Chadian rebels based in Dar Fur attacked N'djamena in an attempt to unseat President Deby. The coup failed and Chad and Sudan later agreed to repair diplomatic ties. A newly released report says credible information suggests that the government of Sudan is arming Janjaweed militias and Chadian rebels who want to overthrow President Idris Deby. The report also mentioned that Weapons are being funnelled from Chad into Dar Fur to support rebels who have refused to sign the Dar Fur Peace Agreement, says a status report on the crisis Sudan.

The UN panel of experts who compiled the document says that an arms embargo in Dar Fur is being routinely violated by all parties to the conflict, giving substance to reports from the African Union Mission in Sudan that say violence between Dar Fur rebels and the Sudan government continues along the Sudan/Chad border.

The arms embargo in Dar Fur is being blatantly violated by all parties operating in the war-torn Sudanese region, including Government forces, allied Janjaweed militias, rebel groups and insurgents from neighbouring Chad, according to the latest report from a panel of experts set up by the United Nations Security Council.

The panel's report, released today, found that Chadian rebels are helping to stoke the conflict in Dar Fur—especially in the region's north and west—by reportedly joining Government forces and the Janjaweed in their operations against rebel groups.

The experts said there are reliable reports that Sudan is re-supplying the Chadian rebels with weapons and vehicles, with weapons and ammunition observed being offloaded at local airports and moved to locations within Dar Fur, where three years of fighting have killed an estimated 200,000 people and forced another 2 million to leave their homes.

There is indicattions that the Sudanese goverment ontinues to support the Janjaweed, providing weapons and vehicles in breach of its commitments, according to the report.

The Janjaweed/armed militias appear to have upgraded their modus operandi from horses, camels and AK-47s to land cruisers, pick-up trucks and rocket-propelled grenades," it stated.

The panel of experts, appointed by the Council last year to monitor the arms embargo and targeted financial and travel-related sanctions, also found that rebel forces have "shown a notable increase in capacity to engage the forces of the Government" since March.

Turning to the financial and travel-related sanctions, the experts said it considered Sudan to have "wilfully avoided" its commitment under the resolution to implement financial sanctions against persons designated by the Council.

They also voiced concern that fighting has increased in recent months because of a major split within rebel movements based on which groups and factions signed the Dar Fur Peace Agreement (DPA) in May and which did not.

Tragically, it is the long-suffering innocent civilians of Dar Fur who continue to bear the brunt of recent events.

Greece's Ambassador Adamantios Vassilakis, Chairman of the Council committee dealing with sanctions concerning Sudan, said in a letter to the Council President that the committee will consider the panel's many recommendations and then present their views to the full Council.

Meanwhile, Under-Secretary-General for Humanitarian Affairs Jan Egeland told a news briefing in Geneva that the violence and insecurity plaguing Dar Fur has escalated in recent months, with the militias stronger than ever. Janjaweed militias are much better armed, they are more brutal than ever and their potential to do badly is better than ever.

Mr. Egeland, who is also the UN Emergency Relief Coordinator, said the escalating fighting has led to surging numbers of internally displaced persons (IDPs) across Dar Fur, a remote and impoverished region the size of France on Sudan's western flank.

Their suffering has been exacerbated because relief workers are unable to reach many of the IDPs due to the insecurity.

Asked by journalists about the recent Human Rights Council session, Mr. Egeland said he thought it was a shame that it did not issue a strong statement on Dar Fur.

Also a UN report confirmed the above mentioned concerning the build-up of arms in Dar Fur has allowed rebels to continue fighting Sudan government forces in the region. Sudan is charged with launching a ground offensive in northern Dar Fur that has displaced tens of thousands of civilians in recent weeks.

The report adds that Janjaweed militias have upgraded from horses and guns to trucks and rocket-propelled grenades. Tens of thousands of civilians have died in the three and a half year conflict that began when rebels attacked government positions in Dar Fur, complaining the remote region remained undeveloped due to neglect by the central government.

Sudan is charged with arming militias to crush the rebellion using a savage campaign of rape and murder in what the United States calls genocide.

Meanwhile, President Omar al-Bashir met in Asmara on October 14 with the chairman of the National Democratic Alliance (NDA) and head of the Democratic Unionist Party Mohamed Osman al-Mirghani. It said that the meeting discussed issues related to solving the questions of Sudan peacefully, expressing their appreciation for the efforts that led to the realisation of Eastern Sudan Peace Agreement.

The UN Security Council adopted a resolution on August 31 calling for the deployment of up to 20,000 peacekeepers to replace an embattled African Union contingent that has failed to restore peace and stability in Dar Fur.

At least 200,000 people have died as a result of fighting, famine and disease, and more than two million have fled their homes since rebels launched an uprising in Dar Fur in early 2003, prompting a scorched earth response from the military and militia allies.

Beshir rejected continually deployment of UN forces, charging the plan was part of a US-engineered plot to invade and plunder resources.
Diplomats and experts see a deployment as crucial to the implementation of an ailing peace deal signed in May, and argue that regime officials fear a UN presence would expose them to war crimes prosecutions.
Sudan expels U.N. envoy after he accused army of mobilizing Arab militias in Dar Fur.

On October, 7, 2006 Sudanese Minister of State for Information and Communications Farh Agar announced that the file of deploying UN peacekeeping forces in the country's western region of Dar Fur had been closed. On 14 August 2006 a Sudanese criminal court convicted a Slovenian president's envoy of espionage and other charges and sentenced him to two years in prison. Tomo Kriznar, a peace activist who traveled to Sudan's troubled Dar Fur region in February 2006, had been in custody since July 20, 2006. The envoy is a well known human rights activist in Slovenia and was arrested in July for not having a valid visa.
Sudanese investigators said Mr Kriznar was taking pictures and shooting video material of villages around Dar Fur.
The court ruled that Kriznar was guilty of espionage, publishing false reports and entering the country without obtaining a visa. It sentenced him to two years in prison and ordered him to pay about US$2,400 (euro1, 887.09) in fines. If Kriznar fails to pay the fine, he could stay in jail for another six months, said Justice Minister Mohamed Ali al Mardhi.
The court also ordered the government to confiscate photographic equipment and film found with Kriznar and ruled that he be deported at the end of his prison term. Ivo Vajgl, an adviser to Slovenian President Janez Drnovsek, acknowledged that Kriznar entered Sudan without a valid visa, though he did not know why. He denied the accusations that Kriznar was a spy. On August, 23, 2006, Slovenian authorities stepped up international lobbying at the European Commission level as well as in other EU states and other international organizations to win the release by Sudanese authorities of Slovenian presidential envoy Tomo Kriznar, jailed for two years on charges of espionage.
The arrest and detention of US journalist Paul Salopek on August 28, 2006, foreign correspondent with the Chicago Tribune Who was on assignment for National Geographic Magazine when he was arrested and charged with espionage and entering the country without a visa in Dar Fur region has spotlighted issues of press freedom in Sudan, a nation with a history of media restriction. Salopek entered Sudan via the Chadian border, a common route for journalists who seek to enter Dar Fur without going through official channels.

He was reportedly writing, not on the Dar Fur crisis, but on the sub-Saharan region known as the Sahel. A Chadian driver and an interpreter were arrested and charged along with Salopek.

At present, journalists are required to apply for permits in the capital, Khartoum; Permits may be delayed for months, or denied altogether.

Sudanese newsmen said they are not surprised by the crackdown on foreign journalists in Dar Fur, and claim that independent media in Sudan routinely face restrictions. Alfred Taban who won the Speaker Abbot award in 2005 for his reporting on the Dar Fur conflict for the BBC said that Sudan is a dangerous place to be a journalist. Taban, a southern Sudanese, founded the independent Khartoum Monitor, a newspaper which supports the ideals of black Christians who have long fought the northern Arab government based in Khartoum.

During Sudan's twenty-one year north/south civil war, the Khartoum Monitor was often shut down for printing material deemed inappropriate by the Khartoum Islamist administration. Taban and his staff faced arrests and harassment regularly, this although the Comprehensive Peace Agreement (CPA) of January 2005, was intended to pave the way for freedom of press in Sudan.

Several independent newspapers have opened in Khartoum since the signing of the accord, but Editor-in-Chief of the Citizen Daily newspaper, Nhial Boll, said the threat of arrest and detention is routine for journalists in Sudan. Boll told dpa that one of his staff photographers was arrested this week and the film in his camera destroyed by security forces, after he took pictures of the flooded Nile River without first obtaining permission.

British-based rights group, the Sudan Organization against Torture (SOAT), also reported the arrest and detention of Sudanese journalists in Khartoum and northern Sudan. Sudanese reporter Nasr al-Din al-Tayib told SOAT he was arrested and beaten by security forces on August 16, 2006 after taking pictures of a government-sponsored demolition of homes of displaced Dar Furis.

Four other reporters were detained at the site of the Merowe Dam project in northern Sudan, before being sent away, SOAT.

The controversial dam project will bring electricity to much of Sudan but flooding caused by the construction of the dam has forced thousands of people from their homes.

The explusion of Pronk to leave was the government's second slap in the face to the United Nations within three months. Pronk angered President Omar al-Beshir's regime by criticising its handling of the crisis in Dar Fur and pushing for deployment of UN peacekeepers and has reported that government forces had suffered two major defeats in fighting in Dar Fur, In an October 14 entry on his Internet blog, Pronk criticised the performance of Sudan's army against Dar Fur rebels, claimed morale among troops was low and linked the military to the infamous Janjaweed militia. The military responded by accusing Pronk of "waging psychological warfare on the armed forces. On October 21, 2006 the Sudanese government decided to expel him. US Secretary of State Condoleezza Rice Monday condemned Sudan's expulsion of a top United Nations envoy as "unfortunate in the extreme," and pledged to consult with UN chief Kofi Annan.

Also the European Union declared deep concern at Khartoum's decision and stressed that United Nations plays a key role which must be reinforced.

British Foreign Office Minister Lord David Triesman also condemned the decision to expel Pronk as "counter-productive.

The departure of Pronk set back efforts to halt the violence in the western region of Sudan where fighting has intensified since then between pro-government and rebel forces.

Sudan government still condemns western media coverage of Dar Fur and denouncing the news spread by western media regarding security in Dar Fur commented that the presence of the African Union forces in Sudan was due to the accusations made against Khartoum. Mr. Abdul Rahman Khalil Ahmad said that GoS believe that the west is no after peace and stability in Dar Fur, because exactly after the peace treaty was signed it tried to start another crisis in Sudan through interfering in Sudan's internal affairs

He condemned the U.S. and the U.K. and that they are after their own economic benefits in Sudan, especially after they understood that the Sudan possesses various unexploited oil and uranium resources, he stressed his support for AU troops presence in Dar Fur and that the African Union forces would be more accustomed to our ways we agreed with their presence, but the U.S. and U.K. after understanding that peace was finding a firm definition in Sudan, cut the African Union forces supplies and asked for the presence of UN forces, which consequently would lead them to a firm place of authority in our country, he added that the Presence of UN forces in Dar Fur with unlimited powers will cease all authority of the government, police, security forces and Sudan's judiciary and so the President, Umar al-Bashir in a speech announced that he preferred to be a resistance group leader than the President of a government which was under the influence of the UN forces. He asserted Sudan capablility of continuing its resistance in the case of sanction he stated that Sudan from 1993 had been placed under various military, political, economical and diplomatic sanctions by the U.S., U.K. and the West. These threats are nothing new, and in addition to this issue, Sudan has no economic or commercial relations with the West, so how can they place us under sanction? Khalil Ahmad also emphasized that his government was after no guarantees regarding the UN Security Council's 1706 resolution and strongly denounced this issue. Regarding when the African Union forces would leave Dar

Fur commented that placing an exact deadline for this issue was difficult, but the Sudan government was placing all its effort in the correct and swift execution of the peace treaty.

Dar Fur has become a byword for horrifying bloodshed with the westernmost war-torn Sudanese province the main subject of discussion at the 61st session of the UN General Assembly this week. Brutal low-level intensity warfare between Sudanese government forces and their local allies, on the one hand, and armed opposition groups on the other, has created a humanitarian catastrophe of frightful proportions. The Sudanese government, meanwhile, is playing down ramifications of the Dar Fur crisis. Sudanese officials claim that Western powers and humanitarian relief groups are conjuring up grossly exaggerated images of death and destruction in Dar Fur as pretext for military intervention. The Sudanese government, supported by a considerable segment of Sudanese and Arab public opinion, is loath to contemplate the idea of another Muslim nation policed by Western troops.

On Sept. 19, 2006, Sudanese President Omar Hassan Al-Beshir addressed the General Assembly and reiterated the Sudanese government position that it was strongly opposed to the deployment of foreign peace-keeping troops in Dar Fur, and stressed that the majority of the peace-keeping troops should be African under the African Union's command. Al-Beshir criticised the international media for "serving ulterior motives". He warned that international media "gives the false impression that the whole of Dar Fur is in chaos". He added: "our position is that the force of the African Union (AU) should continue in Dar Fur.

On August 16, 2006 JEM delegates stationed at the AU headquarters in the North Dar Fur town of El Fasher as part of an effort to bring peace to in Dar Fur have been advised to leave the AU headquarters because they has refused to sign the Dar Fur Peace Agreement a ccording to Sam Ibok AU's chief negotiator in Sudan. He said that the decision had been requested by the government in Khartoum. The move could hinder investigations of truce violations as AU troops may not be able to travel safely in areas controlled by the two factions that did not sign the peace deal. Mohammed Abbasher Ahmed, JEM delegate for the Justice and Equality Movement warned the move could push it to resume full fledged fighting, the AU's decision could lead it to resume open warfare in Dar Fur, thisshould be regarded as a declaration of war, a return to the fighting.

Ibok said the group did not participate in the various cease-fire commissions and that the Sudan Liberation Movement led by main rebel chief Minni Minnawi, who signed the peace deal, refused to sit with them. There is no alternative but to ask them to leave," Ibok said. "It doesn't mean we have lost hope that JEM will eventually join the peace process, but it reflects that we can't fund and host people who are doing nothing.

The AU's order to rebel groups to leave its headquarter includes both the Sudan Liberation Army (SLA) faction led by Abdel Wahed

Mohamed el-Nur and the JEM

On September 18, 2006 People rallied in cities across the world to protest the violence in the war-torn Dar Fur region of Sudan, and urge world leaders to intervene to resolve the conflict. Tens of thousands of people demonstrated in New York City, religious leaders gathered outside Downing Street in London to pray for a resolution, and a candlelight vigil was held in Cambodia to remember Dar Fur victims. In a counter demonstration, about 150 people in Khartoum, Sudan, marched to the United Nations' offices to protest the proposed deployment of U.N. peacekeepers in Dar Fur. Protests and other events for the "Global Day for Dar Fur" were scheduled in four dozen cities worldwide to show support for Dar Fur's people and pressure the Sudanese government to protect its civilians and end the conflict.

Is it all about Oil?

Although the civil war in southern Sudan had started long before sharing Oil fortune dominated interests and peace talks in Sudan but it could be ended with an agreement regulate oil fortune sharing, all others conflicts began after oil exploring became main economical topic and part of each peace talks agenda.

Sudan, which only started exporting oil in 1999, during this year has become sub-Saharan Africa's third largest oil producer, only surpassed by Nigeria and Angola. Peace between the North and South has enabled Sudan to produce around 400,000 barrels per day (bbl/d) of crude oil by now, with government plans to increase this to 600,000 bbl/d by the end of the year. With large undeveloped fields, exports are set to boom.

New statistics presented by US state agencies today indicate that Sudan already has become a bigger oil producer than Equatorial Guinea (330,000 bbl/d), Congo Brazzaville (244,000 bbl/d) and Gabon (237,000 bbl/d)—countries that have shifted on holding sub-Saharan Africa's third place among oil producers during the last decade. Only Nigeria (2.2 million bbl/d) and Angola (1.4 million bbl/d) produce more oil in sub-Saharan Africa.

Also in a North African context, Sudan's oil production is becoming significant. Algeria is estimated to have an oil production of around 2.1 million bbl/d, including condensates and natural gas plant liquids, while Libya's oil production is around 1.8 million bbl/d—both countries experiencing rapid production growth.

Meanwhile, the Egyptian oil production is currently estimated at 579,000 bbl/d, being on a downwards trend since the mid-1990s. Sudan will soon surpass its northern neighbour.

By conservative estimates, Sudan's current oil production is at 382,000 bbl/d, according to figures from the US agency Energy Information Administration (EIA). In 2005, Sudan's crude oil production had averaged 363,000 bbl/d, and rapid growth was registered. It is therefore possible that the Sudanese oil production already has hit the 400,000 bbl/d threshold, sources indicate.

Numbers on Sudanese oil production always are insecure as the Khartoum government and major oil companies operating in the country avoid publicity and do not hand out complete data. Oil production in Sudan is a sensitive issue due to US sanctions against the country and "genocide complicity" allegations against oil companies involved there made by US courts.

Sudan only started producing and exporting oil in July 1999, with the completion of an export pipeline that runs from central Sudan to the Red Sea port of Bashair. North American and European companies have been strongly discouraged from taking part in Sudan's oil adventure—especially by Washington—leaving Sudan open to Chinese, Indian and Malaysian investors. China National Petroleum Corporation (CNPC), India's Oil and Natural Gas Corporation (ONGC) and Malaysia's Petronas are now the biggest players in Sudan's oil sector.

According to the 'Oil and Gas Journal', Sudan contained proven conventional reserves of 563 million barrels in January 2006, which is more than twice the proven estimates of 2001. The Sudanese Energy Ministry estimates total oil reserves at five billion barrels. Exploration efforts have so far covered only a few parts of the country.

Due to civil conflict, oil exploration has been mostly limited to the central and south-central regions of Sudan. Production is centred on the areas bordering the Khartoum-held north and the autonomous government of South Sudan, a region that finally has found peace and thus allows for stable oil production and investments at a larger level.

But the Chinese also operate larger oil fields between the regions of Kordofan and Dar Fur—both under Khartoum's control—which are close to the Dar Fur conflict area. Sudanese sources estimate that Dar Fur and Kordofan may be the areas richest in oil in the entire country. It is further estimated that vast potential reserves are held in the desert regions of north-western Sudan, the Blue Nile Basin, and the Red Sea area in eastern Sudan.

The expansion of the Sudanese oil production is going very quickly, with major investments flowing into the country from Hina's CNPCs. According to local sources, it is the large and controversial concession of Block 6 that is currently experiencing the largest Chinese investments. Block 6 is partly located in Dar Fur.

During the last few months, CNPC has been able to increase the production on Block 6 from 10,000 to 40,000 bbl/d.

With the large increases on Block 6—but also in South Sudan, where North American oil companies meanwhile are able to participate—Sudan's oil production by now probably already is at around 420,000 bbl/d. Khartoum is therefore on a steady road to reach the production target of 600,000 bbl/d it has set for the end of 2006.

Khartoum and the autonomous government of South Sudan—which have signed a revenue-sharing deal on oil production in the south—can make good use of the booming incomes. Since November 2005, oil revenues have streamed into the empty pockets of the South Sudan government, which is in the process of establishing entirely new state structures in a vast region plagued by warfare for over two decades. Revenues are to help finance rebuilding of health and education services.

Also the Khartoum government strongly needs these extra revenues, especially as Western countries increasingly have isolated Sudan. Despite sanctions against Khartoum, the country's GDP grew by 6.4 percent in 2005 and is expected to grow 5.7 percent in 2006, mainly driven by the oil industry. Currently, 70 percent of Sudan's total export revenues come from oil exports, according to EIA. In response to inquiries over the alleged new oil installation in Dar Fur, the Sudanese embassy in Nairobi has provided a dossier on the history of oil exploration and production in Sudan.

Oil exploration in Sudan was started in the late 1950s at the Red Sea coast, but actual digging began 25 years later after an agreement with Chevron Petroleum was signed in 1975.

Encouraging initial results obtained from central Sudan led to the signing of a second agreement with Chevron in 1979 for operations in Muglad and Blue Nile basins. Subsequently, a number of agreements were signed with the French petroleum company Total and Sun Oil of the US in 1982.

Geological and geophysical surveys were conducted at different locations and the results led to the digging of 95 exploratory wells. Of these, 26 were found to be productive, while the remaining 49 were not promising.

Explorations were made at fields in Suakin in East Abu Gabra in the west, and Sharif, Wihda, Talh, Heglig, Adariel and Kaikatif in the south. But there was no oil production.

In 1992, a Blocks System was adopted in the division of the basins, and on the basis of this system, a number of agreements were signed with the Greater Nile Petroleum Company, (GNPOC) the Canadian Petroleum Company, Gulf Petroleum and the China National Petroleum Company.

Petroleum was first produced at the fields of Abu Gabra and Sharif, and was followed by production at Adariel and Heglig. The total production amounted to 220,000 barrels per day (bpd) but research indicated that the volume of reserves was much higher.

Sudan's state-owned petroleum corporation, Sudapet, was established in accordance with the 1998 Law of Petroleum Resources. It is a public corporation whose main functions are to administer and control all petroleum-related activities carried out in Sudan, including offshore exploration operations, and to set specifications for marketing of petroleum products.

The country's import bill for petroleum products had by this time hit $400 million, weighing heavily on the country's balance of trade. This led the government to encourage investment in the exploration, production, refining and distribution of oil.

Among the foreign investors are the China National Petroleum Company (CNPC), which began work as government partners in Blocks 1, 2 and 4 in 1995. They are also in partnership in Blocks 3 and 7 with Petrodar and have been granted an outright concession for Block 6. Petronas Oil Company has the concession for Block 8 and is also a partner in GNPOC.

The Pakistani oil company Zafir has recently been awarded concession rights to Block 9. Currently, Sudan is exporting 300,000 bpd of crude oil.

A number of companies have applied for new oil concessions, particularly Block 11 in central Sudan, and Blocks 15 and 12 in eastern Sudan and western Sudan, respectively.

Already, there is a proposal for the construction of a pipeline—to be named Mina El Khair—for exporting refined oil from Khartoum to Port Sudan and other terminals.

Initially, the marketing of petro-leum products was exclusively undertaken by foreign companies which operated a network of depots and distributions stations. In 1975, the government started importing petroleum, while the companies continued with distribution.

In the early 1990s, local investors started to compete in the field of deposition and distribution. A number of national companies constructed more than 20 depots at Khartoum Refinery.

In May 2003 petroleum production reached 500,000 bpd and petroleum and its derivatives were the leading export items in 2002.

A total of 62.2 million barrels of crude were exported in 2002. According to the foreign trade statistics, the earnings for that year were $1.4 billion.

The statistics also show that 450.7 million metric tonnes of benzene were exported at a value of $93.1 million. Gas exports totalled 92.6 million metric tonnes, earning the country $17.4 million.

Exports of naphta were 32.2 million metric tonnes, worth $2.2 million. Eight million metric tonnes of furnace oil reached foreign markets and fetched $1.1 million. Earnings of $11,000 were made from the export of 95,000 metric tonnes of mixed gas.

PEACE ENFORCEMENT THROUGH UN?

The Role of the African Union in Dar Fur

The African Union (AU) organisation consists of fifty-three African states. Established in 2001, the AU was formed as a successor to the amalgamated African Economic Community (AEC) and the Organisation of African Unity (OAU). Eventually, the AU aims to have a single currency and a single integrated defence force, as well as other institutions of state, including a cabinet for the AU Head of State. The purpose of the union is to help secure Africa's democracy, human rights, and a sustainable economy, especially by bringing an end to intra-African conflict and creating an effective common market

The AU is governed by the AU Assembly of Heads of State and the Pan-African Parliament, which are both assisted by the AU Commission which constitutes one of the secretariats of the Pan African Parliament. The current President of the Pan African Parliament, Gertrude Mongella, is the Head of State of African Union. Denis Sassou-Nguesso, president of the AU state of the Republic of the Congo is the Chair of the AU Assembly of Heads of State and Government. Alpha Oumar Konare is the current Chairman of the African Union Commission, which serves as the Secretariat of the Pan African Parliament and a civil service of the African Union.

The AU covers the entire continent except for Morocco, which opposes the membership of Western Sahara as the Sahrawi Arab Democratic Republic. However, Morocco has a special status within the AU and benefits from the services available to all AU states from the institutions of the AU, such as the African Development Bank. Moroccan delegates also participate at important AU functions, and negotiations continue to try to resolve the conflict with the Polisario Front in Tindouf, Algeria and parts of Western Sahara.

The historical foundations of the African Union originated in the Union of African States, an early confederation that was established by Kwame Nkrumah in the

1960s, as well as subsequent attempts to unite Africa, including the Organisation of African Unity (OAU), which was established on May 25, 1963, and the African Economic Community in 1981. Critics argued that the OAU in particular did little to protect the rights and liberties of African citizens from their own political leaders, often dubbing it the "Dictators' Club".

The idea of creating the AU was revived in the mid-1990s as a result of the efforts of the African Unification Front. The heads of state and government of the OAU issued the Sirte Declaration on September 9, 1999, calling for the establishment of an African Union. The Declaration was followed by summits at Lomé in 2000, when the Constitutive Act of the African Union was adopted, and at Lusaka in 2001, when the plan for the implementation of the African Union was adopted.

The African Union was launched in Durban on July 9, 2002, by its first president, South African Thabo Mbeki, at the first session of the Assembly of the African Union. The second session of the Assembly was in Maputo in 2003, and the third session in Addis Ababa on July 6, 2004.

Its Constitutive Act declares that it shall "invite and encourage the full participation of the African diaspora as an important part of our Continent, in the building of the African Union". The African Union Government has defined the African diaspora as "consisting of people of African origin living outside the continent, irrespective of their citizenship and nationality and who are willing to contribute to the development of the continent and the building of the African Union".

The AU's first military intervention in a member state was the May 2003 deployment of a peacekeeping force of soldiers from South Africa, Ethiopia, and Mozambique to Burundi to oversee the implementation of the various agreements. AU troops are also deployed in Sudan for peacekeeping in the Dar Fur conflict. In 1994 the OAU wasn't aware of the situation of the country and only provided some humanitarian help to the conflict.

The African Union Troops in Dar Fur

The presence of African Union forces in Dar Fur however helped somehow in protecting civilians, at least those in refugees' camps, even to the most disingenuous members of the international community. It will no longer be able alone to undertake the various tasks of civilian and humanitarian protection and provide security for the more than 2 million displaced persons in some 300 camps and concentrations of affected populations; providing security for humanitarian operations and transport corridors; disarming or neutralizing the Janjaweed militia and others rebel groups; protecting vulnerable rural populations that continue to suffer deadly attacks; and providing the security that will enable displaced and bereft persons to return to their villages and lands.

These tasks are and have always been clearly far beyond AU capabilities, even when AU deployment was cynically celebrated by US, European, and UN officials. There is some evidence that at least the language about AU capabilities may be starting to change; but there is even more evidence that self-serving political realities and a lack of real commitment will prevail, and that apparent commitment to an international Dar Fur intervention is merely verbal.

A key summit meeting of the AU's 15-member Peace and Security Council (PSC) called to rule on the status of the AU contingent in Dar Fur took place in New York on Sept. 20, 2006. Sudanese President Omar al-Beshir, who joined the summit, came under intense pressure to accept the UN force.

Beshir claims that UN peace plans are a US-engineered ploy to invade his country and plunder its resources. The United States and Denmark meanwhile called for a ministerial meeting of the UN Security Council on Dar Fur here Friday to discuss Dar Fur.

US Ambassador to the UN John Bolton said the foreign ministers of the council's 15 members were being invited to take part along with their counterparts from Canada, South Africa, Nigeria, Senegal, Rwanda, the Netherlands, Egypt, Chad, Norway and Algeria.

Bolton also announced that he was circulating a draft resolution calling for a six-month extension of the mandate of the 12,273-strong UN force in southern Sudan, which expires September 24.

The draft also reiterated a council call for beefing up the strength of that force to up to 20,000 so it can be shifted to Dar Fur to keep the peace there.

Addressing the UN Security Council, UN envoy Jan Pronk sought to reassure Sudan that the UN aim in Dar Fur was only "to protect the people, while respecting the sovereignty of the Sudanese nation". He reiterated that any UN deployment there would require Khartoum's consent.

The envoy stressed the need to keep the AU force in Dar Fur until Khartoum gives its green light for a UN takeover.

Pronk also made it clear that a peace accord signed by Khartoum and the main Dar Fur rebel group, the faction of the Sudan Liberation Movement (SLM) led by Minni Minnawi, in Nigeria last May was not working because it did not include two other insurgent groups.

A smaller faction of the SLM led by Abdel Wahid Al-Nur and another group the Justice and Equality Movement (JEM) have refused to sign the accord, saying it did not meet all their demands.

At same time, in a related development, US Secretary of State Condoleezza Rice discussed Dar Fur with her Chinese counterpart Li US officials.

Rice urged the Chinese to do everything they could do to allow in the international force, to allow for that transition from the AU mission to the UN force. Despite all efforts of UN Secretary-General Kofi Annan, and seemingly supportive words from

US Secretary of State Condoleezza Rice, and all UN Security Council resolutions the movement toward an international force that will succeed the AU force in Dar Fur has yet to gain any meaningful traction. The AU may have signalled that it is willing in principle to surrender the mission to the UN (chiefly because it is no longer being supported by dismayed donors in Brussels), but there are huge obstacles in Khartoum and within the UN, especially at the Security Council, but also within the UN bureaucracies.

The US government signals GoS that it need not be worry about international humanitarian intervention, nor about sanctions.

The UN Secretary-General declared in December 2005 in his report to the Security Council that Khartoum has "abjectly failed to fulfil its commitments to identify, neutralize and disarm militia groups outside the formal state security forces under its influence, as demanded by the UN Security Council.

The UN Security Council adopted a resolution on August 31 calling for the deployment of up to 20,000 peacekeepers to replace an embattled African Union contingent that has failed to restore peace and stability in Dar Fur.

But GoS rejected as usual the deployment of UN forces, charging the plan was part of a US-engineered plot to invade and plunder resources. Diplomats and experts see a deployment as crucial to the implementation of an ailing peace deal signed in May, and argue that regime officials fear a UN presence would expose them to war crimes prosecutions.

Sudan expels U.N. envoy after he accused army of mobilizing Arab militias in Dar Fur.

On October, 7, 2006 Sudanese Minister of State for Information and Communications Farh Agar announced that the file of deploying UN peacekeeping forces in the country's western region of Dar Fur had been closed.

Sudanese Minister of State for Information and Communications Farh Agar Meanwhile, Sudanese Minister of State for Foreign Affairs Ali hmed Karti also said that the Sudanese government was due to sign new protocol with the United Nations and the African Union (AU) to absorb the new plan for Dar Fur, The three-month mandate of AU forces in Dar Fur is not enough to complete proposals stated in the plan, but it could be helpful for finalizing a resolution in the region.

It was reported that the UN and AU have presented a plan of sending UN experts and technicians besides financial assistance to the AU forces, which have been accepted by the Sudanese government.

In view of Sudan's persistence in its refusal of deploying international peacekeeping forces in Dar Fur, the AU extended on September 21, 2006 the mandate of its 7800-strong forces in Dar Fur further three months. The Sudanese government has welcomed a resolution by the African Union's Peace and Security Council

(PSC) extending the mandate of its forces in Dar Fur for another three months. GoS declared that would have been much better if it had been extended even longer, six months for instance, because the African troops have now got acquainted with the region and its people and their performance has been commended by the international community, State Foreign Minister Al-Sammani al-Wasila al-Sammani told asid that he believes it is easier for the international community to help provide financial and technical assistance to the established AU forces than start from scratch with other forces, like UN forces yet to be forces, He pointed out as important the provision of the PSC resolution calling for the holdout movements to join the Dar Fur peace process. "This provision is very important because security and peace in the region will be guaranteed if those movements sign the Dar Fur peace agreement and it is therefore imperative that the international community endeavour to persuade them to sign the Abuja peace deal. Contrary to the continued calls by some governments for the UN to act unilaterally against Sudan, AU Commission Chairman Alpha Konare is contra this view. Although he is on favour of UN intervention but this has to be done with the Sudanese government's approval, the bulk of the troops would be AU forces, the command would be African and the AU political leadership will be there. He also contradicted certain members of the Security Council, which have consistently placed the blame solely on the Government of Sudan. According to Konare, the current instability in Dar Fur is more the direct result of fighting between the rebel movements themselves than between the rebels and the Government of Sudan.

The situation in the period from 2005 to 2006 Dar Fur has reached a catastrophic stage. The peacekeeping force of the African Union, meant only to monitor a weak, partly and an unstable cease-fire, has proven inadequate to stop the large-scale violence there. African states have shown strong resistance to non-African forces stepping into the crisis, citing broad principles of Non intervention. The UN Security Council has failed to act on the situation and the developed countries have shown little readiness to intervene. Requests from the African Union peacekeeping force for assistance and aid from NATO have been answered, but not fully. The international community's reaction to a potentially genocidal situation has been something more than a gesture, but something less than a clear expression of political will.

This raises numerous questions about public attitudes in both Africa and the United States.

Now the majority of the African countries believe the UN should have the right to intervene to stop human rights abuses such as genocide. The UN is the most popular force to intervene in situations like Dar Fur, followed by the African Union, consistent with a broader attitude of confidence in the United Nations.

Half believe that countries should be able to intervene in the event of such human rights abuses even without UN approval. This attitude about the United Nations reflects a broader confidence in the UN among the African countries also those represented in he AU forces in Dar Fur.

The United Nations Organisation

The organisation of United Nations has been created as result of the experiences resulted from the two World Wars. The main purpose of establishing the organisation is to maintain international peace and security specially the strict limitation of use of force by member states.[33]

However, the United Nations Charter recognizes some exceptions from this rule where the above mentioned prohibition under some conditions shall not be applied.[34] Those exceptions are:

1. The inherent right of individual or collective self-defence under Article 51 of the UN Charter.

2. Enforcement actions authorized by the Security Council in accordance with Chapter VII.

The purposes of the above mentioned exceptions as to the prohibition of use of force can be summarized in the following six points:

---

[33] The term "United Nations" refers to what the preamble to the Charter describes as (an international organisation to be known as the United Nations) the UN consists of six organs: the General Assembly, the Security Council, the Economic and Social Council, the Trusteeship Council, the International Court of Justice and the Secretariat. All of which are based in USA/New York with an exception of the International Court of Justice which seated in the Netherlands/Den Haag. In addition to those main six organs there numerous sub-organisations, Programmes and Funds created to help achieving UN missions, e.g. UNHCR, UNICEF, and UNDP.... etc.

[34] It is beyond the scope of this book to present detailed and complete covering study about to United Nations as Organisation, thus only facts in relation with justifying active UN role in the on-going conflict in Dar Fur shall be considered.
Article 2(4) of the United Nations Charter: All Member States shall refrain in their international relations from the threat of use of force against the territorial integrity or political independence of any state, or in any other manner inconsistent with the purpose of the United Nations.

- to restore or maintain international peace and security in the face of a threat to
the peace, breach of peace or an act of aggression in form of (Peace Enforcement)
action or mission:

The UN Charter tends in this point to create a tied collective security system to
avoid the mistakes made by the creation of the League of Nations. Chapter VII
of the Charter provides that in the case of a threat to the peace, breach of peace
or act of aggression which could not be resolved by peaceful means, the Security
Council could take such action by air, sea or land forces as may be necessary to
maintain or restore international peace and security, the Member Sates are to conclude special agreements with the Security Council by which they would, on call,
make available armed forces, assistance and facilities for the purpose of maintaining international peace and security.[35]

Enforce sanctions imposed by the Security Council (Sanctions Enforcement)

Sanctions imposed in connection of the enforcement of a Security Council
Resolution need also to be enforced otherwise they have no affections. There are
some examples of water-ways related actions to enforce Security Council's sanctions e.g. in 1966 the Security Council called on the United Kingdom to use
force if necessary to prevent the arrival Beira in Mozambique of vessels reasonably
believed to be carrying oil destined for Southern Rhodesia. Warships of the Royal
Navy were deployed for that purpose, also some operations of the US—Navy during the Iraqi invasion of Kuwait in 1990s fall under this category. An actual example is the on-going operations of German-Navy on Lebanese coasts to enforce
weapons smuggling embargo against Hissb-Allah militias.

---

[35] The early case in this regard was the North Korean invasion of South Korea in June
1950. The Security Council recommended Member States should assist the South Korea
to stop the invasion and restore international peace and security. Also the Security Council
decision regarding the Iraqi invasion against Kuwait in August 1990 was such case of
international peace enforcement. However Member States those joining such operations
are mostly such countries with specific (strategic or economic) interests in the on-going
conflict, the region and/or especially in the invaded State.

Defend the personnel of Peacekeeping operations (self-defence)

Whether in national or international rules, self-defence is one of the most clear cases were using force is allowed. The UN Charter provides the same rule in case of self-defence. The UN Armed Forces have instructions to defend themselves in case of falling under attack. The General Assembly tried to summarize a definition for what"self-defenceis. "The Force will be provided with weapons of a defensive character only. It shall not use force except in self-defence. Self-defence would include resistance to attempts by forceful means to prevent it from discharging its duties under the mandate of the Security Council.[36]

Provide physical protection to civilians in a war situation (Protection of Civilians)

Protection of civilians is doubtless a core element in Peacekeeping missions, without the need of express obligation thereto. On the other hand, carrying out this duty of civilians protection was mostly unsuccessful especially in such cases were use of force was abandoned or were this has taken advisory form to the local authority how to carry out civilians protection by themselves.[37]

---

[36] The above mentioned definition came in connection with the building up of the UNEF II in 1973. When the first UN Peacekeeping Force UNEF1 has been built up, the troops were instructed that they never take initiatives of use of fire but they might respond to such an attack. The same instructions has been given to the ONUC operated in Zaire in July 1960, the most important experience in this regard has been made by the Congo's operations.

[37] Examples of which are Congo's and Haiti's Operations. This was demonstrated in Haiti a few days after the arrival of Peacekeeping Forces when a civilian has been beaten to death by Haitian uniformed group before the eyes of UN troops. However, the Security Council could put this behind it in Bosnia by using force measures to actively protect civilians. On Wednesday, August 10 2005 Haitian police, accompanied by a group of men dressed in civilian clothes attacked suspected gang members, bandits, and kidnappers in the neighborhoods of Bel-Air and Cité Soleil. Witnesses say the police fired indiscriminately at the suspects, killing at least five, including a pregnant woman and a teenage boy. The police then stood by as the civilian-looking men they had brought with them proceeded to attack and lynch at least five more victims including one who was burned alive. Currently MINUSTAH, a 7,600 member United Nations peacekeeping force, is in Haiti with the goal of stopping the wave of shootings and violence that is threatening November elections. The upcoming elections will replace the interim government set up after the February 2004 rebellion that forced President Jean-Bertrand Aristide into exile. Despite

Civilian's protection was an issue in Bosnia as well as in Rwanda. Where the Security Council later managed to solve this problem in Bosnia, Bosnia's operation lessons haven't been adopted in Rwanda. The UN force in Rwanda was acting according to Chapter VII of the UN Charter and its mandate was to "contribute to the protections of civilians only in case of riskincluding building up of safe areas, the fact that excluded the use of force.

Protect activities intended to relieve the suffering of civilians in such circumstances (protection of humanitarian activities)

Protection of humanitarian activities is part of or exactly first step to protecting civilians e.g. to use force to protect Airports, convoys, hospitals ... etc has been authorized by the Security Council in many cases.[38]

Such protection operations seem to be easier or less difficult to carry out than civilians' protections missions but still far from being unproblematic.

Problems like land mines, night ambushes, using civilians as human shields ... etc are just few examples of obstacles facing UN Forces carrying out such mandate. Also in cases were Force needn't to be used, political problems like refusal of cooperation from side of local authorities or administrative and legislative objections make the fulfilment of humanitarian activities protection difficult if not impossible in some cases. The cases, where use of force becomes necessary give rise for similar political problems as by the cases of protection of civilians.[39]

---

the U.N. presence, massacres have continued. In a report last month, the human rights group Amnesty international said Haiti's ill-equipped police force executes and arbitrarily arrests people with impunity. It also criticized the U.N. for not preventing such police action. Action must be taken to stop the chaos and killing in Haiti; MINUSTAH must begin challenging the illegal violence of Haiti and initiate genuine action to protect the human rights of Haitian civilians.

[38] Protection of humanitarian activities was the reason behind the Security Council's decision in May 1992 to give UNPROFOR a mandate in Bosnia and Herzegovina after the breakout of civil war there. The same reasons were behind mandates in Angola, Rwanda, Somalia and Haiti.

[39] Enforce relocation of civilians for their own safety. Also the question; whether humanitarian agencies accept protection by military force..? Humanitarian agencies have always relied on their neutrality, political independent and non-military character to successfully carry out their missions.

Restore or maintain peace and security in an internal conflict

UN intervention in domestic civil matters or matters those mainly fall within the domestic jurisdiction of a member state is prohibited by article 2 (7) of the UN Charter, this without prejudice to the application of enforcement measures under Chapter VII.[40] The UN practice show many cases, especially during the Cold War, where the Security Council authorized Peacekeeping actions related to internal conflicts, this practice started by the Congo and Cyprus conflicts and has been continued in the case of Somalia conflict. However all those actions took place within the framework of collective security, with some hesitation concerning the internationality aspects of the Security Council action?

Peace-keeping or peace enforcement..?

The question of Peacekeeping presuppose existing peace which facing a threat of deteriorating, which means preventing the outbreak of a conflict. Although the situation in Dar Fur is far beyond this, it is important to have an overview about UN peacekeeping history and development in this regard.

The history of Peacekeeping operations and Peacekeeping forces after the Cold War shows two categories or divisions of those generations; the so-called traditional or first-generation also known as Cold War peacekeeping and the new or second-generation or multidimensional peacekeeping.[41]

The first-generation operations represent those where a political organ of the UN deploys a military force between two or more armies, with their consent, pending, and in the absence of, a political settlement.[42] Others add helping to create conditions in which political negotiations can start or continue as one of the targets of a first-generation peacekeeping operation. Clearly there is no a united or generally accepted definition, but at least the principles of first-generation operations are

---

[40] Article 2(7) nothing contained in the present Charter shall authorize the United Nations to intervene in matters which are essentially within the domestic jurisdiction of any state or shall require the Members to submit such matters to settlement under the present Charter; but this principle shall not prejudice the application of enforcement measures under Chapter VII.

[41] There are many critical opinions and discussions as to his kind of categorizing. See J. Chopra, Second Generation Multinational Operations, The Washington Quarterly 15, summer 1992; and Steven Ratner, The New UN Peace-keeping, supra FN83 of Chapter 1. Charles Dobbie, A Concept for Post-Cold War Peace-keeping, Survival 36(3), Autumn 1994:121-48. Alan James, Peace-Keeping in the post-Cold War Era.

[42] According to Steven Ratner. Op. cit., p 17.

definitive ones, those has been derived from five principles outlined in regard to UNEF I.[43]

- Consent of the parties to the dispute for the establishment of the mission,
- Non-use of force except in self-defence,
- Voluntary contributions of contingents from small, neutral countries to partici-pate in the force,
- Impartiality and non- intervention,
- Day-to day-control of peacekeeping operations by the Secretary General.

The principles of consent of the parties to the conflict, of the non-use of force and of impartiality has been fundamental principles during the first forty years period of the United Nations, but this hasn't to mean that the existence of them was proofed by every Peacekeeping mission. The above mentioned confirm the below coming theory of necessity of intervention under serious human rights violations especially when such situation threat to reach genocide, which means protection of civilians has priority than question of whether all or some principles are pres-ent, which obviously the case in Dar Fur is.

Some observers speak about a third-generation peacekeeping and remark this with the building up of UNOSOM II as the first UN Peacekeeping operation autho-rized by the council under Chapter VII of the UN Charter to use force in the crucial task of disarming Somali militias. This remark and experience is important here for many reasons; because the similar conditions and nature of the conflict in Somalia and the one in Dar Fur, also because of the necessity of immediate intervention in Dar Fur in which some mistakes happened in Somalia can be avoided. [44]

The UNOSOM was mainly built for the purpose of humanitarian assistance according to the Security Council resolution 751 of 24 April 1992, following the deterioration of situation in Somalia; the United Task Force led by the USA was authorized by the SC to carry out a peace enforcement operation.[45] Later UNOSOM II took over the UNITAF as a Chapter VII operation.

---

[43] The above mentioned principles agreed to by former SC Dag Hammrskjold, and Lester Pearson.

[44] UN operations; not only expanding, but breaking new ground, UN Chronicle, Vol.30 No.3, September 1993, p44.

[45] UNITAF led by the USA during peace enforcement operations in Somalia in accor-dance with the Security Council resolution 794, December 3, 1992.

Worth mention that enforcement measure involving use of force minded by UN Chapter's drafters are such of article 42, although this also applicable under article 39, or 40 of the UN Charter.

The humanitarian intervention right in international public law

Humanitarian Intervention has been a subject of debate for many years. The debate mainly concerns legitimacy and legality of this actions part of international law. But what is Humanitarian Intervention.?

Humanitarian Intervention signifies the use of armed force by a state or states to protect citizens of targeted state from large scale human rights violations. Humanitarian Intervention in the above mentioned sense defer from intervention situation by one state to protect own citizens in targeted state.[46] The nationality of citizens subject to violation is of secondary importance in case of Humanitarian Intervention. Humanitarian Intervention in cases of self-determination conflicts take place on behalf of a self-determination movement within the targeted state to protect human rights and prevent violations against human rights not create a new state.

Using armed force for the above mentioned purpose of Humanitarian Intervention is subject to many restrictions and prohibitions, the most important of them are outlined in the UN Charter. On the other side, the increase of human rights violations on the one hand and of the conventional and customary norms of human rights protection enforce such norms on the other hand raise many questions as to such limits and restrictions and extensions.[47]

The changes within the international law from a law governing relations between states themselves to a law governing how those states to treat their citizens came gradually but surely. The UN Charter originally was silent as to description of rights and freedoms which are be protected, but its provisions in this respect has been later developed and supplemented by the Universal declaration of Human Rights adopted by the General Assembly on December, 10, 1948 and the International Covenant on Civil and Political Rights from March, 23, 1976

---

[46] Interventions actions to protect nationals are mainly based on self-defence principle

[47] UN Secretary General Kofi Annan seems to stand behind the above mentioned by his declaration on January 26, 2004 by the Stockholm International Forum on Preventing Genocide; Genocide … is particularly always, if not by definition, a threat to the peace. It must be dealt with as such by strong and united political action and, in extreme cases, by military action".

and the International Covenant on Economic, Social and Cultural Rights from January, 3, 1976.

Intervention and sovereignty

The origin of the sovereignty doctrine which originally concerned the internal structure of the absolute monarchies found its origin in the European Middle Ages. According to it, there has to be an organ in the state which possessed absolute legislative and political power. The head of this organ was totally independent in exercising such power without duty answer higher power (being sovereign)[48]. The principle of non-intervention resulted in respect of the doctrine of sovereignty as described above. The difficulty with the principle of non-intervention is to define the degree of interference that constitutes impermissible intervention.[49]

---

[48] The king, the prince or governor … etc

[49] the Pugwash study group discussed in it's second meeting took place in Como, Italy, from 28-30 September 2000 which this topic concerning Intervention, Sovereignty and International Security. The debate over humanitarian intervention has been shaped by the ongoing crisis in Sierra Leone at that time, most notably the arrival and failure of the UN intervention force, the 17 August publication of the Brahimi report; UN Secretary General Kofi Annan's call at the Millennium Summit for an extended UN role in the protection of human rights; and continued post-conflict tensions in Kosovo. For some, the implications of these events are that international legal case law is reinforced for humanitarian intervention and that the success of the UK's Operation Palliser in Sierra Leone demonstrates a need to think more expansively of how to conduct military interventions (e.g., strategic raids that can change the political equation on the ground without necessarily having to achieve victory). On the political side, however, the recommendations of the Brahimi report are caught in a vice, with there being no means to implement them. It seems clear that the UN is incapable of commanding and conducting the type of military intervention (deploying quick reaction forces) that could be effective in reversing a deteriorating situation. Within the UN, Cuba and North Korea have blocked efforts at giving the Department of Peacekeeping Operations (DPKO) greater military competence (e.g., by appointing seconded officers). Combined with the UN's bureaucratic nature and the absence of strong US involvement, the Kofi Annan initiative at the Millennium Summit raises more questions than answers regarding the UN's ability to be an effective command operation. Accordingly, many in the group felt that the 'franchising' of military operations will be necessary if the international community is to have the resources it needs for timely and effective intervention; more thought is needed on how to efficiently subcontract military operations, especially to deal with perceptions of double standards when it comes to committing troops. One problem of many with subcontracting; however, is that those who provide peacekeepers often expect to reap the economic benefits of reconstruction (a form of neocolonialism). In the case of Sierra Leone, for example, there is the problem of

British troops providing training to local troops who are led by a former warlord. In a discussion of how concepts of state sovereignty and individual human rights are evolving, one participant noted that both have been integrated since their origins in the 12th century, and that what is new is the concept of international security, beginning with League of Nations in 1919, and evolving through the 20th century. What China, Cuba, North Korea, and others defend is a concept of absolute sovereignty, but sovereignty has never been absolute. In western countries, sovereignty is maligned by stressing its negative connotations, but sovereignty is a positive concept when grounded in equality (extending to both territory and the individual). Human rights in both international law and the UN charter have now become a "major legal net" of rules, procedures, statutes, albeit of a different character than the body of international law surrounding sovereignty. Another view stressed that the right of rebellion and self-determination, as epitomized by the American Revolution, is based on universal rights; in a similar way, the spirit of the UN Charter is in its preamble. Problems arise with the tendency of powerful states to export their values, however worthy, through illegitimate means (e.g., the messianism of the French Revolution in exporting democracy). Comparisons today would be countries exporting free-market and democratic values through trading policies (globalization) or through military means; noteworthy ends not always implemented by legitimate means. How far can states go in acting without official UN sanction? The use of force in international affairs was not prohibited until the creation of the UN Charter (article 2), so there was a tradition of humanitarian intervention that evolved prior to 1945 that did not need the official sanction of a body like the UN. Some argue for a concept of legitimate countermeasures that can be considered lawful in counteracting blatant abuses of human rights and violations of humanitarian law; the corollary is that the actions of Russia and China in blocking effective action to deal with a situation such as Kosovo were illegitimate. Other participants agreed that there are no absolutes regarding concepts of human rights, sovereignty, and intervention; the problem is one where western countries are seeking to impose their will on the majority. Moreover, the consequences of military interventions often end up making the situation worse. What measures could in fact strengthen UN humanitarian action? Changing the Security Council veto process was thought unrealistic, as was allowing the General Assembly to substitute itself for the Security Council (e.g., the 1950s Dean Acheson proposal). More feasible would be strengthening the UN's early warning and conflict prevention mechanisms. Some suggested a more active Secretary General (a lá article 99) who acts as the conscience of the Security Council. In response, it was noted that Kofi Annan has been encouraged by the Security Council to act according to article 99, but is then reminded to be more of a Secretary and less of a General. In addition, as was evident during the Kosovo crisis, there is a fundamental split in the UN between the legal and political departments (anti-intervention) and humanitarian affairs (pro). Regarding the *Millennium Report*, one should turn the question around, asking those with doubts about intervention—just how should the international community respond to Rwanda, Srebrenica, etc.? One problem in forging an international consensus is that support for interventions among developing countries is not helped by the fact that the

Balkans receive a majority share of UN post-reconstruction funds. Plus, the UN will never support interventions against the major regional powers, much less against the P-5. And, despite the moral imperative cited by Annan, the logistics difficulties of intervening in a country like the Democratic Republic of Congo (where seven different militaries are currently operating) will block that prospect. Oftentimes, the UN's problem in calling upon member states is that the willing are not able, and the able are not willing. Taking but the most recent example, India joins what it thinks is a peacekeeping force, not an intervention force, its relations with Nigeria sour, so it leaves Sierra Leone. Where does the UN go from here? As noted in the Brahimi report, interventions/peacekeeping must be based on a well-defined mandate and backed by appropriate resources, or they shouldn't be undertaken. The notion of an all-volunteer UN force is a non-starter; the G-77 won't agree to it, because they say it will be used against them, and the US won't agree because it will have to bear the cost. So, there will continue to be problems in getting timely authorization to use standby forces. Looking at the larger picture, the UN has not even done proper reviews of how to conduct successful preventive diplomacy (only one success cited, between Iran and Afghanistan) and post-conflict reconstruction. Sentiments were expressed that humanitarian intervention does not have to be military intervention; a wide range of options and agencies are available, and early warning can be more effective than it has been. Regarding US attitudes towards the UN, one participant expressed understanding for the criticisms of American exceptionalism, but thought that Americans should turn the question around—why is the US so often called in at the last minute to resolve problems that have been festering for years? Only through more effective UN mechanisms for conflict prevention and collective intervention will the US not be the 'force of last resort.' Another participant asked if groups like Pugwash could help the process by defining the criteria for intervention, which could then make humanitarian interventions more timely, more of an automatic process, and of a nature that targets those responsible rather than injures innocent civilians. One response was that the Security Council would never agree on "rules of the road" beforehand, but perhaps could reach agreement on general principles. The primary problem is that the number of UN mandates is increasing, but not the resources to carry them out. A particular problem is that, although the US is willing to pay 25% of the costs of authorized peacekeeping operations, it is billed by the UN for 30%, thus increasing the US debt and locking in an incentive for the US not to join peacekeeping efforts. Politically, humanitarian interventions seem to be focusing at present on protecting ethnic minorities (and in a selective manner), rather than on protecting individual human rights (as in Somalia), which undermines the possibility of reaching consensus. The point was made that the essential failure of the League of Nations was that it was asked to do more than it could; we should avoid the same problem with the UN. The UN and the Secretary General should be 'norm setters.' Sovereignty is about both power and legitimacy. The UN focus should be on peace-building, not continuing to fight battles over where and when to intervene. This means less focus on chapters 6 and 7, and more on chapter 12. And wouldn't this be the best way to re-engage Russia, China and others in a collective UN effort? The commissioned paper by Vladimir Baranovsky, "Humanitarian Intervention:

Russia's Approaches," noted a diversity of Russian views on these issues, but stressed that criticisms of such interventions are similar to those found in other countries, particularly in regard to normative, messianic strains of humanitarian intervention "making the world safe for human rights" (ironically recalling how the Soviet Union imposed its values on others in the past). Feeling insecure and relatively weak, Russia will remain wary of humanitarian intervention. While Russia's approach to humanitarian intervention is evolving, its course will be largely determined by how self-confident Russia feels about itself. The discussion that followed noted how the intervention/sovereignty debate is becoming one of "the West vs. the Rest", the rest including both countries who are intervened against, and the other great powers (the dissident great powers) who disagree with western concepts. The problem thus becomes one of: where do we disagree, why do we disagree, and what do we do about it? To a large extent, the problem isn't one of humanitarian intervention per se, but of peace building and state building, and that a consensus is forming among the great powers on these issues. Humanitarian intervention confuses and confounds the issues of human rights, democratization, etc., of the west imposing its values on others, which issues really come into play in post-conflict reconstruction. Why do we disagree? There are four reasons: (1) the impact of history (and the Soviet legacy), which makes the Russians neuralgic about Western interventions once seen as the tool of "imperialism" and which de-sensitizes them to the implications of their own interventions in nearby states. The latter then opens them to the charge of hypocrisy and clumsy double-standards. (2) Self-interested fears, that NATO unilateralism might be applied to Russia, or in Russia's immediate vicinity, something which, while utterly implausible to most Western observers, figures easily in Russia's prevalent worst-case analysis. (3) Humanitarian interventions and the reasons for them tend to be a low priority among Russian politicians and the elite, given the scale of problems with which they are wrestling at home and in their own neighborhood. (4) While the first three factors have parallels for China and India as well, the fourth factor is unique to the Russian case: Russian disaffection with the West and the United States' approach to humanitarian intervention owes in part to the steady deterioration in the overall relationship with the West and the United States. General frustration finds expression in tangible cases like Kosovo. What then to do? One needs to surmount the problem of great power irresponsibility in the first decade of the post-Cold War era. That is, one needs to overcome the unwillingness of the great powers— whether the US, Japan, China, Russia or major European states—to make major sacrifices and run substantial risks to address the underlying problems at the root of what become crises requiring "humanitarian intervention." In short, the great powers have done far too little to aid with the formidable state building and rebuilding tasks that, when beyond the wit and resources of societies caught in their grip, serve as the single most important threat to international peace and stability. As for the case of humanitarian intervention itself, there should be a basis for consensus between the West and the 'dissident major powers.' Provided the West is prepared to respect their concern over procedure and agency, they are likely to accept the legitimacy of forceful intervention to stop massive violations of fundamental human rights, including genocide. Discussion of Russia noted its attributes as both a superpower and a super problem (with the former deriving in part from the latter). Russia is a critical actor in a critical region (the post-Soviet space). This, along with two other attributes (its UN veto, nuclear weapons) makes Russia a great power. Russian (and other) criticism of the US is that the US is being a superpower on the cheap, engaging in unilateralism when and where it wants. A second can of worms is that the high threshold of genocide and ethnic cleansing on which you might get agreement beforehand doesn't cover all the cases of peace and state building on which the great powers and the UN should devote their resources (the post-Soviet space among many others). We have an extraordinary moment where the absence of strategic rivalry makes possible new dynamics of great power relations for peace building. Strategic rivalry is reappearing, however, especially in the post-Soviet space. The discussion noted how NATO's Kosovo operation was one of several reasons why Russia used more force in the second Chechen war. Also, Moscow could point to human rights abuses in Chechnya between the first and second conflicts as a legitimate pretext for Russia intervening. For most Russians, Kosovo did little to promote the validity of humanitarian intervention. There is also the downside of overloading the concept of humanitarian intervention, of trying to have it do too much. While one can sympathize with the normative values underlying the concept of humanitarian intervention, one should be equally cautious about wreaking too much collateral damage (to civilians, to the international system) in carrying out such interventions. We should adhere to the medical edict of 'do no harm', and more rigorously analyze concepts of the 'legitimate use of force.' To the two current variants permitted by the UN Charter (in self-defense and to ensure international peace), a third variant is needed that better defines and circumscribes the use of force for humanitarian aims. One should be especially cautious of defining modes of humanitarian intervention as a means of fighting terrorism. In short, cooperation, responsibility, and accountability need to be essential components of humanitarian interventions. China's attitude is based on historical experience (19th and 20th century imperial incursions into China) and it's multi-national composition (56 nationalities, with many minorities living in border areas). Demands for independence for Tibet, Xingjing and other areas heighten Chinese sensitivity to issues of intervention and sovereignty. While neighboring India accepts that Tibet is an autonomous region of China, for example, many in India protest Chinese policy in Tibet. Above all, there is the issue of Taiwan, which is sine qua non considered an internal Chinese affair. Taiwan remains the most important and sensitive issue to be resolved, and the one that could most easily spark conflict in East Asia. And, China's stand on Taiwan influences its positions on other matters, as when China blocked Macedonia's request for the stationing of UN troops during the Kosovo crisis (to which one participant wondered whether the Chinese veto itself wasn't a denial of Macedonia's sovereign right to self-defense). Despite China's sensitivities on Tibet, Taiwan and other issues, it was thought that processes of globalization and of China becoming integrated into the international economy are leading to changes in Chinese policy and attitudes regarding modalities of intervention. Others noted that the international community has a vested interest in facilitating Chinese integration into the world community, and of demonstrating that the security interests of the Middle Kingdom are best served by enhancing human security in the rest of the world. China is evaluating different types of conflicts on their own merits and making decisions as to the legitimacy of its involvement in international actions. While China has legitimate concerns about intervention, stemming from its historical experience and humiliation, these concerns are less valid regarding anxieties that other countries will interfere in its internal affairs. There is a need to think of intervention in the context of enhancing individual and human security more broadly, not in legalistic terms of humanitarian intervention. Yet Kofi Annan's emphasis on human security (as opposed to borders, territorial integrity, etc.) was not well received by the G-77. While there is a need for a UN human security report (similar to its human development report), G-77 sensitivities are too great. In this vein, several participants took issue with the premise that the West can somehow 'help' China move toward a greater acceptance of humanitarian intervention. It was noted that the concept of human security will be slow to take root in China, given less emphasis on the individual in Chinese society. In terms of regional dynamics, opinions were expressed that ASEAN/ARF is a particularly ineffective institution on security issues (cases cited were Indonesia, the South China Sea, the Koreas). The commissioned paper by Radha Kumar, "Sovereignty and Intervention: Opinions in South Asia," noted that, while attitudes regarding intervention and sovereignty in South Asia are changing, such notions are still largely defined within the context of de-colonization. Positions taken on international issues have been rather formal and not deeply felt, unlike sentiments regarding regional South Asia issues that are of interest to the international community. Two prime examples are Bangladesh (East Pakistan) and Sri Lanka (and lessons learned in the latter are seen as applicable to Bosnia and Kosovo). When peacekeeping turns to kingmaking, however, disaster happens. Following its experience in Sri Lanka, India has gradually withdrawn from the international peacekeeping arena, the latest example being the removal of Indian troops from Sierra Leone. In Pakistan, a previous emphasis given to alliances over unilateralism and sovereignty is changing due to the experience over Afghanistan. This is also seen in a Pakistani shift over Kashmir from advocating international involvement to stressing that Kashmir is more a bilateral issue with India. Within South Asia, Sri Lanka is the most open to international mediation. The notion of exceptionalism is fading, that conflicts in South Asia are unique, though the consequences of this are more for notions of sovereignty (i.e., greater acceptance for devolution of political power to defuse internal conflicts) than support for intervention. Comments included the point that South Asia has no regional forum or architecture in which to try and resolve regional problems. Pakistan and India have both engaged in unilateral acts which have exacerbated problems between them (Bangladesh, Jammu/Kashmir). India's fear that Sri Lanka might gravitate to the west led to interventions in that country, which worsened the situation and helped contribute to the defeat of the Indian peacekeeping measure. A new element is the nuclear factor and the introduction of delivery vehicles and advanced conventional weapons. India's acquisition from Russia of conventional weapons that Pakistan sees as excessive and which Pakistan can't match, increases its reliance on nuclear deterrence. For this reason, one participant hoped that Pakistan and India might be more willing to accept international initiatives on Kashmir, and possibly on nuclear stability as well. Yet how does the nuclear factor affect Indian and Pakistani perceptions of intervention and sovereignty? Would India joining the Security Council make it more, or less, willing to support peace enforcement? Given resentment over western intervention to prevent Pakistan and India from acquiring nuclear weapons, and the feeling of many in the subcontinent that the acquisition of nuclear weapons is the supreme expression of the sovereign right to self-defense, the nuclear factor only complicates the picture. Participants thought it difficult to imagine any kind of regional security arrangement for South Asia. This is an important point regarding Afghanistan, where Pakistani dependence on the Taliban is becoming increasingly worrisome, given terrorism in Pakistan, possible mischief against China, and the Taliban exporting its ideology to central Asia. Pakistan is conferring with Russia on Afghanistan, while some in Russia are calling for intervention to deal with the Taliban. The point was made here that support for terrorist groups can often come back to bite the hand of the supporter (Iraq-Iran; Israeli support to Hamas). It was noted that Indian policy is one of strong support for sovereignty as a cornerstone of the UN, while also actively involved in UN peacekeeping missions, as well as unilateral peacekeeping with the concurrence of the target state (Nepal-1950; Sri Lanka-1971 and 1987; Maldives-1988). While mistakes were made in Sri Lanka, the intervention was requested by the Sri Lanka government, and India's aim was to maintain Sri Lanka as unitary state. Mention was also made of cases of Indian intervention without consent; Junagadh (1947), Hyderabad (1948), Goa (1968), East Pakistan (1971), which some saw as illegitimate. Recently, India has become very uneasy with mission creep in UN operations that verge more on peace enforcement than consensual peacekeeping. Yet if the UN can only undertake peacekeeping with the consent of the target country, how can it respond to a situation like Rwanda? The commissioned paper by Adekeye Adebajo and Chris Landsberg, "The Heirs of Nkrumah: Africa's New Interventionists," noted how, with Africa just emerging from its colonial past, the founders of the Organization of African Unity in 1963 put a premium on consolidating sovereignty, even at the expense of freezing colonial borders. Strongly emphasizing the principles of sovereignty and non-intervention, the OAU Charter permitted exceptions only for support of national liberation movements. Interventions even partially related to the defense of human rights, such as that by Tanzania to topple Idi Amin, were rare indeed. Today, the situation is very different. First came the end of the Cold War, with its legacy of superpower and post-colonial interventions, There has also been the break-down of two post-colonial taboos: the inviolability of borders and secessions through the use of force (Eritrea, 1993). While the continent is still grappling with the legacy of artificial borders, a combination of moral imperatives (decolonisation, apartheid, genocide) and strategic aims (economic, political) is propelling the case for interventions, by Africans, in Africa. Accordingly, in recent years the OAU has been reviewing the need for military capabilities, reviving the 1960s dream of Kwame Nkrumah that the OAU set up an African high command. OAU conflict management and early warning capabilities are being developed, along with the increased use of electoral observer missions, and even small military observer missions (though with mixed results), in Rwanda,

Burundi, and the Comoro Islands. At the subregional level, ECOWAS and SADC are likewise seeking to develop conflict mediation and prevention mechanisms. Yet the current situation in Africa is that small states are more willing to intervene, but lack the necessary resources. Among the larger states, South Africa for most of the 1990s was unwilling to support and/or participate in interventions because of its apartheid past (e.g., Mandela resisted US pressure to commit South African forces in the Great Lakes). Only recently has South Africa, aided by the emergence of a legitimate Nigeria, become more pro-active in the role it plays throughout the continent. Some participants cautioned, though, about overstating South Africa's ability, resources, leverage, and influence. President Mbeki's diplomacy is grounded in the fact that other African states aren't going to automatically respond to South Africa's wishes or lead. For its part, Nigeria's main aim in West Africa has been to limit regional instability from Liberian conflict (750,000 refugees spilling outside borders), though its role did fuel regional concerns over Nigerian hegemony, especially during the period when Gen. Sani Abachi was essentially blackmailing the international community in return for Nigeria's role in West Africa. Elsewhere, Lesotho was cited as an example of a benign intervention (legitimate, but not effectively carried out), where Zaire/DRC is a malignant intervention, essentially becoming Africa's first 'world war.' Discussion focused on how Africa has attempted to deal with problems requiring intervention, most often on its own, with limited resources and without the help of international community. In addition to ECOWAS and SADC, there is a third subregional organization, IGAD, comprised of seven East African countries. Though the IGAD emphasis was originally on drought and desertification, the organization has developed conflict resolution mechanisms and sought to apply them to Somalia and Sudan. Several participants noted that the UN Security Council has not interpreted African conflicts in same way that Kosovo was defined, as threats to international peace and security requiring UN action. For others, the sad reality is that the P-5 doesn't see a need for African involvement, as no national interests are at stake. For the US, a Somalia syndrome has replaced the Vietnam syndrome. Impartial peacekeepers may be preferred, but in the case of Africa, many UN Security Council members are so impartial that they have no vested interest in providing needed capabilities. For most participants, then, the solution for effective intervention would appear to be a mixed model of direct involvement by regional organizations, supported by international resources. While interventions under a UN mandate are to be preferred, subregional capacity will have to be strengthened as the UN and international community can not always be counted on. A final point was that human rights is hardly a Eurocentric concept, especially with Africa's experience of colonialism. In the end, however, the definition of terms is not as important as having a clearer understanding of what we want the concepts to convey and how to act on them. One participant cited the four criteria for intervention listed in the study group's Venice workshop report as a useful starting point for seeking greater international consensus. The question remains, however, what happens after the intervention in terms of political reconstruction? Intervention is often necessary, but not often successful. Yet how should the international community respond when criminals hijack the state? Participants cited the duty of the entire international community to become involved; through international organizations, legal channels, the media, NGOs, trans-national companies, and the scientific community. The toughest issue will remain that of intervention, with military force, carried out against the will of the target. One participant listed three main criteria for such interventions: (1) clear threats to international peace and security; (2) gross violations of human rights; while it will be difficult to develop hard and fast criteria (and these can be manipulated for political reasons), general principles can be adumbrated; and (3) legitimacy (to what extent does international humanitarian law transcend the UN Charter?). Customary law recognizes that the world evolves, and differing perspectives need to be aired if consensus is to be reached. The political objectives necessary for peace-building need to be clarified, as the military's main role is but to create the conditions for successful peace-building. This is a critical period in which to show support for the UN and implement the Brahimi report. While the veto will continue to be a factor in Security Council deliberations, the question is how to minimize its use and maximize consensus. When it comes to intrastate conflict, intervention is a case of the international community putting itself between the problem and the solution. In terms of the work of the study group, there is a need to focus on the three Ps: principles, publics, and process. One participant cautioned about moving too quickly to process issues (e.g., modalities of intervention), without having fully explored principles and publics. Regarding the latter, there is a vital need for developing arguments that can persuade politicians and public opinion as to why interventions serve both national and international security interests. Also useful could be further analysis of the distinction between constructive intervention (conflict mediation) and coercive intervention (whether military or economic), and the differing stages of a crisis/conflict in which these can be applied. The work of Bruce Jentleson was cited regarding how an early resort to coercive preventive diplomacy might have been highly effective in preventing widespread misery in Rwanda, Kosovo, and East Timor. Participants also noted that it is important to broaden our notions of what constitutes the 'international community' and of how different actors (the private sector, civil society, the media) can help contribute to long-term success. The problem should not be seen as one of intervention per se, but of continued tension between sovereignty and intervention and the fact that intervention only takes place in countries where state structures are eroding: i.e., in developing countries, in precisely those countries that need sovereignty the most. What is needed are steps to support the state-building process. Intervention should be seen as a rare contingency; the less it's used, the more successful and stable the international community. Stable states are important as well because the very decision to intervene is a sovereign decision (in terms of contributing troops and funds to peacekeeping missions). A more pointed criticism of sovereignty, however, is the "West failure" descriptor of Susan Strange, where the social contract inherent in state sovereignty has (1) failed to prevent governments from killing its own citizens (genocide); (2) failed to equitably manage the international economy; and (3) failed to care for the global commons. There is an inherent conditionality of sovereignty that must be recognized. In reviewing the workshop discussion and thinking of the future work of the Pugwash study group, four levels can be discerned: The descriptive,

The right to intervene as previously explained conflicts with an international law principle that is of sovereignty which added somewhat contradictory concerns for contemplations. It is clear that the state has long occupied the central role in international law and one of the derivatives of this fact is the principle of sovereignty. But one must remember that the international law is gradually developing from a state centred idea to a more individual-centred concept.[50]

The development of international law has also been characterised by state-centralised features that is the consolidation of sovereign and independent states contributed to the development of their relations from an individual, state-centred to bilateralist-centred. The obvious consequent of such a bilateralist approach was the evolution of international legal obligations merely at the level of individual states, the consequent of which, the international law dose not oblige states to adopt a certain conduct in absolute terms, but only in the context of relations with the particular state or states or other international legal subjects to which a specific obligation under conventional or customary law are owed. The development of

---

of explicating differing national/regional views of intervention and sovereignty, which this workshop focused on; The conceptual, of more sharply defining concepts of sovereignty, intervention, international security, and the international community; The operational, of setting principles and criteria for when intervention is called for; devising mechanisms for increasing the legitimacy of intervention (changes to the Security Council); proposing ways for intervention to be more timely and effective (UN volunteer force, standby forces, regional forces); non-military means of intervention (pre-conflict engagement, targeted economic sanctions, etc.); Larger issues of international peace and security, of recognizing that intervention is an admission of failure, of a breakdown in security that was not solved by diplomatic and political means between the disputants themselves. Thus there is a need to go beyond intervention to think of structures and mechanisms that promote peace building, collective security, and global governance (especially given our current window of opportunity to do something about this during an absence of strategic rivalry). In this regard there is a link between this intervention and sovereignty study group and Pugwash efforts to analyze the political and security requirements (security guarantees, conflict resolution mechanisms, and modalities of collective security) that would facilitate the transition to a non-nuclear world. Thus caution is warranted about moving too quickly to issues of process and policy (#3), when more work is needed on conceptual issues and for ways of thinking less in terms of intervention per se than in thinking of strategies for peace and state building. It is these types of issues that many thought should form the agenda for the next meeting of the study group, in Castellón de la Plana, Spain, in May 2001.

[50] The doctrine of natural law in the sixteenth and seventeenth centuries sees the mistreatment by a sovereign of his own subjects as iusta causa for war, implying the corresponding right to intervene against a government at the request of an oppressed individuals.

international law contributed towards more cooperative non-state international legal subjects, which are focused someway on international solidarity (e.g. United Nations, International Court of Justice.... etc).

This shows the importance of collective interests of the international community and their priority in protection as to those of individual states. Such interests are not necessarily in conflict with bilateralist interests, they exist along with them, but what then if there is a conflict?

Solving this conflict depends on the answer to the following question: what is more important to be protected or which interest has priority? The preservation of international stability and order or the prevention of suffering of threatened individuals..? To make it more clear ... Let us ask ... is there any stability or order when human rights violations are happening? Can stability and order stand side by side with violating human rights?

The fact is, in such cases where human rights violations taking place on daily bases there is no stability, instability in one region extends to whole state and includes neighbouring states, the conflict in Dar Fur in Sudan is live example for such situation as described in foregoing chapters.

The reasons for humanitarian intervention of the UN

The UN Charter in itself contains no article dealing expressly with the principle of non-intervention but the principle's existence can be deducted from many different provisions e.g. articles 2(4) and 2(7). This issue has also been addressed by the General Assembly in many different resolutions.[51]

---

[51] Article 2

The Organisation and its Members, in pursuit of the Purposes stated in Article 1, shall act in accordance with the following Principles.

1. The Organisation is based on the principle of the sovereign equality of all its Members.

2. All Members, in order to ensure to all of them the rights and benefits resulting from membership, shall fulfil in good faith the obligations assumed by them in accordance with the present Charter.

3. All Members shall settle their international disputes by peaceful means in such a manner that international peace and security, and justice, are not endangered.

4. All Members shall refrain in their international relations from the threat or use of force against the territorial integrity or political independence of any state, or in any other manner inconsistent with the Purposes of the United Nations.

There are many arguments regarding the justification of intervention. An argument in favour of the legality of humanitarian intervention is based on the literal interpretation of article 2(4). The article obliges member states to refrain in their international relations from the threat or use of force against the territorial integrity or political independence of any state, or in any other manner inconsistent with the Purposes of the United Nations. Many ideas the restrictions as to the use of force are limited to the above mentioned situations and allowed in others unforeseen circumstances. A second argument in favour of the legality of humanitarian intervention is based on the clausal rebus sic stantibus, asserts that the prohibition of use of force is conditioned by the proper functioning of the collective security system.

Where international community expectations on the United Nations during the Cold War period were limited to Peace Keeping missions, those has been changed through experiences international community made by human rights violations occurred in Bosnia, Kosovo, Rwanda and Somalia, which are recent examples where states relied on UN's reluctance to act without consent of violating state. Among those examples are also the situation in Ethiopia and Sudan. At that time both governments blocked international humanitarian access to areas under insurgent control during the nineteen eighties the matter which contributed to the death of more than 500.000.

The Exceptions to the principle of (non-use of force)

Beside the above mentioned humanitarian intervention principle as exception to non-use of force principle there others exceptions in this regard, those are the

---

5. All Members shall give the United Nations every assistance in any action it takes in accordance with the present Charter, and shall refrain from giving assistance to any state against which the United Nations is taking preventive or enforcement action.
6. The Organisation shall ensure that states which are not Members of the United Nations act in accordance with these Principles so far as may be necessary for the maintenance of international peace and security.
7. Nothing contained in the present Charter shall authorize the United Nations to intervene in
matters which are essentially within the domestic jurisdiction of any state or shall require the Members to submit such matters to settlement under the present Charter; but this principle shall not prejudice the application of enforcement measures under Chapter VII. Cf. Bring, supra n. 9, pp.125 ff. The declaration on principles of international law concerning friendly relations and co-operation among states in accordance with charter of the United Nations. GA Res. 2625 (XXV), 24 Oct. 1970.

cases of self-defence, peace threat (collective security), armed attack and invitation right of the opposition.

Self-defence and right of collective self-defence

Although self-defence is not directly relevant to the case of humanitarian intervention but it has been invoked in many cases to justify the use of armed force. The right of self-defence as implemented in article 51 was meant to be a temporary right until the Security Council has taken necessary measures to maintain international peace and security; also the implementation of the collective self-defence right is governed by same conditions.

Article 51 of UN Charter although mentioning armed attack as a situation giving rise for right of self-defence but contains no definition of self-defence.[52]

The application of this right came in questions by many international crisis rose by different United Nations bodies, e.g. during the Cuban Missiles Crisis in 1962, and during the Israeli attack on Iraqi nuclear sites in 1981 by the UNAEC. The new circumstances under war against terror helped developing this principle and gave rise for far more many cases, at same time giving it wider definition than ever before. The central issue concerning collective self-defence is that, individual states or groups of States should be allowed to take protective measures without the prior authorisation of the Security Council.

Bearing the above mentioned in mind, and implementing it on the situation in Dar Fur it is probably for countries neighbouring the region to claim using such, especially Chad regarding newly spread of violence and rebels attacks to Chadian territories. This will surely extend the right of decision upon UN involvement to Chad instead of putting it in the hand of the GoS alone.

Peace threat

A threat to international peace and security is one of the previously mentioned reasons giving rise for UN intervention to prevent or end such threat. But what constitutes a threat to international peace and security? Article 39 of the UN Charter

---

[52] Nothing in the present Charter shall impair the inherent right of individual or collective self-defence if an armed attack occurs against a Member of the United Nations, until the Security Council has taken measures necessary to maintain international peace and security. Measures taken by Members in the exercise of this right of self-defence shall be immediately reported to the Security Council and shall not in any way affect the authority and responsibility of the Security Council under the present Charter to take at any time such action as it deems necessary in order to maintain or restore international peace and security.

doesn't contain fixed definition as to this. According to the above mentioned it is a question of interpretation, the matter which gives the Security Council wider implementation possibilities.[53] It is beyond the purpose of this book to analyses the principle in itself or related article 39 of UN Charter. We just would only like to consider the principle of "threat to the peaceto find an evidence that an international situation characterised by gross human rights violations or by the existence of humanitarian disaster may be seen as amounting to such threat, to bring it more closely let us take known examples like Rwanda, Haiti and Somalia, is there any difference with the situation now in Dar Fur, doesn't it constitute peace threat??.

Collective use of force for humanitarian reasons

United Nations intervention for humanitarian reasons which also justify use of force when necessary has been discussed previously. Added to the above mentioned, article 2(7) of UN Charter expressly provides that it doesn't prejudice the application of enforcement measures under Chapter VII. This means that the invocation of Chapter VII in itself removes the principle of non-intervention as obstacle to coercive UN action by making article 2(7) inapplicable and any action based on that Chapter need therefore not rely on the not within the domestic jurisdiction argument at all.

Armed attack

Armed attack gives reason for the previously mentioned self-defence principle although self-defence can take place priory to an attack, as we have seen, as protective measure to prevent attack being taking place. The term "Armed Attackin itself hasn't been mentioned in the Covenant of the League of Nation but aggression which has been considered as an opposite of self-defence.

An example of intervention based on armed attack argument is the Tanzanian intervention in Uganda in 1979; the Tanzanian came after period of tension between Uganda and Tanzania. In 1978 Ugandan troops attacked Tanzania and occupied the Ugandan region of Kagera Salient, however the occupation lasted for few weeks till November 1978, Tanzanian Army together with the later became to be known as Ugandan National Liberation Front lunched two months later on January 1979 an attack on Ugandan territories, and flowingly captured the capital

---

[53] The General Assembly adopted in 1974 a resolution on the definition of aggression, but although this text sets out a set of objective criteria, it also states that it dose not prejudice the discretion of the Council. GA Res3314 (XXIX) on the definition of aggression article 2 and 4.

of Kampala making an end to the Edi Amin's regime. The declaration has been given to UN and to OAU for the attack is that it was a response of the Ugandan aggression. The Tanzanian action provoked little reaction from international community and was not debated within United Nations. The incident was considered at an OAU summit in July 1979, but although the action violated basic principles of OAU Charter Tanzania wasn't been condemned, not only that, two states were in favour of such a course of action.[54]

Invitation right of Opposition or government

The experiences made in Congo shows that a democratically elected government or opposition has the right to invite UN for intervention in cases of attack and necessity of self-defence. After Congo declared independence from Belgium on June 30, 1960 an elected Congolese government was formed headed by Patrice Lumumba. Few days later tribal riots broke out and there was mutiny within the Congolese army. Belgium sent troops to protect Belgians and others aliens. The Congolese Government accused Belgium of committing an act of aggression and preparing the secession of Katanga. On July 12, 1960, the president and the prime Minister of Congo messaged the Secretary General for help. The Security Council adopted a resolution calling on Belgium to withdraw its troops from Congo without delay. The resolution also authorized the Security Council to take steps to provide with necessary military assistance. Although this action, mainly tends to the protection of a member state or country against external intervention, given the official request of to that effect addressed by the government of that country to the United Nations, but UN forces most important mission was to prevent a civil war in Congo, the UN forces mainly operated and used force against Katangese mercenaries those repeatedly violated cease-fire agreements.[55]

---

[54] The Edi Amin regime in Uganda was marked by extraordinary cruelty. During its eight years in power an estimated number of more that 300.000 were killed, many after having suffered terrible torture, the Tanzanian military action although somehow justified as self-defence and response to Ugandan aggression and occupation of Tanzanian territories marked as brought an end to the atrocities and human rights violation took place by Amin regime. Such acts of aggression and provocative over-boarder operations taking place on daily based on Chadian and Libyan boarders to Sudan.

[55] The Security Council resolution 146 of August, 9, 1960 expressed that the entry of UN forces into Katanga was necessary, paragraph A2 of resolution 161 gave ONUC explicit authorization for the mission in Congo.

Protection of own citizens

Protection of own citizens is one of international intervention reasons in internal conflict, although it mainly tends to protect or evacuate own citizens from conflict region, but it remains as an international interfering measure in on-going internal conflict especially when it comes to use of force to protect own citizens or when a longer stay in the conflict state is necessary within such protection mission. This right was regarded as the exercise of the right of self-preservation, as exercise of the right of self-defence, as one of several justifiable forms of intervention, or as action justified in terms of necessity. Examples of such are many, evacuation of European citizens from Rwanda during the Rwandan genocide, evacuation of Belgians citizens during the Congo conflict … etc. such scenario can take place in Dar Fur by Chadian and others African forces from neighbouring states those have citizens in the region, not evacuate them but to protect since such evacuation seems to be impossible under recent unrest situation.

The comparison and experiences with UN mission in Somalia

The collapse of the Siad Barre military regime in 1991 led to a clan power struggle in many parts of Somalia. The increasing hostilities resulted in brutal civil war which killed more than 350.000 Somalis and left 2 million facing the risk of starvation. The political chaos, deteriorating security situation and wide spread armed rubbery and looting aggravated by collapse of structure and institutions of government led to total lawlessness situation.

The UN's early response to the crisis in Somalia was ineffective in many respects, the matter which put the status of the whole humanitarian intervention program in question.

In January 1992 the Security Council declared its concern about the deterioration of humanitarian situation in Somalia and that it present threat to the peace and accordingly imposed weapons import embargo under Chapter VII. Negotiations during the following months led to a cease—fire agreement between the two main rebel groups. In April 1992 the Security Council decided sending the UNOSOM to Somalia, the mission of which as previously mentioned was traditionally peacekeeping mission to help by the delivery of humanitarian assistance with the authorisation to use of force only for self-defence purposes. But further deterioration of humanitarian situation there and lack of cooperation from all war parties led to the necessary change of the peacekeeping mission to peace enforcement mission.

In November 1992 it was necessary to take immediate steps, the Secretary General suggested the Security Council that it might become necessary to review the basic premises of the United Nations efforts in Somalia. Acting under Chapter VII the Security Council adopted Resolution 794 stating that the situation in Somalia requires immediate and exceptional response authorised the use of "all necessary meansby the Secretary General and United Nations member states to build a secure environment for humanitarian relief operations in Somalia and authorising the use of force beyond that necessary for self-defence.

This led to sending the UNITAF (although under Chapter VII but as a non-UN operation), during this period from December 1992 to May 1993 UNOSOM elements remained operating beside UNITAF working together to enable handing back responsibility to UNOSOM. On May 1993 UNOSOM II in has been taken over in accordance with Security Council Resolutions 814 of March 1993. During the handover phase, while it did not have the same capability as UNITAF, UNOSOM II was still accepted by the majority of Somalis as being the primary authority in the area it occupied. The situation became complicated through the nature of command relationship within the forces at the deposal of UNOSOM. While logistic troops came under UN command the crucial combat support of Quick Reaction Forces QRF, with its tremendous firepower was, and remained at all times under US command. This also applied to the Ranger and Delta Force troops that deployed during the hunt for Warlord General Aideed.

The nature of the UNOSOM operations changed dramatically after October, 3 1993 following the killing of Malaysian and US soldiers. The US administration under decided the withdrawal of its troops under the domestic pressure which took place on March 1995.

The United Nations secretariat officials, including then Secretary General Boutrus Ghali, permanent representatives at the Security Council, the United States diplomatic, military and political establishment claimed opposing sometimes simplistic and often mistaken interpretations and conclusions about what works and what dose not in particularly fostering peace.

Somalia experience made clear the missing of a political capability in operations field, also the failure of international efforts depending on UNOSOM alone to solve the problem is a further mistake. Another problem during the transition phase from UNITAF to UNOSOM II was how to deal with serious offences against the mission and against humanitarian law. Although could be mastered successfully e.g. the prosecution of Warlord Gutaale in Baidoa and Australian led investigations in incidents involving the deaths of aid workers and the assassinations of moderate elders, it is necessary to have international investigation teams to trace crimes committed in Dar Fur.

The necessity of international criminal court for Dar Fur

Sudan set up a special court in 2005, in response to demands by the international community that war-crimes suspects be sent to the International Criminal Court in The Hague. Sudan forcefully resisted the demands and insisted it could try war criminals internally.

The special court set up by Sudan to try war criminals has failed to bring justice to victims and has had little effect in the region. A war crimes court in the volatile northern region has only seven cases pending, while there are no cases before the western Dar Fur court. The ICC is designed to be a court of last resort, used when a nation's own justice system is unable or unwilling to investigate and prosecute war crimes which now the case in Sudan

U.N. Commission on Human Rights special investigator in Sudan urged on August 17, 2006, after visiting Dar Fur that persons involved in human rights violations in the conflict-wracked area of western Sudan be brought to trial. Khartoum's efforts to ensure accountability, including trying persons suspected of killing civilians, rape, looting and destruction of property, "have so far proved inadequate. Unless action is taken to protect civilians from attacks, "there will be a further deterioration in the coming months. A top U.N. envoy to Sudan has charged that the nation's human rights record in Dar Fur remains poor, despite the signing of a peace deal aimed at ending violence in the region. The U.N. said human rights abuses have continued with impunity in Dar Fur, and a special court set up by Sudan to try Dar Furi war criminals has failed to bring justice to victims. She said that Sudan has done little to improve its human rights record in Dar Fur and that local authorities have done little to protect civilians in the region from rape, murder and looting, and have failed to deter violence against vulnerable populations. She also criticised government restrictions which hindering the delivery of humanitarian aid to some parts of Dar Fur. she expressed concern that a special court set up by Sudan to try war criminals has failed to bring justice to victims and has had little effect in the region. A war crimes court in the volatile northern region has only seven cases pending, while there are no cases before the western Dar Fur court.

There is no express mention in the United Nations Charter to create an international criminal tribunal to try individuals charged with crimes against humanity or for violations against human rights. In February 1993 the Security Council decided; that an international tribunal shall be established for the prosecution of persons responsible for the serious violations of international humanitarian law committed in the territory of the former Yugoslavia since 1991, after concluding that wide spread violations of international humanitarian law constituted a threat to international peace and security. The Security Council took the steps regarding genocide and human rights violations committed in Rwanda 1994.[56] As above mentioned the main purpose of both tribunals is to investigate and prosecute persons responsible for the genocide, atrocities and crimes against international humanitarian law, violations, atrocities and crimes which more or less as the same as those committed and still taking place on daily basis in Dar Fur. One must admit that an international criminal tribunal has efficiency, neutrality, independence, flexibility, responsibility, financial and legal abilities that a domestic court never has.

Investigation is an important pre-trial procedure to enable the international criminal court to exercise its duties. It is also important to solve relevant case and identify the problem of justice system and to enable hearing victims or prepare witnesses for court-hearing. A United Nations criminal investigation is important; it should be conducted separately by specialised and authorised investigators for the purpose of trial, in spite of the human rights investigation.

A special United Nations commission of inquiry that has been investigating war crimes in Dar Fur submitted its report to U.N. Secretary General Kofi Annan on Janauery, 25, 2005 found that war crimes had indeed been committed and to further recommended that the case be handed over to the International Criminal Court (ICC) in The Hague

The Bush administration has been pushing for the Security Council to establish an ad hoc tribunal similar to those set up for trying war crimes in Rwanda and the former Yugoslavia, even though U.S. officials have long complained about their expense and duration.

But the European Union (EU) has adamantly opposed this alternative, noting that the original decision to establish the ICC derived from frustrations over the costs and delays involved in setting up and running separate tribunals.

As the EU dug in, despitelong discussion no final decision had yet been made, while Rep. Frank Wolf, a Bush loyalist who has also pushed hard for action in Sudan, called publicly for the administration to show greater flexibility. At the same time, several prominent attorneys who have defended the administration's scepticism about multilateral treaties suggested that the case was still open. A former Justice Department official who has roundly criticised the ICC on the editorial pages of the staunchly neo-conservative Wall Street Journal and Weekly Standard said "One should never cut off one's nose to spite one's face. But the

---

[56] Both International Criminal Tribunals has been established under Chapter VII of United Nations Charter.

appearance of a column in the Washington Post calling for the administration to support an ICC referral by the former head of the Justice Department's Office of Legal Counsel, Jack Goldsmith, offered new hope that the administration might indeed come around. "We see this as very significant," said Heather Hamilton, vice president of programmes for Citizens for Global Solutions (CGS), formerly the World Federalist Association, in a reference to the column by Goldsmith who was known to be ideologically compatible with the administration's unilateralist tendencies.

In his article, Goldsmith conceded the administration may indeed find itself "in a bind" given its strenuous efforts to negotiate bilateral agreements that ban other nations from transferring U.S. citizens to the ICC's jurisdiction, even as it leads international efforts to hold Sudan accountable for war crimes and even "genocide in Dar Fur.

But Goldsmith went on to argue that a Security Council referral would be perfectly consistent with the long-held U.S. policy that only the Security Council, where Washington has a veto, should have the authority to initiate ICC prosecutions against citizens or officials from non-ratifying nations. Under the Rome Statute, the ICC's chief prosecutor may initiate actions on his own, as well.

The Dar Fur case allows the United States to argue that Security Council referrals are the ONLY valid route to ICC prosecutions and that countries that are not parties to the ICC (such as the united States) remain immune from ICC control in the absence of such a referral.

With respect to Prosper's remarks, Goldsmith argued that "fears of 'legitimising' the ICC are overstated, for better or worse, the ICC is not going away anytime soon.

In addition to winning political support among the Europeans, U.S. backing for a referral would give the U.S. leverage in seeking tougher sanctions against Sudan if it were part of a larger package, he continued, and make it politically more difficult for China and Russia to veto such a measure.

A strong United Nations force is needed to halt the genocide in Sudan's Dar Fur region. If it is not sent soon, it may be too late for many thousands of potential victims. The immediate cause of the delay is the refusal by Sudan's president, Omar Hassan al-Bashir, to agree to a U.N. force, which he preposterously claims would attempt to recolonize the Sudan. He is able to get away with this largely because China, a permanent member of the Security Council, continues to protect him with the threat of using its veto.

One reason Beijing stands behind Mr. Bashir is oil. China is trying to diversify its oil sources beyond the crisis-prone Middle East, and Africa is one obvious alternative. Already, some 7 percent of China's imported oil comes from Sudan.

Another factor is Beijing's extreme sensitivity to any U.N. encroachments on national sovereignty. China fears that by assenting to U.N. intervention in Dar Fur over the protests of the Sudanese government, it might open the door to unwanted meddling in its own affairs, with regard to Tibet, for example. No such precedent would be established, however, if China used its influence with Mr. Bashir to win his agreement to a U.N. force.

China is generally pretty thick-skinned about human-rights criticisms. Its practices at home leave much to be desired, and it does business with more than its share of unsavory regimes abroad. But genocide is different, and Beijing knows it. China is already embarrassed by its support for Mr. Bashir. When Prime Minister Wen Jiabao visited Africa recently, he pointedly did not go to Sudan.

Surely Beijing does not want the world to see it as the main obstacle to sending a U.N. force to end the killing in Dar Fur. But right now, that is exactly the case. Other countries, like Russia, are also hanging back. But if China dropped its objections, they would probably follow its lead.

Washington, for its part, needs to build up its own pressure on Mr. Bashir. With the recent departure from government of Robert Zoellick, the administration's highest-ranking diplomat working on Dar Fur, there is a real danger that crucial momentum will be lost. President Bush needs to appoint an envoy to Sudan right away, before the genocide's toll, already more than 200,000 deaths, grows still larger.

Bush might be more inclined to veto an ICC referral if the case had not involved Sudan, according to one Congressional aide who noted that some right-wing lawmakers like Wolf, while generally hostile to the ICC, are even more opposed to Khartoum.

The Christian Right has done more on Sudan than any other single constituency, if an ICC referral is the best way to get serious sanctions imposed against the regime, they will support it, regardless of what Bush thinks about the ICC.

Also helpful at this point is the decline in influence within the administration of the outgoing undersecretary of state for arms control and international security, John Bolton.

Bolton saw in the ICC a major threat to Washington's sovereignty, and conceived the strategy of canceling tens of millions of dollars in military and economic aid for poor countries that ratified the Rome Statute without signing an accord with Washington promising that they would never submit a U.S. citizen to the ICC's jurisdiction.

Bolton, who once told the Wall Street Journal that signing the letter to the U.N. renouncing Washington's signature on the treaty establishing the ICC, the Rome Stature, was "the happiest moment of my government service", had hoped to be promoted to deputy secretary of state or deputy national security adviser in Bush's second term but now appears headed either to Vice President Dick Cheney's office or to the private sector.

U.N. Commission on Human Rights special investigator in Sudan urged on August 17, 2006, after visiting Dar Fur that persons involved in human rights violations in the conflict-wracked area of western Sudan must brought to trial. Khartoum's efforts to ensure accountability, including trying persons suspected of killing civilians, rape, looting and destruction of property, have so far proved inadequate. Unless action is taken to protect civilians from attacks, there will be a further deterioration in the coming months. A top U.N. envoy to Sudan has charged that the nation's human rights record in Dar Fur remains poor, despite the signing of a peace deal aimed at ending violence in the region. The U.N. said human rights abuses have continued with impunity in Dar Fur, and a special court set up by Sudan to try Dar Furi war criminals has failed to bring justice to victims. She said that Sudan has done little to improve its human rights record in Dar Fur and that local authorities have done little to protect civilians in the region from rape, murder and looting, and have failed to deter violence against vulnerable populations. She also criticised government restrictions which hindering the delivery of humanitarian aid to some parts of Dar Fur.

Khartoum's efforts to ensure accountability, including trying persons suspected of killing civilians, rape, looting and destruction of property, have so far proved inadequate. Unless action is taken to protect civilians from attacks, "there will be a further deterioration in the coming months.

The U.N. said human rights abuses have continued with impunity in Dar Fur, and a special court set up by Sudan to try Dar Furi war criminals has failed to bring justice to victims. She said that Sudan has done little to improve its human rights record in Dar Fur and that local authorities have done little to protect civilians in the region from rape, murder and looting, and have failed to deter violence against vulnerable populations. She also criticised government restrictions which hindering the delivery of humanitarian aid to some parts of Dar Fur

According to the UN Children's Fund (UNICEF) the situation in Dar Fur region has steadily worsened on 18 September 2006, with Government forces, allied militias and rebel groups committing widespread abuses, civilians are being specifically targeted and sexual violence is rising. [57]

In Dar Fur, where over 400,000 people have lost their lives and some 2 million more have been driven from their homes in three years, the Government refuses the international assistance Civilians have been displaced on some occasions for a second and third time. Humanitarian access is more restricted than ever.

---

[57] United Nations High Commissioner for Human Rights Ms. Louise Arbour

The level of sexual violence in Dar Fur continues to rise, while no progress is made in holding anyone accountable for these and other crimes.

The ICC must be able to exercise the full force of its mandate; cases of violence are often inadequately investigated and remain unpunished. Existing mechanisms for preventing and redressing violations are still insufficient due to the abysmal security situation and a lack of adequate resources, sexual abuses continue on a large scale, human rights violations by State security forces, and the failure of the Government to provide the protection of the rule of law to all its citizens also generate serious concerns.

The Government's public commitment to investigate these crimes, including the killings of 17 humanitarian workers of Action Contre la Faim, is welcome. In too many cases, however, investigations have failed to produce results and victims have been denied justice and redress.

European Union foreign ministers warned Sudan government and rebel fighters on September 15, 2006 that they would be "held accountable" for war crimes in Dar Fur and called on both sides to end violations of a cease-fire there. The EU ministers said the Sudanese government had a "responsibility to protect its citizens from all violence and to guarantee respect for human rights," and should accept a U.N. peacekeeping force in Dar Fur. They also called on both sides of the conflict "to permit the unhindered delivery of humanitarian assistance." In a declaration adopted after talks on the Dar Fur crisis, they warned "those who decide and carry out policies leading to death and suffering in Dar Fur will be held accountable," backing similar comments by U.N. Secretary General Kofi Annan earlier this week.

However, the EU ministers made no reference to the possibility European governments would file cases at the International Criminal Court in The Hague, Netherlands

The Chief Prosecutor of the International Criminal Court (ICC), Luis Moreno-Ocampo informed the Security Council on December 14, 2006 that he is almost ready to bring cases about some of the worst war crimes committed in the Sudanese region of Dar Fur during the past three years.

Luis Moreno-Ocampo will submit evidence to ICC judges by February 2007, at the latest and, ahead of that step, he is now introducing measures to protect victims and witnesses. According to the text of his statement to the closed-door Council meeting, Mr. Moreno-Ocampo said that his first case will focus on a series of incidents in 2003 and 2004, when conflict emerged in Dar Fur as Government forces and allied militia clashes with rebel groups seeking greater autonomy.

The evidence provides reasonable grounds to believe that the individuals identified have committed crimes against humanity and war crimes, including the crimes of persecution, torture, murder and rape, during a period in which the gravest crimes occurred in Dar Fur.

In a press statement released following his briefing, the Prosecutor said perhaps most significant, the evidence reveals the underlying operational system that enabled the commission of these massive crimes."

The Council referred the Dar Fur issue, along with the names of 51 suspected perpetrators, to the recently established ICC in March 2005, after a UN inquiry into whether genocide occurred in Dar Fur found the Government responsible for crimes under international law and strongly recommended referring the dossier to the court.

The probe also found credible evidence that rebel forces were responsible for possible war crimes, including the murder of civilians and pillage.

Mr. Moreno-Ocampo said that his office had taken more than 100 formal witness statements and screened hundreds of potential witnesses since the start of its investigation, travelling to 17 different countries to pursue inquiries. He also said that his office is closely following recent reports of continuing violence in Dar Fur, despite the signing of the Dar Fur Peace Agreement (DPA) in May by some of the parties to the conflict, and an apparent spillover into neighbouring Chad and the Central African Republic (CAR).

Violent clashes between factions inside the rebel groups, as well as between the different movements, have led to significant numbers of civilians being killed. There are also disturbing reports of a repetition of similar patterns associated with earlier crimes, including reports of attacks on civilian locations by armed militias, supported by elements of the Sudanese security forces. Incidents of rape and sexual assaults continue to be reported at very high levels.

During his briefing the Prosecutor said the information he had received so far from the Sudanese Government about individuals who had been arrested "do not appear to render the current ICCcase inadmissible.

The US Role in Sudan's Conflicts

The change in the US policy to Sudan began in February 2006, when Washington and London succeeded in getting an agreement in principle that the UN Security Council would transform the existing AMIS peacekeeping force into a UN-controlled mission.

Until recently, US official policy had been to support the African Union (AU) peacekeeping mission in Dar Fur region in February in meeting with United Nations Secretary General Kofi Annan, US President George Bush called for the number of troops in the Dar Fur region of western Sudan to be doubled. He said the troops would be "probably under the United Nations,but called for a greater role to be played by NATO in planning and facilitating the intervention.

His statements indicate that the US administration, after little comment on Dar Fur for the last year, has now decided to more aggressively pursue its policy on Sudan. In his remarks, Bush said that the AU had failed to provide security; he remarked that the effort was noble, but it didn't achieve the objective.

There is a deteriorating humanitarian situation in Dar Fur, with attacks on civilians continuing, some 2 million people have fled their homes and are living in camps, relying on food aid from the UN and NGOs.

Cross-border raids by militias from Dar Fur into neighbouring Chad are increasing, with crops and villages attacked and cattle and livestock looted. Chad and Sudan are accusing each other of backing anti-government militias, and there is a real risk of trans-border tribal ties internationalising the Dar Fur conflict, with a potential for open confrontation between the neighbouring countries. On October, 10, 2006 some hundred Sudanese soldiers fled a rebel attack in western Dar Fur took refuge in neighbouring Chad over the weekend, 103 Sudanese soldiers including three officers crossed the border to take refuge in Chad. Six wounded soldiers were taken into the care of Chadian authorities and treated in Bahai in eastern Chad along the Sudanese border. The 97 others were taken to Iriba, another town in eastern Chad, said the statement. The GoS said it was still deciding what to do about returning the soldiers to Sudan. Chad was not in any way involved in these clashes which took place on Sudanese territory. GoS started heavy attacks against rebel positions in the region during the weekend belong to the Justice and Equality Movement, which still active after it refused to join other factions in signing an agreement with the Sudanese government in May to bring peace to the province. The fithing left at least 80 people injured.

As reply to this change in US government politics to Sudan, on September 25, 2006, Sudan's president accused U.S. plans to create a "new Middle East" were behind an international push to replace African Union peacekeepers with U.N. forces in war-ravaged Dar Fur.

In a speech to cabinet ministers and journalists gathered in Khartoum, he said the United States and Britain wanted to recraft the region in Israel's interests.

Omar Hassan al-Bashir announced later a travel ban on U.S. officials, significantly restricting their movement in the Eastern African country.

Under the measures, no American official in Sudan is allowed to travel more than 25 km away from the presidential palace in Khartoum without a special permit, Bashir told a press conference. Any American official who comes to Sudan, his passport will be stamped for only 25 km from the presidential palace. Bashir said the move was in response to similar restrictions imposed by the U.S. administration on Sudanese officials in the United States. The US government also started many efforts to bring an end to the southern Sudan conflict and played a role in signing the agreement between the Sudan government and the southern Sudan People's Liberation Movement (SPLM) reached in January 2005 brought to an end the country's 21-year-old civil war.

A key part of the deal was to allow Sudan's oil wealth to be shared with the south and open up possibilities for US and European corporations. Sudan's oil reserves are estimated at between 660 million and 1.2 billion barrels. According to Africa Confidential, the Khartoum regime has blocked oil revenues going to the south and has also refused to disband the government-backed militias that operate in the southern area key parts of the CPA. But one must remark that the newfound interest of the Bush administration in western Sudan has nothing to do with humanitarianism, however, but is bound up with the geo-political interests of US imperialism especially because the new role of China in Sudan and this region of Africa. In the USA a majority of Americans show support for a variety of possible steps in response to the crisis in Dar Fur and see that the UN should step in with military force to stop the violence in Dar Fur. A large majority also favour NATO, including the US, contributing equipment and logistical support to the African Union peacekeeping force in Dar Fur. The same about USA can be said about Europe. The US government called an emergency international meeting to push for a stronger international peace force that could put down factional killing in Sudan's Dar Fur region, despite objections from Sudan's central government.

Secretary of State Condoleezza Rice was hosting the session on the sidelines of the United Nations opening session.

A group of Dar Fur-born exiles called Rice's efforts a good first step, but it also criticized the United States and other world powers for doing too little too late to stop a daily tide of killings and rapes in Dar Fur's ravaged villages and teeming refugee camps.

President Bush repeated the charge of genocide in one of the most pointed portions of his address to world leaders at the United Nations earlier this week. He named a special U.S. envoy to bring added pressure on the Khartoum government of President Omar al-Bashir.

The U.S. approach is hitting some resistance, especially from nations that argue that Sudan will respond best if it does not feel that its sovereignty or authority is being challenged.

Arab League Secretary General Amr Moussa commented to the difference of opinion in remarks saying that he really want to contribute to the creation of a quiet atmosphere, a working atmosphere but they have suffered at certain stages of this problem of either exaggeration or misinformation, he added, there is a major problem in Dar Fur, but not all what you hear, not all the information circulated, are really accurate. On August 20, 2006 The Arab League continued to back Sudan's refusal of a UN peacekeeping force in Dar Fur region A League committee on Sudan voiced its support for Khartoum's rejection of a US-British draft UN resolution that would pave the way for the deployment of UN troops to Dar Fur, the diplomats said. Instead the committee called for a reinforcement of the African Union mission already on the ground in the western Sudanese region, which has been devastated by a three-year conflict between rebels and government forces.

Till August, 2006 the Bush administration was divided about whether to name special envoy on Sudan or not. Two U.S. lawmakers said that the Bush administration continues to resist appointment of a special envoy on Sudan, without which they the situation in the strife-torn region of Dar Fur threatens the complete breakdown of efforts for peace.

Two of the most outspoken members of Congress on Dar Fur, Frank Wolf and Chris Smith, said bold action is needed to avert a breakdown of both the Dar Fur peace agreement and the larger Comprehensive Peace Agreement for Sudan. Both point to what they said is a void created by the departure of Robert Zoellick, the former Deputy Secretary of State who recently resigned. Zoellick played a crucial role in negotiations leading to a Dar Fur peace agreement last May, which, however, was signed only by one of the Dar Fur rebel groups. Congressman Wolf said only a special envoy can re-focus attention of the Bush administration and prevent the situation in Dar Fur and Sudan generally from deteriorating: There is no one U.S. point person focusing on Sudan, Wolf notes that Salva Kir, and Minni Minnawi, leader of one of only three Dar Fur rebel factions to sign the May accord, met with President Bush in the White House. Appointing a special envoy, he said would send a clear message to Khartoum of continuing U.S. determination to bring peace to Sudan. Congressman Smith refers to what he calls a "gaping hole" in U.S. leadership on Dar Fur and Sudan, as Washington's attention has focused on the Middle East and North Korea. Smith said that a special envoy would meet with the key players in Sudan and Dar Fur with the aim of preventing the collapse of peace efforts: We look around, whether it be the problems in the Middle East or the problems with North Korea, there is always something clamoring for attention. But in Dar Fur, every day men and women and children die a needless death because of that inattention. In a conversation with Jendayi Frazer, the top U.S. official for Africa, Congressman Wolf said he received strong negative resistance to his renewed call for a special envoy, which is not acceptable, noting that Congress provided 250-thousand dollars for the administration to pay the costs of an envoy. Wolf urges President Bush and Secretary of State Condoleezza Rice to help overcome such resistance: Secretary of State Condoleezza Rice has been there in Dar Fur, she confirmed she cared about it, the president has also personally confirmed he cared about it, they should appoint special envoy and get this person moving quickly to deal with the issue.

Appearing with lawmakers was David Rubenstein, with the Save Dar Fur Coalition: Rubenstein said; by allowing our focus to move away from this, by not maintaining the leadership that the U.S. and this administration has held, we are saiding to the world that genocide is no longer as important to us as it once was, and that we can step away from the commitments and obligations we made, the U.N. Security Council must quickly approve an effective international force with a clear mandate to protect civilians in Dar Fur, along with steps to bolster the existing 77-hundred strong African Union force.

U.N. Secretary-General Kofi Annan proposed an international force with as many as 24-thousand troops and police.

However, the government in Khartoum continues to resist any transformation of the African force to U.N. control, and Annan said securing such consent will require intensive discussions with Khartoum.

Finally the Bush administration named on September 19, 2006 the former director of the U.S. Agency for International Development, Andrew Natsios as a special envoy for Sudan, the White House has been reluctant to name a special envoy, in part because State Department diplomats disliked the idea, and hoped that international pressure would force the Sudanese government to make concessions in its proxy battle, using militias rather than the Sudanese army, with rebels in Dar Fur.

US President George W. Bush discussed on, Sept 20, 2006 with Egyptian President Hosni Mubarak the need to deploy a UN force in Sudan's Dar Fur region. They both expressed a strong commitment to effecting the transition to a UN force.

UN Secretary General Efforts

on August 2, 2006, Annan said in a report to the UN Security Council that a UN-led force for Dar Fur would need up to 18,600 troops and intense international pressure has to be put on Sudan to accept the intervention, UN Secretary General Kofi Annan said. The new force should take over from the current African Union peacekeepers as soon as possible, adding more troops from mainly African and Asian countries. The UN chief said "the international community's message should make clear that the costs of rejecting the transition could be serious and lasting.

Referring to Khartoum's oppositon, Annan stressed that the UN force was not intended to occupy the country. He appealed to the Sudanese authorities to ensure that the aims and the ideals of the United Nations are neither contorted nor misrepresented to suit political ends

Annan proposed three alternatives to replace the 7,000 strong African Union force in the western Sudanese region, where up to 300,000 people have been killed and more than two million displaced since civil war erupted in 2003.
- The first would have about 17,600 troops, consisting of 14 infantry battalions and a divisional reserve of two Special Forces companies, backed by three reconnaissance aircraft, eight tactical helicopters and 18 utility helicopters.
UN Secretary General Annan said this force would be the best equipped and likely offers the fastest route to a secure environment and eventual return to normality.
- The second option would be for 18,600 troops with two additional infantry battalions but fewer aircraft.
Because of the reduced ability to respond to incidents by air, it was described as "the most challenging option to deploy and sustain.
- The third plan was for 15,300 troops to be backed by six additional helicopters and three extra rapid reaction companies.
With fewer troops deployed, it carries a higher degree of risk on the protection of civilians" and will also be more vulnerable to bad weather.

Position of Sudanese Government

It is clear that GoS is fighting hard to keep U.N. peacekeepers out of Dar Fur by accusing western "crusaders" of trying to take over the country. But what he really fears may be more basic: Losing control over a key political stronghold in the troubled region.
Observers say that determination to keep tight control of Dar Fur and prevent any loosening of his regime's grip on the large, sprawling country overall could complicate the West's efforts to help Dar Fur's suffering millions.
The United Nations, United States, Europe and African nations insist they have no hidden agenda and merely want to help get humanitarian aid to Dar Fur. They believe only a strong U.N. peacekeeping force can end the violence in the western region, where more than 200,000 people have been killed and 2.5 million chased from their homes in fighting between rebels and the army.
But Sudanese President Omar al-Bashir has warned he would personally lead a jihad, or holy war, against any U.N. troops, he warned that Dar Fur would become a "graveyard" for United Nations forces if they were deployed in the western region.
And Khartoum has continuously sought to feed into widespread conspiracy theories of a western "crusade" against Arab countries, pointing to the invasion of Iraq and the killing of Lebanese civilians by Israel as proof that the U.N. is biased against Arabs.

Khartoum also claims the mounting American outcry over Dar Fur is fueled by "Zionist groups" and says that charities hype the crisis for political gain.

The issue was throw into stark relief recently when, on a visit to Cairo, U.S. Secretary of State Condoleezza Rice spent much of her time with Arab officials lobbying them to intercede with Sudan, rather than on Arab-Israeli peace efforts or the Lebanon war.

Despite such high-profile efforts, the West has been unable to persuade Sudan that its intentions are purely humanitarian. Sudan has refused to consider allowing a U.S. peacekeeping force now in the south to move to Dar Fur in the west, or to allow the United Nations to take over a current, feeble Dar Fur peacekeeping mission by the Africa Union.

It also recently rejected an Arab League overture to allow Arab peacekeepers, although Arab diplomats said al-Bashir promised to offer a counterproposal.

Al-Bashir did send a letter to U.S. Secretary General Kofi Annan last week reiterating that he would consent to the U.N. providing support to the AU mission.

Supporters of a U.N. force have tried to point out that both victims and perpetrators in Dar Fur are in many cases Muslims, although pro-government Arab militias are accused of most atrocities against ethnic African villagers.

They also point out that the sprawling, landlocked desert region would be of little strategic value to anybody.

Majzoub al-Khalifa there is no trust left Sudan's top official for Dar Fur there is no trust left, how can the international community guarantee that America will not use the U.N. to turn Sudan into a new Iraq?

Sudanese contend that rumored oil and uranium fields under Dar Fur, and even Pope Benedict XVI's recent comments on Islam, are the real reasons the West wants to move in. Such arguments probably hold some weight in a part of the world where Arabs have high mistrust of American motives.

But the top U.S. diplomat in Sudan dismisses them. Indeed, the harsh rhetoric has come even as the Sudanese regime has collaborated with the Bush administration on terror issues. But it has a weak spot in the rebellions that often break out across its vast expanse.

The fact is that the government isn't going toward more democracy, and rebellions across the country reflect this, Dar Fur, though underdeveloped, has long been a power base for Khartoum political parties, unlike the south, where Sudan agreed to U.N. peacekeepers as part of a 2005 peace treaty.

AU leaders are finalizing plans to add 1,200 soldiers to the existing 7,000-strong force. The AU would send more peacekeeping troops to Dar Fur region and toughen the soldiers' role in protecting civilians until the U.N. reaches a compromise with the Sudanese government.

Even more soldiers could come if NATO provided adequate logistics support and the Arab League and other international donors provided funding. AU peace-keepers would soon have new rules of engagement, under which they would not only monitor violence and investigate incidents, but also actively interfere to prevent attacks on civilians by the multiple rebel groups and pro-government militias that plague the region.

The AU's spokesman in Sudan, Nouredinne Mezni, said the new rules would enable peacekeepers to better implement the Dar Fur Peace Agreement signed in May between Sudan and the main rebel group there.

Infighting among splinter rebel factions is a major cause of the violence, along with a new offensive by the Sudanese military against rebels who refuse to join the peace deal. Khartoum is accused of bombing villages where these groups hide, in effect causing more civilian casualties.

GoS will deploy new integrated forces in Dar Fur to work alongside African Union peacekeepers in providing security in the region, President Omar al-Beshir said that the integrated units of the army, police and security forces will be responsible for keeping peace and stability in Dar Fur region.

These units will operate in the presence of the African Union forces to which he said his government will not accept any substitute, reiterating his opposition to a proposed transition to a UN force, they will continue supporting the African forces and the UN can support those forces logistically and materially, describing ng the UN force as "an American-engineered conspiracy to turn the Sudan into another Iraq".

This came after the Security Council approved the dispatch of a 20,000-strong UN contingent to replace an ill-equipped and cash-strapped African Union force which has failed to end more than three years of violence sparked by a revolt among Dar Fur's mostly black African population.

A meeting of potential troop contributors to the UN mission was expected to take place Monday at UN headquarters in New York.

The Sudanese president disputed allegations that the situation in the region was worsening, and challenged reported casualty figures for the conflict.

Those parties which allege 300,000 people were killed in the conflict are lying and I defy anyone to prove that figure. The number of the dead all through the conflict has not exceeded 10,000 on both government and rebel sides. He said that he defy anyone to show him a single village that has been bombarded as those parties claim, he said, adding that those allegations are intended to find justifications for deployment of UN forces in Dar Fur.

Beshir claimed that security situation is now calm in most parts of the region and that his government would endeavor to "rally all political forces, including the opposition, around our national cause" of blocking the deployment of UN forces in the country.

The president stressed that his government would not accept UN peacekeepers, even if the resolution is amended to drop provisions such as those calling for reorganization of the police and judiciary, to which he is particularly opposed.

Beshir also said his government had decided to impose travel restrictions on US diplomats in the country, limiting them to movement within 25 kilometers (15 miles) of the center of the capital Khartoum, in response to similar restrictions imposed on Sudanese diplomats in the United States.

U.S. calls emergency session as Dar Fur killing goes on

By now, Sudanese President Omar al-Beshir finds him increasingly isolated as his peace partners rally the growing consensus in favour of a UN peacekeeping force for Dar Fur. The Sudan People's Liberation Movement, which formed a national unity government with Beshir's long-ruling National Congress after signing a landmark peace deal last year, confirmed its acceptance of UN troops in Dar Fur. After a three-day meeting in the southern capital of Juba, the former rebel movement's leadership justified its position and confirmed that Sudan needed to avert confrontation with the international community. SPLM leader Salva Kiir, also Sudan's first vice president, was quoted in a Sudanese paper asserting the necessity of a UN deployment to protect civilians from the atrocities of the pro-government Janjaweed militia.

It seems that the government of Khartoum will face an internal crisis in the coming phase as a result of disagreements with the SPLM over the deployment of international troops in Dar Fur. [58] If this happened, the SPLM's split from Beshir on the issue of peacekeeper is one of the most serious cracks in the unity government since its inception last year.

The Security Council's approach's concerning Dar Fur

The Security Council envisaged AMIS being absorbed into the existing UN mission (UNMIS), which was established in mid-2004 to enforce the CPA. It was estimated that a UN mission for Dar Fur would need four years and up to 20,000 soldiers to complete. AMIS currently has around 7,000 peacekeepers.

Bush's meeting with Kofi Annan appears to have been an attempt to speed up this process. According to Annan, it was agreed that the UN force would need to be "a much more effective force on the ground, current rules of engagement for the AU

---

[58] According to independent Sudanese analyst Mohammed Abu Sid told AFP

force preclude active policing operations that could lead them into conflict with both Sudanese troops and rebel forces.

In February 2006, US Ambassador to the United Nations John Bolton used the one-month US presidency of the UN Security Council to raise concern over Sudan and press for the UN peacekeeping force to be sent to Dar Fur in the immediate future. He was opposed by all other Security Council members, including Britain, which advised more diplomacy and waiting for the African Union to make the official request for transition to a UN force. It is expected that the AU will agree to the transition, but the fact that the Sudan government is lobbying hard against it may cause delays.

Bolton also attempted to get the Security Council to agree to sanctions against key individuals for their roles in the continuing military conflict in the region. The UN agreed last year to such sanctions and set up a panel of experts to draw up a list of individuals to be targeted, including Sudan's interior and defence ministers and national intelligence chief. But China, Russia and Qatar have rejected the panel's proposals.

NATO was already involved in providing transport for AMIS, but the US is now pushing for its role to be extended. Robert Zoellick, deputy to Secretary of State Condoleezza Rice, said that NATO is needed while the UN prepares its force, since the UN force could take up to a year to get off the ground. Such a role for NATO is not supported by all the Western powers, however. French diplomats are arguing that the European Union (EU) is better placed than NATO for an African operation and have suggested that a NATO mission would reduce the European Security and Defence Policy's role and visibility in a vital and sensitive arena.

The United Nations must take over the guard job in Dar Fur, otherwise the slaughter, suffering and starvation would continue, is the common refrain. The United Nations has acted, with the Security Council passing resolution 1706 that would mandate inserting 20,000 blue helmets in the damning Dar Fur. But the problem is that Sudanese government would have none of that. From the rostrum of the United Nations general assembly at its 61st session last month, Sudanese president, General Omar Bashir said that a UN force would mean that "Sudan in under a mandate, a sort of trustship.

However, even though that the UN security council has authorized sanctions against Sudan, including an oil embargo and a no-fly zone over Dar Fur, no country has made any serious effort to implement them. Meanwhile most African countries have threaten to pull out their forces from the existing AU force in Dar Fur and urged Sudan to accept the deployment of the United Nations peace keepers.

But Sudan insists that any deployment of the blue helmets, will easily amount to the West Imposing its brand of solution on essentially African problems. Khartoum's sympathizers point to Iraq and Afghanistan, where western intervention using the

UN as a pretext has worsened the situation. Khartoum warns of outright civil war, should the west impose its will.

Sudanese Vice President Ali Osman Taha expressed on Sept., 18, 2006 that U.N. forces would not enter Dar Fur without his government's permission.
Taha's comments came as international pressure official and public increased on Sudan to accept United Nations peacekeepers in Dar Fur, two weeks before AU amnadate was due to expire. Taha also dismissed the position declared earlier this week by First Vice President Salva Kiir Mayardit and his Sudan People's Liberation Movement welcoming U.N. troops. "The government is a grouping of a number of political parties and it is not strange that there may be different positions.
A British Foreign Office official commented that the international community should consider all options in handling Sudan's refusal of troops. Comments by David Triesman to reporters at the U.N. implied that military intervention had not been ruled out as a means to address Khartoum's rejection of international peacekeepers.
Hundreds of thousands of people already rallied around the globe to protest against the violence in Dar Fur.
But analysts argue that without a much more robust peace keeping, the 2.5 million refugees camped out in the squalid camps would remain in a critical danger, with aid agencies, increasingly unable to access them. But the west's policy in the Middle East as much as in the developing world is viewed with enormous suspicion in Sudan. In Sudan itself, government prodded several groups to protest at the local UN office any suggestion of deploying the blue helmets in Dar Fur. However, most African countries contributing to the inept A.U force are threatening to pullout, if the UN does not weigh in. The new Nigerian foreign minister, Mrs Joy Ogwu told the 61st UN general assembly that Khartoum will bear all responsibility for the tragedy of Dar Fur should it continue to obstruct the deployment of UN force.
Her conclusion suggests explicitly that the A.U venture in Dar Fur is definitely over. But should it be so? The transformation of the former Organization for African Unity (OAU) to the African Union (AU) raised great hope. The hope was more when the AU dumped the clause of the former OAU unconditional non interference in the internal affairs of member states in favour of greater involvement. Dar Fur was AU first hard test which indicated that weak institutional capacity and capability continues to hamper Africa's best diplomatic intentions.
Also the Arab League has supported Sudan in rejecting the deployment of western troops in Dar Fur and called for further dialogue between Khartoum and the United Nations on the issue. Qatar was the first country to contribute to the

150-million-dollar pledge made by the Arab League to beef up the African Union monitoring force deployed in Sudan's war-torn Dar Fur region.

Qatar paid 2.3 million dollars out of the seven million it promised, sources at the Arab League said. The pan-Arab body made a total pledge of 150 million dollars during its latest summit in Khartoum on March 2006.

Secretary-General Kofi Anan has clearly said that "without the consent of the Sudanese Government, the transition will not be possible", reported Pronk, directly contradicting the position of unilateral action. However, getting the consent of the Government requires consultations. A transition to a United Nations force has to be made attractive to the Sudanese leadership in order to get its support. That also requires trust, confidence-building and time. It requires that those in favor of a transition and those against it should refrain from the present collision course." It is clear that hostile rhetoric by certain members of the Security Council have continued the crisis in Dar Fur and raise suspicions by the Government of Sudan.

Diplomatic efforts to persuade Sudan to admit United Nations peacekeepers to Dar Fur intensified on August 17 2006 as Britain introduced a draft Security Council resolution that could lead to the deployment of up to 20,000 UN troops and police in the troubled region. The draft resolution came as the Security Council met to discuss the continuing violence in Dar Fur, despite a peace agreement signed in May by the government and one of the three main rebel groups. Omar Hassan al-Bashir, Sudan's president, has continued to oppose the deployment of a UN force in Dar Fur, although there are 10,000 UN peacekeeping troops assigned to support a peace agreement in the south of the country. The draft resolution would require the consent of President Bashir for the force to be deployed to Dar Fur, but is seen as a way of increasing the pressure on him to do so. It proposes extending the existing UN mission in Sudan to cover Dar Fur as well, and giving its military commander the ability to move troops between the two regions as required.

Under the draft resolution, the African Union force would be transferred to the UN's authority by the end of mandate, with UN members providing additional logistical and transport support that would increase its ability to move across a region the size of France.

Amnesty International and Human Rights Watch have both urged the UN to approve a force capable of protecting civilians in Dar Fur, and criticised President Bashir's opposition to the force. Amnesty said that government aircraft were continuing to bomb groups opposed to the May peace agreement, in defiance of a UN ban on offensive military flights.

On August 22, 2006 Sudan's government has proposed sending some 10,000 of its own troops to quell the violence in the troubled region of Dar Fur instead of the United Nations peacekeeping force that it has repeatedly refused.

The Sudanese plan was already presented to the United Nations Security Council. The plan sees that the Sudanese government would use the troops to "gain control of the security situation and achieve stability in Dar Furand to "deal with the threats posed by the activities of groups that have rejected the Dar Fur peace agreement. The plan does not explicitly reject a United Nations force, which the United States and others have advocated to secure the shaky peace agreement. But it makes clear that Sudan believes it should be responsible for stabilizing the worsening crisis in Dar Fur. Bashir asserted in a letter to Kofi Annan, the secretary general of the United Nations, that the restoration of stability and the protection of civilians are central responsibilities of the government of the Sudan. But the Sudanese proposal, taken with what advisers for the African Union, human rights groups and aid organizations describe as a large buildup of military forces in Dar Fur, indicates that the government may intend to deal with the escalating crisis in its western provinces by force. on Aug 28, 2006 a divided Security Council met behind closed doors to debate the deteriorating situation in Dar Fur as the United States accused China of blocking a deal to deploy UN peacekeepers in Sudan's war-torn western region. On the other hand China will send second peacekeeping team to Sudan composed of 435-member, engineering, transport and medical sections to be dispatched in January 2007. It would replace the first team sent in June for six and half years, the longest United Nations peacekeeping mission that China has even taken on.

The meeting of the 15-member body came as Sudan rejected US pressure to accept a US-British draft resolution calling for the deployment of a robust UN force in Dar Fur. Also the talks between Sudanese President Omar al-Beshir and Washington's top Africa envoy Jendayi Frazer on August 29, 2006 Washington's top Africa envoy were fruitless

US Assistant Secretary of State Jendayi Frazer, who travelled to Khartoum to soften Sudanese government opposition to the UN force, looked set to leave empty-handed but for a letter addressed to US President George W. Bush in which Sudanese President Omar al-Beshir reiterated his firm opposition to the deployment of UN troops. Now Sudanese government has been given a deadline till January 1, 2007 deadline to accept the deployment of UN peacekeepers to Dar Fur or face coercive international action to halt violence in the region. [59] Sudanese

---

According to [59] US Presidential envoy Andrew Natsios

government must allow an initial group of 60 UN peacekeeping staff currently "marooned" in the Sudanese capital to deploy to Dar Fur by year's end. Natsios said that there is a Plan B" which had been discussed with key partners dealing with the crisis, which include the European Union, China and the Arab League.
Sudanese President Omar al-Bashir said in a recent letter to outgoing U.N Secretary-General Kofi Annan that Sudan was ready to immediately implement agreements endorsing a three-step U.N. plan to strengthen the beleaguered 7,000-strong African union force in the vast western region of Sudan.
Sudanese government has responded "favourably" to this UN compromise plan drafted after Khartoum consistently rejected any UN troop deployment and aimed at bolstering an embattled contingent of African observers in war Dar Fur. Mr. Mulki, Mauritanian UN diplomat was dispatched to Sudan last week in a bid to clinch Khartoum's approval for a three-phase UN plan aimed at bolstering the struggling AU force.
According to a joint statement issued on December, 26, 2006 by U.N. and African Union offices in Sudan, the first group of more than 175 U.N. advisers and staff supporting peacekeepers in Dar Fur will deployed in the first week of Janaur 2007. The United Nations and African Union offices in Sudan provided the Sudanese government with a list of the names of the 43 U.N. military staff officers and 24 police advisers making up the first U.N. group to be deployed to Dar Fur. This action opens the way for sending the personnel to the troubled area of western Sudan. The Sudanese government confirmed that it was permitting the first U.N. experts to head to Dar Fur. But the numbers it gave were lower than those mentioned by the U.N. statement. Sadeq Al-Magli, a spokesman for the Foreign Ministry said that 18 military experts and 20 policemen would soon head to Al Fasher, capital of North Dar Fur. The discrepancy could not be accounted for immediately. Most of the experts come from African and Asian countries.
According to the statement released Wednesday U.N. staff officers and police advisers will wear their national uniforms with blue U.N. berets and an African Union Mission in Sudan (AMIS) arm band.

The right concept to solve the conflict

UN Secretary General plan is to reinforce African Union (AU) peacekeepers in Dar Fur, while pressuring Sudan to accept a UN force.
He gave three options for the UN, with Sudan's approval, to bring peace.
One scheme would involve 18,600 African and Asian troops, making it the world's largest UN peace force. The main problem is to find a solution which acceptable for all parties and at same time would solve the conflict.

It is clear that AU troops in their actual situation will never help stopping the conflict, which means better equipped, and organized peacekeepers are necessary, it is only the UN which can provide such troops, Sudanese government insists to have African troops, so let those UN African troops wear blue helmets. The duties those troops will have and steps of their mission can be summarised in the following points:

1. Securing the Region: dispatching enough, well equipped troops those are also authorised to use force and return fire not only for self-defence purposes in all burn points of Dar Fur region to secure them,

2. Withdrawal of government troops from Dar Fur region to avoid provocations and complicating peace process.

3. Disarmament; as soon as the above mentioned presence of UN troops has been guaranteed all over the region, all conflicts parties have to give up all their weapons within specified period otherwise, this should be enforced against unwilling group(s).

4. Peace Talks: after carrying out above mentioned steps, all concerned parties have to meet for peace talks which have to be observed by UN.

5. Implementing Peace steps: points and steps agreed to in peace agreement have to be implemented under international sanctions for party who will breach or violate peace agreement.

6. Resettling civilians: necessary and immediate measures to resettle civilians and rebuild infrastructure have to be taken to avoid economical immigration and rubbery.

7. International criminal tribunal prosecutions: International criminal tribunal prosecutions can then take place to prosecute criminals.

Refrences

1. Operation Allied Force, a case of humanitarian intervention, Katarilna Saariluoma, Garmisch-Partnerkirchen, Consortium, 2004.

2. Die unilaterale humanitäre Intervention im "zerfallenen Staat (failed state) Ingo Liebach, Köln, Heymann, 2004.

3. International law and the use of force, Christine Gray. 2. ed., Oxford Oxford Univ. Press, 2004.

4. You, the people, the United Nations, transitional administration, and state-building, Simon Chesterman. Oxford. Oxford Univ. Press, 2004

5. Die Staatengemeinschaft und das Kosovo, humanitäre Intervention und Internationale Übergangsverwaltung unter Berücksichtigung einer Verpflichtung des Intervenierten zur Nachsorge, Philipp A. Zygojannis.,Berlin, Duncker & Humblot, 2003

6. Recourse to force, state action against and armed attacks, Thomas M. Franck., 4. Print., Cambridge, Cambridge Univ. Press, 2003

7. International Interventionen und Crisis Response Operations, Charakterstika, Bedingungen und Konsequenzen für das Internationale und nationale Krisenmanagement, Karl Schmidseder., Frankfurt am Main, Peter Lang, 2003

8. Democracy and UN-intervention, a stud of state commitment to UN-interventions 1991, t999, Andreas Andersson., Karlstad, Univ., Dep. of Political Science, 2002

9. Military intervention and peacekeeping, the reality, Richard Michael Connauhton. Adlershot u.a., Ashgate, 2002

10. Human rights functions of United Nations peacekeeping operations, Mari Katayangai, The Hague u. a. Martinus Nijhoff publ., 2002

11. "Kilo two, Belgische speziale troapen infiltreren in burgeroorlogen Somalië, Johan Goyvaerts., Erpe-Mere, De Krijger, 2000 Ausleibsystem

12. Gescheiterter Staat-gescheiterte Intervention?, die humanitäre Intervention der UNO in Somalia, Natali Rezwanian-Amiri, Glienicke Berlin u.a. Galda & Wilch, 2000

13. Friedenssicherung und Völkerrecht, Markus Kaim., Erfurt, Landeszentrale für Politische Bildung Thuringen, 2000

14. The United Nations and anew world order for a new millennium, self-determination, state succession, a humanitarian intervention, Edward MacWhinney, The Hague, Kiuwer Law International, 2000

15. The legality of the UN humanitarian intervention under chapter VII of the UN Charter : Somalia and beyond, **Abdiwahid Osman Haji**, Ottawa, Univ, Diss., 1999

16. The Question of intervention, statements by the Secretary-General, Kofi Atta Annan, New York, United Nations Dept. of Public Information, 1999

17. Restoring and operations, the search for a legal framework, Michael J. Kelly. The Hague u. a., Kluwer, 1999

18. Die humanitäre Intervention_durch den Sicherheftsrat der Vereinten Nationen im "faded state, das Beispiel Somalia, Jürgen Barti, Frankfurt am Main, Peter Lang, 1999

19. Die UNO-Friedensoperation in Kambodscha Vorgeschichte, Konzept, Verlauf und kritische Evaluierung des international Engagements, Peter Hazdra, Frankfurt am Main, Peter Lang, 1997

20. Humanitarian action and peace-keeping operations debriefing and lessons; report and recommendations of the international conference, Singapore, Februray 1997,Institute of Policy Studies, London u.a. Kluwer Law International, 1997

21. Der kriegerische Konflikt in Somalia und die internationale Intervention 1992 bis 1995, eine entwicklungsgenetische und multidimensionale Analyse, Ron H. Herrmann, Frankfurt am Main, Peter Lang,   1997

22. The conceit of innocence losing the conscience of the West in the war against Bosnia, Stjepan Gabriel Mestrovi 'c. 1. ed.—College Station, Texas A&M University Press, c 1997

23. Humanitarian intervention, the United Nations in an evolving world order, Sean D. Murphy, Philadelphia, Penn, Univ. of Pennsylvania Press, 1996

24. UNO, Weltpolizei auf dem Prüfstand, 38 Jahre Friedensmissionen vom Suez bis Kambodscha, Imke Keil & Sabine Lobner, Münster, Lit, 1994

25. Kingdoms of the Sudan, R.S. O'Fahey and J.L. Spaulding, Methuen & Co. Ltd., London, Methuen, 1974.

26. International Law and the Use of Force, Christine Gray, Oxford university press, 2ed., 2004.

27. The Legality of the UN Humanitarian Intervention under Chapter VII of the UN Chapter, Somalia and Beyond, Osman Haji, Abdiwahid, UMI Dissertation Service. MI, USA. 1997.

Restoring and Maintaining Order in Complex Peace Operations, Michael J. Kelly, Kluwer Law International, Den Haag, Netherlande, 1999.

War and intervention, issues for contemporary peace operations, Michael V. Bhatia., 1.Print, Bloomfield, CT, Kumarian Press, 2003

The use of force in UN peace operations, Trevor Findlay, Oxford, Oxford Univ. Press u.a., 2002

United Nations peacekeeping operations, ad hoc missions, permanent engagement, Ramesh Thakur,Tokyo u.a., United Nations Univ. Press, 2001

Keeping the peace, the United Nations and the maintenance of international peace and security,Nigel D. White.,2. ed., Manchester u.a., Manchester Univ. Press, 1997

United Nations peace-keeping, United Nations, New York, NY, United Nations, Dep. of Publ. Information, 1996

Keeping the peace, conflict resolution in the twenty-first century, School of International and Public Affairs, New York, NY, 1993

Human rights functions of United Nations peacekeeping operations, Mari Katayanagi.,The Hague [u.a], Martinus Nijhoff Publ., 2002

Democratic accountability and the use of military force in international law, Charlotte Ku. 1Ed., Cambridge [u.a.], Cambridge Univ. Press, 2003

UN Resolutions on Dar Fur

United Nations S/RES/1547 (2004)
Security Council Distr.: General
11 June 2004
04-38626 (E)
0438626
Resolution 1547 (2004)
Adopted by the Security Council at its 4988th meeting, on 11 June 2004
The Security Council,
Welcoming the signature of the Declaration on 5 June 2004 in Nairobi, Kenya, in which the parties confirmed their agreement to the six protocols signed between the Government of Sudan and the Sudan People's Liberation Movement/ Army(SPLM/A), and reconfirmed their commitment to completing the remaining stages of negotiations,

Commending the work, and continued support of the Intergovernmental Authority on Development (IGAD), in particular the Government of Kenya as Chair of the Subcommittee on Sudan, in facilitating the peace talks, and recognizing the efforts of the Civilian Protection Monitoring Team, the Joint Military Commission in the Nuba Mountains and the Verification and Monitoring Team supporting the peace process, and *expressing* its hope that IGAD will continue to play a vital role during the transitional period, *Reaffirming* its support for the Machakos Protocol of 20 July 2002 and subsequent agreements based on this Protocol,

Reaffirming its commitment to the sovereignty, independence and unity of Sudan,

Recalling the statements by its President (S/PRST/2003/16) of 10 October2003 and (S/PRST/2004/18) of 25 May 2004,

145

Condemning all acts of violence and violations of human rights and international humanitarian law by all parties and *expressing* its utmost concern at the consequences of the prolonged conflict for the civilian population of Sudan, including women, children, refugees and internally displaced persons,

Urging the two parties involved to conclude speedily a Comprehensive Peace Agreement and *believing* that the progress now being made in the Naivasha Process will contribute to improved stability and peace in Sudan,

Welcoming the Secretary-General's report (S/2004/453) of 7 June 2004,

1. *Welcomes* the Secretary-General's proposal to establish, for an initial period of three months and under the authority of an SRSG, a United Nations advance team in Sudan as a special political mission, dedicated to preparation of the international monitoring foreseen in the 25 September 2003 Naivasha Agreement on Security Arrangements, to facilitate contacts with the parties concerned and to prepare for the introduction of a peace support operation following the signing of a Comprehensive Peace Agreement;

2. *Endorses* the Secretary-General's proposals for the staffing of the advance team and *requests* in this regard the Secretary-General to conclude all necessary agreements with the Government of Sudan as expeditiously as possible;

3. *Declares* its readiness to consider establishing a United Nations peace support operation to support the implementation of a Comprehensive Peace Agreement, and *requests* the Secretary-General to submit to the Council recommendations for the size, structure, and mandate of this operation, as soon as possible after the signing of a Comprehensive Peace Agreement;

4. *Requests* the Secretary-General, pending signature of a Comprehensive Peace Agreement to take the necessary preparatory steps, including, in particular, prepositioning the most critical logistical and personnel requirements to facilitate the rapid deployment of the above-mentioned possible operation principally to assist the parties in monitoring and verifying compliance with the terms of a Comprehensive Peace Agreement as well as to prepare for the Organization's role during the transitional period in Sudan;

5. *Underlines* the need for an effective public information capacity, including through local and national radio, television and newspaper channels, to promote understanding of the peace process and the role a United Nations peace support operation will play among local communities and the parties;

6. *Endorses* the conclusions of the Secretary-General with regard to the situation in Sudan, in particular Dar Fur and the Upper Nile set out in paragraph 22 of his report, *calls* upon the parties to use their influence to bring an immediate halt to the fighting in the Dar Fur region, in the Upper Nile and elsewhere, *urges* the parties to the Ndjamena Ceasefire Agreement of 8 April 2004 to conclude a political agreement without delay, *welcomes* African Union efforts to that end, and *calls* on the international community to be prepared for constant engagement including extensive funding in support of peace in Sudan;

7. *Requests* the Secretary-General to keep it informed of developments in Sudan, particularly on the Naivasha negotiation process, the implementation of the peace process and the execution by the advance team of its mandate, and to submit a report to the Council no later than three months after adoption of this resolution;

8. *Decides* to remain seized of the matter.

United Nations S/RES/1556 (2004)
Security Council Distr.: General
30 July 2004
04-44602 (E)
0444602
Resolution 1556 (2004)
Adopted by the Security Council at its 5015th meeting, on 30 July 2004
The Security Council,
Recalling its Statement by its President of 25 May 2004 (S/PRST/2004/16), its resolution 1547 (2004) of 11 June 2004 and its resolution 1502 (2003) of 26 August 2003 on the access of humanitarian workers to populations in need, *Welcoming* the leadership role and the engagement of the African Union to address the situation in Dar Fur and *expressing* its readiness to support fully these efforts,

Further welcoming the communiqué of the African Union Peace and Security Council issued 27 July 2004 (S/2004/603),

Reaffirming its commitment to the sovereignty, unity, territorial integrity, and independence of Sudan as consistent with the Machakos Protocol of 20 July 2002 and subsequent agreements based on this protocol as agreed to by the Government of Sudan,

Welcoming the Joint Communiqué issued by the Government of Sudan and the Secretary-General of the United Nations on 3 July 2004, including the creation of the Joint Implementation Mechanism, and acknowledging steps taken towards improved humanitarian access,

Taking note of the Report of the Secretary-General on Sudan issued 3 June 2004 and welcoming the Secretary-General's appointment of a Special Representative for Sudan and his efforts to date, *Reiterating* its grave concern at the ongoing humanitarian crisis and widespread human rights violations, including continued attacks on civilians that are placing the lives of hundreds of thousands at risk, *Condemning* all acts of violence and violations of human rights and international humanitarian law by all parties to the crisis, in particular by the Janjaweed, including indiscriminate attacks on civilians, rapes, forced displacements, and acts of violence especially those with an ethnic dimension, and expressing its utmost concern at the consequences of the conflict in Dar Fur on the civilian population, including women, children, internally displaced persons, and refugees,
Recalling in this regard that the Government of Sudan bears the primary responsibility to respect human rights while maintaining law and order and protecting its

population within its territory and that all parties are obliged to respect international humanitarian law,

Urging all the parties to take the necessary steps to prevent and put an end to violations of human rights and international humanitarian law and underlining that there will be no impunity for violators,

Welcoming the commitment by the Government of Sudan to investigate the atrocities and prosecute those responsible,

Emphasizing the commitment of the Government of Sudan to mobilize the armed forces of Sudan immediately to disarm the Janjaweed militias,

Recalling also in this regard its resolutions 1325 (2000) of 31 October 2000 on women, peace and security, 1379 (2001) of 20 November 2001, 1460 (2003) of 30 January 2003, and 1539 (2004) of 22 April 2004 on children in armed conflict, and 1265 (1999) of 17 September 1999 and 1296 (2000) of 19 April 2000 on the protection of civilians in armed conflict,

Expressing concern at reports of violations of the Ceasefire Agreement signed in N'Djamena on 8 April 2004, and reiterating that all parties to the ceasefire must comply with all of the terms contained therein,

Welcoming the donor consultation held in Geneva in June 2004 as well as subsequent briefings highlighting urgent humanitarian needs in Sudan and Chad and reminding donors of the need to fulfil commitments that have been made,

Recalling that over one million people are in need of urgent humanitarian assistance, that with the onset of the rainy season the provision of assistance has become increasingly difficult, and that without urgent action to address the security, access, logistics, capacity and funding requirements the lives of hundreds of thousands of people will be at risk,

Expressing its determination to do everything possible to halt a humanitarian catastrophe, including by taking further action if required,

Welcoming the ongoing international diplomatic efforts to address the situation in Dar Fur,

Stressing that any return of refugees and displaced persons to their homes must take place voluntarily with adequate assistance and with sufficient security, *Noting with grave concern* that up to 200,000 refugees have fled to the neighbouring State of Chad, which constitutes a serious burden upon that country, and expressing grave concern at reported cross-border incursions by Janjaweed militias of the Dar Fur region of Sudan into Chad and also taking note of the agreement between the Government of Sudan and Chad to establish a jointmechanism to secure the borders,

Determining that the situation in Sudan constitutes a threat to international peace and security and to stability in the region,

Acting under Chapter VII of the Charter of the United Nations,

1. *Calls on* the Government of Sudan to fulfil immediately all of the commitments it made in the 3 July 2004 Communiqué, including particularly by facilitating international relief for the humanitarian disaster by means of a moratorium on all restrictions that might hinder the provision of humanitarian assistance and access to the affected populations, by advancing independent investigation in cooperation with the United Nations of violations of human rights and international humanitarian law, by the establishment of credible security conditions for the protection of the civilian population and humanitarian actors, and by the resumption of political talks with dissident groups from the Dar Fur region, specifically the Justice and Equality Movement (JEM) and the Sudan Liberation Movement and Sudan Liberation Army (SLM/A) on Dar Fur;

2. *Endorses* the deployment of international monitors, including the protection force envisioned by the African Union, to the Dar Fur region of Sudan under the leadership of the African Union and *urges* the international community to continue to support these efforts, *welcomes* the progress made in deploying monitors, including the offers to provide forces by members of the African Union, and *stresses* the need for the Government of Sudan and all involved parties to facilitate the work of the monitors in accordance with the N'Djamena ceasefire agreement and with the Addis Ababa agreement of 28 May 2004 on the modalities of establishing an observer mission to monitor the ceasefire;

3. *Urges* member states to reinforce the international monitoring team, led by the African Union, including the protection force, by providing personnel and other assistance including financing, supplies, transport, vehicles, command support, communications and headquarters support as needed for the monitoring opera-

tion, and *welcomes* the contributions already made by the European Union and the United States to support the African Union led operation;

4. *Welcomes* the work done by the High Commissioner for Human Rights to send human rights observers to Sudan and *calls upon* the Government of Sudan to cooperate with the High Commissioner in the deployment of those observers;

5. *Urges* the parties to the N'Djamena Ceasefire Agreement of 8 April 2004 to conclude a political agreement without delay, notes with regret the failure of senior rebel leaders to participate in the 15 July talks in Addis Ababa, Ethiopia as unhelpful to the process and calls for renewed talks under the sponsorship of the African Union, and its chief mediator Hamid Algabid, to reach a political solution to the tensions in Dar Fur and *strongly urges* rebel groups to respect the ceasefire, end the violence immediately, engage in peace talks without preconditions, and act in a positive and constructive manner to resolve the conflict;

6. *Demands* that the Government of Sudan fulfil its commitments to disarm the Janjaweed militias and apprehend and bring to justice Janjaweed leaders and their associates who have incited and carried out human rights and international humanitarian law violations and other atrocities, and *further requests* the Secretary General to report in 30 days, and monthly thereafter, to the Council on the progress or lack thereof by the Government of Sudan on this matter and *expresses its intention* to consider further actions, including measures as provided for in Article 41 of the Charter of the United Nations on the Government of Sudan, in the event of non-compliance;

7. *Decides* that all states shall take the necessary measures to prevent the sale or supply, to all non-governmental entities and individuals, including the Janjaweed, operating in the states of North Dar Fur, South Dar Fur and West Dar Fur, by their nationals or from their territories or using their flag vessels or aircraft, of arms and related materiel of all types, including weapons and ammunition, military vehicles and equipment, paramilitary equipment, and spare parts for the aforementioned, whether or not originating in their territories;8. *Decides* that all states shall take the necessary measures to prevent any provision to the non-governmental entities and individuals identified in paragraph 7operating in the states of North Dar Fur, South Dar Fur and West Dar Fur by their nationals or from their territories of technical training or assistance related to the provision, manufacture, maintenance or use of the items listed in paragraph 7 above;

9. *Decides* that the measures imposed by paragraphs 7 and 8 above shall not apply to:—supplies and related technical training and assistance to monitoring, verification or peace support operations, including such operations led by regional organizations, that are authorized by the United Nations or are operating with the consent of the relevant parties; supplies of non-lethal military equipment intended solely for humanitarian, human rights monitoring or protective use, and related technical training and assistance; and supplies of protective clothing, including flak jackets and military helmets, for the personal use of United Nations personnel, human rights monitors, representatives of the media and humanitarian and development workers and associated personnel;

10. *Expresses* its intention to consider the modification or termination of the measures imposed under paragraphs 7 and 8 when it determines that the Government of Sudan has fulfilled its commitments described in paragraph 6;

11. *Reiterates* its support for the Naivasha agreement signed by the Government of Sudan and the Sudan People's Liberation Movement, and *looks forward to* effective implementation of the agreement and a peaceful, unified Sudan working in harmony with all other States for the development of Sudan, and *calls on* the international community to be prepared for constant engagement including necessary funding in support of peace and economic development in Sudan;

12. *Urges* the international community to make available much needed assistance to mitigate the humanitarian catastrophe now unfolding in the Dar Fur region and calls upon member states to honour pledges that have been made against needs in Dar Fur and Chad and underscoring the need to contribute generously towards fulfilling the unmet portion of the United Nations consolidated appeals;

13. *Requests* the Secretary-General to activate inter-agency humanitarian mechanisms to consider what additional measures may be needed to avoid a humanitarian catastrophe and to report regularly to the Council on progress made; 14. *Encourages* the Secretary-General's Special Representative for Sudan and the independent expert of the Commission on Human Rights to work closely with the Government of Sudan in supporting independent investigation of violations of human rights and international humanitarian law in the Dar Fur region;

15. *Extends* the special political mission set out in resolution 1547 for an additional 90 days to 10 December 2004 and *requests* the Secretary-General to incorporate into the mission contingency planning for the Dar Fur region;

16. *Expresses* its full support for the African Union-led ceasefire commission and monitoring mission in Dar Fur, and *requests* the Secretary-General to assist the African Union with planning and assessments for its mission in Dar Fur, and in accordance with the Joint Communiqué to prepare to support implementation of a future agreement in Dar Fur in close cooperation with the African Union and *requests* the Secretary-General to report to the Security Council on progress;

17. *Decides* to remain seized of the matter.

United Nations S/RES/1564 (2004)
Security Council Distr.: General
18 September 2004
04-51547 (E)
0451547
Resolution 1564 (2004)
Adopted by the Security Council at its 5040th meeting, on 18 September 2004
The Security Council, Recalling its resolution 1556 (2004) of 30 July 2004, the statement of its President of 25 May 2004 (S/PRST/2004/18), its resolution 1547 (2004) of 11 June 2004 and resolution 1502 (2003) of 26 August 2003, and *taking into account* the Plan of Action agreed by the Secretary-General's Special Representative to Sudan and the Government of Sudan, *Welcoming* the Secretary-General's report of 30 August 2004 (S/2004/703) and the progress achieved on humanitarian access, and expressing concern that paragraphs 59-67 indicate that the Government of Sudan has not fulfilled the entirety of its commitments under resolution 1556 (2004) and taking into account the need to foster and restore the confidence of vulnerable populations and to improve radically the overall security environment in Dar Fur; and *welcoming* the recommendations contained in the report, particularly those concerning the desirability of a substantially increased African Union Mission presence in the Dar Fur region of Sudan,

Welcoming the leadership role and the engagement of the African Union in addressing the situation in Dar Fur,

Welcoming the 6 September 2004 letter to the President of the Security Council from the President of the African Union, Nigerian President Olusegun Obasanjo, including his appeal for international support for the extension of the African Union Mission in Dar Fur,

Reaffirming its commitment to the sovereignty, unity, territorial integrity, and independence of Sudan, as consistent with the Machakos Protocol of 20 July 2002 and subsequent agreements based on this Protocol as agreed to by the Government of Sudan,

Recalling the Joint Communiqué of 3 July 2004 of the Government of Sudan and the United Nations Secretary-General, and *recognizing* the efforts undertaken by the Joint Implementation Mechanism (JIM) and the Special Representative of the Secretary-General to advance the aims of the communiqué and the requirements of resolution 1556 (2004),

Welcoming that the Government of Sudan has taken a number of steps to lift administrative obstructions to the delivery of humanitarian relief, which has resulted in access for an increased number of humanitarian personnel in Dar Fur as well as international human rights non-governmental institutions, and *recognizing* that the Government of Sudan has broadened its cooperation with United Nations humanitarian agencies and their partners,

Urging the Government of Sudan and the rebel groups to facilitate this humanitarian relief by allowing unfettered access for humanitarian supplies and workers, including across Sudan's borders with Chad and Libya by land and by air as may be required,

Expressing grave concern at the lack of progress with regard to security and the protection of civilians, disarmament of the Janjaweed militias and identification and bringing to justice of the Janjaweed leaders responsible for human rights and international humanitarian law violations in Dar Fur,

Recalling that the Sudanese Government bears the primary responsibility to protect its population within its territory, to respect human rights, and to maintain law and order, and that all parties are obliged to respect international humanitarian law,

Stressing that the Sudanese rebel groups, particularly the Justice and Equality Movement and the Sudanese Liberation Army/Movement, must also take all necessary steps to respect international humanitarian and human rights law, *Emphasizing* that the ultimate resolution of the crisis in Dar Fur must include the safe and voluntary return of internally displaced persons and refugees to their original homes, and *noting* in that regard the 21 August 2004 Memorandum of Understanding between the Government of Sudan and the International Organization for Migration (IOM),

Expressing its determination to do everything possible to end the suffering of the people of Dar Fur,

Determining that the situation in Sudan constitutes a threat to international peace and security and to stability in the region,

Acting under Chapter VII of the United Nations Charter,1. *Declares* its grave concern that the Government of Sudan has not fully met its obligations noted in resolution 1556 (2004) and the 3 July Joint Communiqué with the Secretary-General to improve, as expected by the Council, the security of the civilian population of

Dar Fur in the face of continued depredations, and *deplores* the recent ceasefire violations by all parties, in particular the reports by the Cease Fire Commission of Government of Sudan helicopter assaults and Janjaweed attacks on Yassin, Hashaba and Gallab villages on 26 August 2004;

2. *Welcomes* and *supports* the intention of the African Union to enhance and augment its monitoring mission in the Dar Fur region of Sudan, and encourages the undertaking of proactive monitoring;

3. *Urges* Member States to support the African Union in these efforts including by providing all equipment, logistical, financial, material, and otherresources necessary to support the rapid expansion of the African Union Mission and by supporting the efforts of the African Union aimed at a peaceful conclusion of the crisis and the protection of the welfare of the people of Dar Fur, *welcomes* the Government of Sudan's request to the African Union to increase its monitoring presence in Dar Fur in its 9 September 2004 letter to the Security Council, and *urges* the Government of Sudan to take all steps necessary to follow through with this commitment and to cooperate fully with the African Union to ensure a secure and stable environment;

4. *Calls upon* the Government of Sudan and the rebel groups, particularly the Justice and Equality Movement and the Sudanese Liberation Army/Movement, to work together under the auspices of the African Union to reach a political solution in the negotiations currently being held in Abuja under the leadership of President Obasanjo, *notes* the progress made to date, *urges* the parties to the negotiations to sign and implement the humanitarian agreement immediately, and to conclude a protocol on security issues as soon as possible, and *underscores* and *supports* the role of the African Union in monitoring the implementation of all such agreements reached;

5. *Urges* the Government of Sudan and the Sudan People's Liberation Movement to conclude a comprehensive peace accord expeditiously as a critical step towards the development of a peaceful and prosperous Sudan;

6. *Affirms* that internally displaced persons, refugees and other vulnerable peoples should be allowed to return to their homes voluntarily, in safety and with dignity, and only when adequate assistance and security are in place;

7. *Reiterates* its call for the Government of Sudan to end the climate of impunity in Dar Fur by identifying and bringing to justice all those responsible, including

members of popular defense forces and Janjaweed militias, for the widespread human rights abuses and violations of international humanitarian law, and *insists* that the Government of Sudan take all appropriate steps to stop all violence and atrocities;

8. *Calls on* all Sudanese parties to take the necessary steps to ensure that violations reported by the Cease Fire Commission are addressed immediately and that those responsible for such violations are held accountable;

9. *Demands* that the Government of Sudan submit to the African Union Mission for verification documentation, particularly the names of Janjaweed militiamen disarmed and names of those arrested for human rights abuses and violations of international humanitarian law, with regard to its performance relative to resolution 1556 (2004) and the 8 April 2004 N'djamena ceasefire agreement;

10. *Demands* all armed groups, including rebel forces, cease all violence, cooperate with international humanitarian relief and monitoring efforts and ensure that their members comply with international humanitarian law, and facilitate the safety and security of humanitarian staff;

11. *Reiterates* its full support for the 8 April 2004 N'djamena ceasefire agreement, and in this regard *urges* the Government of Sudan to refrain from conducting military flights in and over the Dar Fur region in accordance with its commitments;

12. *Requests* that the Secretary-General rapidly establish an international commission of inquiry in order immediately to investigate reports of violations of international humanitarian law and human rights law in Dar Fur by all parties, to determine also whether or not acts of genocide have occurred, and to identify the perpetrators of such violations with a view to ensuring that those responsible are held accountable, *calls on* all parties to cooperate fully with such a commission, and *further requests* the Secretary-General, in conjunction with the Office of the High Commissioner for Human Rights, to take appropriate steps to increase the number of human rights monitors deployed to Dar Fur;

13. *Calls on* Member States to provide in an urgent manner generous and sustained contributions to the humanitarian efforts under way in Dar Fur and Chad to address the shortfall in response to continued United Nations appeals, *emphasizes* the need for Member States to fulfil their pledges forthwith, and *welcomes* the substantial contributions made to date;

14. *Declares* that the Council, in the event the Government of Sudan fails to comply fully with resolution 1556 (2004) or this resolution, including, as determined by the Council after consultations with the African Union, failure to cooperate fully with the expansion and extension of the African Union monitoring mission in Dar Fur, *shall consider* taking additional measures as contemplated in Article 41 of the Charter of the United Nations, such as actions to affect Sudan's petroleum sector and the Government of Sudan or individual members of the Government of Sudan, in order to take effective action to obtain such full compliance or full cooperation;

15. *Requests* that, in the monthly reports pursuant to resolution 1556 (2004), the Secretary-General report to the Council on the progress or lack thereof by the Government of Sudan in complying with the Council's demands in this resolution and the effort by the Government of Sudan and the Sudan People's Liberation Movement to conclude a comprehensive peace accord on an urgent basis;

16. *Decides* to remain seized of the matter.

United Nations S/RES/1574 (2004)
Security Council Distr.: General
19 November 2004
04-61689 (E)
0461689
Resolution 1574 (2004)
Adopted by the Security Council at its 5082nd meeting, on 19 November 2004
in Nairobi
The Security Council,
Recalling its resolutions 1547 (2004) of 11 June 2004, 1556 (2004) of 30 July
2004 and 1564 (2004) of 18 September 2004 and the statements of its President
concerning Sudan,
Reaffirming its commitment to the sovereignty, unity, independence and territorial integrity of Sudan, and *recalling* the importance of the principles of good-
neighbourliness, non-interference and regional cooperation,

Reaffirming also its support for the Machakos Protocol of 20 July 2002 and subsequent agreements based on this protocol,

Expressing its determination to help the people of Sudan to promote national
reconciliation, lasting peace and stability, and to build a prosperous and united
Sudan in which human rights are respected and the protection of all citizens is
assured,

Recalling that it welcomed the signature of the Declaration on 5 June 2004 in
Nairobi, Kenya, in which the parties confirmed their agreement to the six protocols signed between the Government of Sudan and the Sudan People's Liberation
Movement/Army, and reconfirmed their commitment to completing the remaining stages of negotiations,

Commending again the work and continued support of the Intergovernmental
Authority on Development (IGAD), in particular the Government of Kenya as
Chair of the Sub-Committee on Sudan, in facilitating the peace talks in Nairobi,
recognizing the efforts of the Civilian Protection Monitoring Team, the Joint
Military Commission in the Nuba Mountains and the Verification and Monitoring
Team supporting the peace process, and *expressing* its hope that IGAD will con-
tinue to play a vital role during the transitional period,

Encouraging the parties to conclude speedily a Comprehensive Peace Agreement,
and stressing the need for the international community, once such an agreement

has been signed and implementation begins, to provide assistance towards its implementation,

Emphasizing that progress towards resolution of the conflict in Dar Fur would create conditions conducive for delivery of such assistance, *Expressing* its serious concern at the growing insecurity and violence in Dar Fur, the dire humanitarian situation, continued violations of human rights and repeated breaches of the ceasefire, and *reiterating* in this regard the obligation of all parties to implement the commitments, referred to in its previous resolutions on Sudan,
Condemning all acts of violence and violations of human rights and international humanitarian law by all parties, and *emphasizing* the need for perpetrators of all such crimes to be brought to justice without delay,
Recalling in this regard that all parties, including the Sudanese rebel groups such as the Justice and Equality Movement and the Sudanese Liberation Army, must respect human rights and international humanitarian law, and *also recalling* the primary responsibility of the Sudanese Government to protect its population within its territory and to maintain law and order, while respecting human rights,

Stressing the importance of further progress towards resolving the crisis in Dar Fur, *welcoming* the vital and wide-ranging role being played by the African Union towards that end, and *welcoming* the Government of Sudan's decision in favour of the expansion of the African Union Mission,

Taking note of the Secretary-General's reports of 28 September 2004 (S/2004/763) and 2 November 2004 (S/2004/881),

Deeply concerned by the situation in Sudan and its implications for international peace and security and stability in the region,

1. *Declares* its strong support for the efforts of the Government of Sudan and the Sudan People's Liberation Movement/Army to reach a Comprehensive Peace Agreement, *encourages* the parties to redouble their efforts, *welcomes* the signing of the Memorandum of Understanding in Nairobi on 19 November 2004 entitled "Declaration on the conclusion of IGAD negotiations on peace in the Sudan", attached to this resolution, and the agreement that the six protocols referredto in the Nairobi Declaration of 5 June 2004 constitute and form the core Peace Agreement, and *strongly endorses* the parties' commitment to reach a finalcomprehensive agreement by 31 December 2004 and *expects* that it will be fully and transparently implemented, with the appropriate international monitoring;

2. *Declares* its commitment, upon conclusion of a Comprehensive Peace Agreement, to assist the people of Sudan in their efforts to establish a peaceful, united and prosperous nation, on the understanding that the parties are fulfilling all their commitments, including those agreed in Abuja, Nigeria and Ndjamena, Chad;

3. *Urges* the Joint Assessment Mission of the United Nations, the World Bank and the parties, in association with other bilateral and multilateral donors, to continue their efforts to prepare for the rapid delivery of an assistance package for the reconstruction and economic development of Sudan, including official development assistance, possible debt relief and trade access, to be implemented once a Comprehensive Peace Agreement has been signed and its implementation begins;

4. *Welcomes* the initiative of the Government of Norway to convene an international donors' conference for the reconstruction and economic development of Sudan upon the signing of a Comprehensive Peace Agreement;

5. *Welcomes* the continued operations of the Joint Military Commission, the Civilian Protection Monitoring Team, and the Verification and Monitoring Team, in anticipation of the implementation of a Comprehensive Peace Agreement and the establishment of a United Nations peace support operation;

6. *Reiterates* its readiness, upon the signature of a Comprehensive PeaceAgreement, to consider establishing a United Nations peace support operation to support the implementation of that agreement, and *reiterates* its request to the Secretary-General to submit to the Council, as soon as possible after the signing of a Comprehensive Peace Agreement, recommendations for the size, structure, mandate of such an operation, including also a timetable for its deployment;

7. *Welcomes* the preparatory work already carried out by the United Nations Advance Mission in Sudan (UNAMIS), established by its resolution 1547 (2004), *endorses* the proposals in the Secretary-General's reports of 28 September 2004 and 2 November 2004 to increase its staffing, *extends* the mandate of UNAMIS by a further three months until 10 March 2005, and *calls on* the Sudan People's Liberation Movement/Army to commit to full cooperation with UNAMIS,

8. *Calls on* all countries in the region to do their utmost to support actively the full and timely implementation of a Comprehensive Peace Agreement;

9. *Emphasizes* that a Comprehensive Peace Agreement will contribute towards sustainable peace and stability throughout Sudan and to the efforts to address the crisis in Dar Fur, and *underlines* the need for a national and inclusive approach, including the role of women, towards reconciliation and peace-building;

10. *Underlines* the importance of progress in peace talks in Abuja between the Government of Sudan and the Sudanese Liberation Army and the Justice and Equality Movement towards resolving the crisis in Dar Fur, *insists* that all parties to the Abuja peace talks negotiate in good faith to reach agreement speedily, *welcomes* the signature of the Humanitarian and Security Protocols on 9 November 2004, *urges* the parties to implement these rapidly, and looks forward to the early-signature of a Declaration of Principles with a view to a political settlement;

11. *Demands* that Government and rebel forces and all other armed groups immediately cease all violence and attacks, including abduction, refrain from forcible relocation of civilians, cooperate with international humanitarian relief and monitoring efforts, ensure that their members comply with internationalhumanitarian law, facilitate the safety and security of humanitarian staff, and reinforce throughout their ranks their agreements to allow unhindered access and passage by humanitarian agencies and those in their employ, in accordance with its resolution 1502 (2003) of 26 August 2003 on the access of humanitarian workers to populations in need and with the Abuja Protocols of 9 November 2004;

12. In accordance with its previous resolutions on Sudan, *decides* to monitor compliance by the parties with their obligations in that regard and, subject to a further decision of the Council, to take appropriate action against any party failing to fulfil its commitments;

13. *Strongly supports* the decisions of the African Union to increase its mission in Dar Fur to 3,320 personnel and to enhance its mandate to include the tasks listed in paragraph 6 of the African Union Peace and Security Council's Communiqué of 20 October 2004, *urges* Member States to provide the required equipment, logistical, financial, material, and other necessary resources, and *urges* the Government of Sudan and all rebel groups in Dar Fur to cooperate fully with the African Union;

14. *Reiterates* its call on Member States to provide urgent and generous contributions to the humanitarian efforts under way in Sudan and Chad;

15. *Calls on* all parties to cooperate fully with the International Commission of Inquiry stablished by the Secretary-General, as described in his letter of 4 October 2004 to the President of the Security Council (S/2004/812), the outcome of which will be communicated to the Security Council;

16. *Reiterates* the importance of deploying more human rights monitors to Dar Fur;

17. *Requests* the Secretary-General to keep it regularly informed of developments in Sudan, and to make any recommendations for action to ensure implementation of this resolution and its previous resolutions on Sudan;

18. *Decides* to remain seized of the matter.

Annex
DECLARATION ON THE CONCLUSION OF IGAD NEGOTIATIONS ON PEACE IN THE SUDAN
Gigiri, Nairobi: *Friday 19th November 2004*
WHEREAS the Government of the Republic of the Sudan and the Sudan People's Liberation Movement/Army (the Parties) reconfirmed in the Nairobi Declaration of 5th June, 2004 on the Final Phase of the IGAD led negotiations on Peace in the Sudan, their agreement on the six texts, including the Machakos Protocol as well as the texts relating to Power Sharing, Wealth Sharing, Security Arrangements, and resolution of the Conflict in Southern Kordofan/Nuba Mountains, Blue Nile, and Abyei Area;
WHEREAS the Parties in a Joint Press Statement on October 16, 2004, "recommitted themselves to finalize and conclude the Comprehensive Peace Agreement in recognition that prompt completion of the Peace Process is essential for all the people of the Sudan as it will help in resolving all challenges facing the country";
ACKNOWLEDGING the progress made to date on the Security Arrangements and Ceasefire Details including the extensive work that has been accomplished in the Implementation Modalities annexes; and DECLARING that the conclusion of the IGAD led initiative is central to a comprehensive Peace Agreement in the Sudan including the resolution of the Conflict in Dar Fur;
NOW HEREBY THE PARTIES AFFIRM that the six Protocols referred to in the Nairobi Declaration of 5th June, 2004, constitute and form the core Peace Agreement and therefore invite the UN Security Council in this its Nairobi sitting to pass a resolution endorsing the six Protocols.
FURTHER the Parties declare their commitment to expeditiously complete Negotiations on the two annexes on Ceasefire Agreement and Implementation

Modalities so as to conclude and sign the Comprehensive Peace Agreement no later than 31st December, 2004.
(*Signed*) (*Signed*)

Hon. Yahya Hussein Babikar Cdr. Nhial Deng Nhial
For the Government For the Sudan People's Of the Republic of the Sudan Liberation Movement/Army Witnessed By:
(*Signed*)

Lt. Gen. Lazaro K. Sumbeiywo (Rtd.)
On Behalf of the IGAD Envoys
(*Signed*)

Dr. Jan Pronk
Special Representative of the Secretary-General of the United Nations In the Presence of:
The United Nations Security Council.
(*Signed*) (*Signed*)

Ambassador Abdallah Baali Ambassador Ismael Gaspar Martins
Permanent Representative of Algeria Permanent Representative of Angola to the United Nations to the United Nations
(*Signed*) (*Signed*)

Ambassador Joel Adechi Ambassador Ronaldo Sardenberg
Ambassador Joel Adechi Ambassador Ronaldo Sardenberg
Permanent Representative of Benin Permanent Representative of Brazil to the United Nations to the United Nations
(*Signed*) (*Signed*)

Ambassador Heraldo Muñoz Ambassador Wang Guangya
Permanent Representative of Chile Permanent Representative of China to the United Nations to the United Nations
(*Signed*) (*Signed*)

Ambassador Jean-Marc de La Sablière Ambassador Gunter Pleuger
Permanent Representative of France Permanent Representative of Germany to the United Nations to the United Nations 7
S/RES/1574 (2004)
(*Signed*) (*Signed*)

Ambassador Munir Akram Ambassador Lauro Baja, Jr.
Permanent Representative of Pakistan Permanent Representative of the Philippines
to the United Nations to the United Nations
(*Signed*) (*Signed*)

Ambassador Mihnea Motoc Ambassador Andrey Denisov
Permanent Representative of Romania Permanent Representative of the Russian
Federation to the United Nations to the United Nations
(*Signed*) (*Signed*)

Ambassador Juan Antonio Yáñez-Barnuevo Ambassador Emyr Jones Parry
Permanent Representative of Spain Permanent Representative of the United
Kingdom to the United Nations to the United Nations
(*Signed*)

Ambassador John Danforth
Permanent Representative of the United States to the United Nations

United Nations S/RES/1585 (2005)
Security Council Distr.: General
10 March 2005
05-26638 (E)
0526638
Resolution 1585 (2005)
Adopted by the Security Council at its 5137th meeting, on 10 March 2005
The Security Council,
Recalling its resolutions 1547 (2004) of 11 June 2004, 1556 (2004) of 30 July
2004 and 1574 (2004) of 19 November 2004,

Reaffirming its readiness to support the peace process, *Decides* to extend the mandate of the United Nations Advance Mission in Sudan (UNAMIS), established by
its resolution 1547 (2004), until 17 March 2005, *Decides* to remain actively seized
of the matter ...

United Nations S/RES/1588 (2005)
Security Council Distr.: General
17 March 2005
05-27444 (E)
0527444
Resolution 1588 (2005)
Adopted by the Security Council at its 5143rd meeting, on 17 March 2005
The Security Council,
Recalling its resolutions 1547 (2004) of 11 June 2004, 1556 (2004) of 30 July
2004, 1574 (2004) of 19 November 2004, and resolution 1585 (2005) of 10
March 2005,
Reaffirming its readiness to support the peace process, *Decides* to extend the mandate of the United Nations Advance Mission in Sudan (UNAMIS), established by
its resolution 1547 (2004), until 24 March 2005, *Decides* to remain actively seized
of the matter.

United Nations S/RES/1590 (2005)
Security Council Distr.: General
24 March 2005
05-28408 (E)
0528408
Resolution 1590 (2005)
Adopted by the Security Council at its 5151st meeting, on
24 March 2005

The Security Council,

Recalling its resolutions 1547 (2004) of 11 June 2004, 1556 (2004) of 30 July 2004, 1564 (2004) of 18 September 2004, and 1574 (2004) of 19 November 2004, 1585 of 10 March 2005 and 1588 (2005) of 17 March 2005, and statements of its President concerning Sudan, *Reaffirming* its commitment to the sovereignty, unity, independence and territorial integrity of Sudan, and recalling the importance of the principles of good neighbourliness, non-interference and regional cooperation,

Welcoming the signing of the Comprehensive Peace Agreement between the Government of Sudan (GOS) and the Sudan People's Liberation Movement/ Army (SPLM/A) in Nairobi, Kenya on 9 January 2005,

Recalling the commitments made by the parties in the 8 April N'djamen Ceasefire Agreement and the 9 November 2004 Abuja Humanitarian and Security Protocols between the Government of Sudan, the Sudan People's Liberation Movement/ Army (SPLM/A) and the Justice and Equality Movement (JEM), and recalling the commitments made in the Joint Communiqué of 3 July 2004 between the Government of Sudan and the Secretary-General,

Expressing its determination to help the people of Sudan to promote national reconciliation, lasting peace and stability, and to build a prosperous and united Sudan in which human rights are respected, the protection of all citizens assured, *Taking note* of the statements of Vice-President Ali Osman Taha of the Government of Sudan and Chairman Garang of the SPLM/A at the meeting of the Council on 8 February 2005, and the strong will and determination they expressed to find a peaceful resolution to the conflict in Dar Fur as expressed at the meeting, *Recognizing* that the parties to the Comprehensive Peace Agreement must build on the Agreement to bring peace and stability to the entire country, and calling on all Sudanese parties in particular those party to the Comprehensive Peace Agreement, to take immediate steps to achieve a peaceful settlement to the conflict in Dar Fur and to take all necessary action to prevent further violations of human rights and international humanitarian law and to put an end to impunity, including in the Dar Fur region,

Expressing its utmost concern over the dire consequences of the prolonged conflict for the civilian population in the Dar Fur region as well as throughout Sudan, in particular the increase in the number of refugees and internally displaced persons, *Considering* that the voluntary and sustainable return of refugees and internally displaced persons will be a critical factor for the consolidation of the peace process, *Expressing also* its deep concern for the security of humanitarian workers and their access to populations in need, including refugees, internally displaced persons and other war-affected populations,

Condemning the continued violations of the N'djamena Ceasefire Agreement of 8 April 2004 and the Abuja Protocols of 9 November 2004 by all sides in Dar Fur and the deterioration of the security situation and the negative impact this has had on humanitarian assistance efforts,

Strongly condemning all violations of human rights and international humanitarian law in the Dar Fur region, in particular the continuation of violence against civilians and sexual violence against women and girls since the adoption of resolution 1574 (2004), urging all parties to take necessary steps to prevent further violations, and expressing its determination to ensure that those responsible for all such violations are identified and brought to justice without delay,

Recalling the demands in resolutions 1556 (2004), 1564 (2004), and 1574 (2004), that all parties to the conflict in Dar Fur refrain from any violence against civilians and cooperate fully with the African Union Mission in Dar Fur,

Commending the efforts of the African Union, in particular its Chairman, acknowledging the progress made by the African Union in the deployment of an international protection force, police, and military observers, and calling on all member States to contribute generously and urgently to the African Union Mission in Dar Fur,
Commending also the efforts of the Intergovernmental Authority for Development (IGAD), in particular the Government of Kenya as Chair of the Subcommittee on Sudan,

Reaffirming its resolutions 1325 (2000) on women, peace, and security, 1379 (2001) and 1460 (2003) on children in armed conflicts, as well as resolutions 1265 (1999) and 1296 (2000) on the protection of civilians in armed conflicts and resolution 1502 (2003) on the protection of humanitarian and United Nations personnel,

Welcoming the efforts by the United Nations to sensitize United Nations personnel in the prevention and control of HIV/AIDS and other communicable diseases in all its established operations,

Expressing grave concern at the allegations of sexual exploitation and misconduct by United Nations personnel in United Nations established operations, and welcoming the Secretary-General's 9 February 2005 letter to the Council in this regard, affirming there will be a zero-tolerance policy of sexual exploitation and abuse of any kind in all United Nations peacekeeping missions,

Recognizing that international support for implementation of the Comprehensive Peace Agreement is critically important to its success, emphasizing that progress towards resolution of the conflict in Dar Fur would create conditions conducive for delivery of such assistance, and alarmed that the violence in Dar Fur nonetheless continues,

Taking note of the Secretary-General's reports of 31 January 2005 (S/2005/57 and Add.1), 4 February 2005 (S/2005/68), and 4 March 2005 (S/2005/140) as well as the report of 25 January 2005 of the International Commission of Inquiry (S/2005/60),
Taking note of the request of the parties to the Comprehensive Peace Agreement for the establishment of a peace support mission,

Expressing appreciation for the important contributions of the Standby High Readiness Brigade (SHIRBRIG) towards the planning, preparation, and initial deployment of a peacekeeping operation, as well as the preparatory work by the United Nations Advance Mission in Sudan,

Determining that the situation in Sudan continues to constitute a threat to international peace and security,

1. *Decides* to establish the United Nations Mission in Sudan (UNMIS) for an initial period of 6 months and further decides that UNMIS will consist of up to 10,000 military personnel and an appropriate civilian component including up to 715 civilian police personnel;

2. *Requests* that UNMIS closely and continuously liaise and coordinate at all levels with the African Union Mission in Sudan (AMIS) with a view towards expeditiously reinforcing the effort to foster peace in Dar Fur, especially with regard to the Abuja peace process and the African Union Mission in Sudan;

3. *Requests* the Secretary-General, through his Special Representative for Sudan, to coordinate all the activities of the United Nations system in Sudan, to mobilize resources and support from the international community for both immediate assistance and the long-term economic development of Sudan, and to facilitate coordination with other international actors, in particular the African Union

and IGAD, of activities in support of the transitional process established by the Comprehensive Peace Agreement, and to provide good offices and political support for the efforts to resolve all ongoing conflicts in Sudan;

4. *Decides* that the mandate of UNMIS shall be the following:
(a) To support implementation of the Comprehensive Peace Agreement by performing the following tasks:
(i) To monitor and verify the implementation of the Ceasefire Agreement and to investigate violations;
(ii) To liaise with bilateral donors on the formation of Joint Integrated Units;
(iii) To observe and monitor movement of armed groups and redeployment of forces in the areas of UNMIS deployment in accordance with the Ceasefire Agreement;
(iv) To assist in the establishment of the disarmament, demobilization and reintegration programme as called for in the Comprehensive Peace Agreement, with particular attention to the special needs of women and child combatants, and its implementation through voluntary disarmament and weapons collection and destruction;
(v) To assist the parties to the Comprehensive Peace Agreement in promoting understanding of the peace process and the role of UNMIS by means of an effective public information campaign, targeted at all sectors of society, in coordination with the African Union;
(vi) To assist the parties to the Comprehensive Peace Agreement, in addressing the need for a national inclusive approach, including the role of women, towards reconciliation and peacebuilding;
(vii) To assist the parties to the Comprehensive Peace Agreement, in coordination with bilateral and multilateral assistance programmes, in restructuring the police service in Sudan, consistent with democratic policing, to develop a police training and evaluation programme, and to otherwise assist in the training of civilian police;
(viii) To assist the parties to the Comprehensive Peace Agreement in promoting the rule of law, including an independent judiciary, and the protection of human rights of all people of Sudan through a comprehensive and coordinated strategy with the aim of combating impunity and contributing to long-term peace and stability and to assist the parties to the Comprehensive Peace Agreement to develop and consolidate the national legal framework;
(ix) To ensure an adequate human rights presence, capacity, and expertise within UNMIS to carry out human rights promotion, civilian protection, and monitoring activities;

(x) To provide guidance and technical assistance to the parties to the Comprehensive Peace Agreement, in cooperation with other international actors, to support the preparations for and conduct of elections and referenda provided for by the Comprehensive Peace Agreement;

(b) To facilitate and coordinate, within its capabilities and in its areas of deployment, the voluntary return of refugees and internally displaced persons, and humanitarian assistance, inter alia, by helping to establish the necessary security conditions;

(c) To assist the parties to the Comprehensive Peace Agreement in cooperation with other international partners in the mine action sector, by providing humanitarian demining assistance, technical advice, and coordination;

(d) To contribute towards international efforts to protect and promote human rights in Sudan, as well as to coordinate international efforts towards the protection of civilians with particular attention to vulnerable groups including internally displaced persons, returning refugees, and women and children, within UNMIS's capabilities and in close cooperation with other United Nations agencies, related organizations, and non-governmental organizations;

5. *Requests* the Secretary-General to report to the Council within 30 days on options for how UNMIS can reinforce the effort to foster peace in Dar Fur through appropriate assistance to AMIS, including logistical support and technical assistance, and to identify ways in liaison with the AU to utilize UNMIS's resources, particularly logistical and operations support elements, as well as reserve capacity towards this end;

6. *Calls upon* all parties to cooperate fully in the deployment and operations of UNMIS, in particular by guaranteeing the safety, security and freedom of movement of United Nations personnel as well as associated personnel throughout the territory of Sudan;

7. *Emphasizes* that there can be no military solution to the conflict in Dar Fur, and calls upon the Government of Sudan and the rebel groups, particularly the Justice and Equality Movement and the Sudanese Liberation Army/Movement to resume the Abuja talks rapidly without preconditions and negotiate in good faith to speedily reach agreement, and urges the parties to the Comprehensive Peace Agreement to play an active and constructive role in support of the Abuja talks and take immediate steps to support a peaceful settlement to the conflict in Dar Fur;

8. *Calls upon* all Member States to ensure the free, unhindered and expeditious movement to Sudan of all personnel, as well as equipment, provisions, supplies

and other goods, including vehicles and spare parts, which are for the exclusive and official use of UNMIS;

9. *Calls upon* all parties to ensure, in accordance with relevant provisions of international law, the full, safe and unhindered access of relief personnel to all those in need and delivery of humanitarian assistance, in particular to internally displaced persons and refugees;

10. *Requests* that the Secretary-General transfer all functions performed by the special political mission in Sudan (UNAMIS) to UNMIS, together with staff and logistics of the office as appropriate, on the date when UNMIS is established, and to ensure a seamless transition between the United Nations and existing monitoring missions, namely the Verification Monitoring Team, the Joint Monitoring Mission, and the Civilian Protection Monitoring Team;

11. *Requests* the Secretary-General to keep the Council regularly informed of the progress in implementing the Comprehensive Peace Agreement, respect for the ceasefire, and the implementation of the mandate of UNMIS, including a review of the troop level, with a view to its adjusted reduction, taking account of the progress made on the ground and the tasks remaining to be accomplished and to report to the Council in this regard every three months;

12. *Requests* that the Secretary-General continue to report on a monthly basis on the situation in Dar Fur;

13. *Urges* the Joint Assessment Mission of the United Nations, the World Bank, and the parties, in association with other bilateral and multilateral donors, to continue their efforts to prepare for the rapid delivery of an assistance package for the reconstruction and economic development of Sudan, including official development assistance and trade access, to be implemented once implementation of the Comprehensive Peace Agreement begins, and welcomes the initiative of the Government of Norway to convene an international donors' conference for the reconstruction and economic development of Sudan, and urges the international community accordingly to donate generously, including to address the needs of internally displaced persons and refugees;

14. *Requests* the Secretary-General to take the necessary measures to achieve actual compliance in UNMIS with the United Nations zero-tolerance policy on sexual exploitation and abuse, including the development of strategies and appropriate mechanisms to prevent, identify and respond to all forms of misconduct, includ-

ing sexual exploitation and abuse, and the enhancement of training for personnel to prevent misconduct and ensure full compliance with the United Nations code of conduct, *requests* the Secretary-General to take all necessary action in accordance with the Secretary-General's Bulletin on special measures for protection from sexual exploitation and sexual abuse (ST/SGB/2003/13) and to keep the Council informed, and *urges* troop-contributing countries to take appropriate preventive action including the conduct of pre-deployment awareness training, and to take disciplinary action and other action to ensure full accountability in cases of such conduct involving their personnel;

15. *Reaffirms* the importance of appropriate expertise on issues relating to gender in peacekeeping operations and post-conflict peacebuilding in accordance with resolution 1325 (2000), recalls the need to address violence against women and girls as a tool of warfare, and encourages UNMIS as well as the Sudanese parties to actively address these issues;

16. *Acting* under Chapter VII of the Charter of the United Nations,
(i) Decides that UNMIS is authorized to take the necessary action, in the areas of deployment of its forces and as it deems within its capabilities, to protect United Nations personnel, facilities, installations, and equipment, ensure the security and freedom of movement of United Nations personnel, humanitarian workers, joint assessment mechanism and assessment and evaluation commission personnel, and, without prejudice to the responsibility of the Government of Sudan, to protect civilians under imminent threat of physical violence; and

(ii) Requests that the Secretary-General and the Government of Sudan, following appropriate consultation with the Sudan People's Liberation Movement, conclude a status-of-forces agreement within 30 days of adoption of the resolution, taking into consideration General Assembly resolution 58/82 on the scope of legal protection under the Convention on the Safety of United Nations and Associated Personnel, and notes that pending the conclusion of such an agreement, the model status-of-forces agreement dated 9 October 1990 (A/45/594), shall apply provisionally;

17. *Underscores* the immediate need to rapidly increase the number of human rights monitors in Dar Fur, and urges the Secretary-General and the High Commissioner for Human Rights to undertake to accelerate the deployment of human rights monitors to Dar Fur and augment their numbers and also to move forward with the formation of civilian monitoring protection teams, and expects

that the Secretary-General will report on progress on the formation of these teams in his reports to the Security Council as outlined in paragraph 11;

18. *Decides* to remain seized of the matter.

United Nations S/RES/1591 (2005)
Security Council Distr.: General
29 March 2005
05-28789 (E)
0528789
Resolution 1591 (2005)
Adopted by the Security Council at its 5153rd meeting, on
29 March 2005
The Security Council,
Recalling its resolutions 1547 (2004) of 11 June 2004, 1556 (2004) of 30 July
2004, 1564 (2004) of 18 September 2004, 1574 (2004) of 19 November 2004,
1585 (2005) of 10 March 2005, 1588 (2005) of 17 March 2005, and 1590 of 24
March 2005, and statements of its President concerning Sudan,
Reaffirming its commitment to the sovereignty, unity, independence and territo-
rial integrity of Sudan, and recalling the importance of the principles of good
neighbourliness, non-interference and regional cooperation,

Recalling the commitments made by the parties in the 8 April N'djamena Ceasefire
Agreement and the 9 November 2004 Abuja Humanitarian and Security Protocols
between the Government of Sudan, the Sudan Liberation Movement/Army (SLM/
A) and the Justice and Equality Movement (JEM), and recalling the commit-
ments made in the Joint Communique of 3 July 2004 between the Government
of Sudan and the Secretary-General,
Welcoming the signing of the Comprehensive Peace Agreement between the
Government of Sudan (GOS) and the Sudan People's Liberation Movement/
Army (SPLM/A) in Nairobi, Kenya on 9 January 2005,

Recognizing that the parties to the Comprehensive Peace Agreement must build
on the Agreement to bring peace and stability to the entire country, and calling
on all Sudanese parties, in particular those party to the Comprehensive Peace
Agreement, to take immediate steps to achieve a peaceful settlement to the conflict in Dar Fur and to take all necessary action to prevent further violations of
human rights and international humanitarian law and to put an end to impunity,
including in the Dar Fur region,

Expressing its utmost concern over the dire consequences of the prolonged conflict
for the civilian population in the Dar Fur region as well as throughout Sudan, in
particular the increase in the number of refugees and internally displaced persons,
Considering that the voluntary and sustainable return of refugees and internally displaced persons will be a critical factor for the consolidation of the peace process,

Expressing also its deep concern for the security of humanitarian workers and their access to populations in need, including refugees, internally displaced persons and other war-affected populations,

Condemning the continued violations of the N'djamena Ceasefire Agreement of 8 April 2004 and the Abuja Protocols of 9 November 2004 by all sides in Dar Fur and the deterioration of the security situation and negative impact this has had on humanitarian assistance efforts,

Strongly condemning all violations of human rights and international humanitarian law in the Dar Fur region, in particular the continuation of violence against civilians and sexual violence against women and girls since the adoption of resolution 1574 (2004), urging all parties to take necessary steps to prevent further violations, and expressing its determination to ensure that those responsible for all such violations are identified and brought to justice without delay,

Recognizing that international support for implementation of the Comprehensive Peace Agreement is critically important to its success, emphasizingthat progress towards resolution of the conflict in Dar Fur would create conditions conducive for delivery of such assistance, and alarmed that the violence in Dar Fur nonetheless continues, *Recalling* the demands, in resolutions 1556 (2004), 1564 (2004), and 1574 (2004), that all parties to the conflict in Dar Fur refrain from any violence against civilians and cooperate fully with the African Union Mission in Dar Fur,

Welcoming the 16 February 2005 N'djamena Summit on Dar Fur and the continued commitment of the African Union to play a key role in facilitating a resolution to the conflict in Dar Fur in all respects, and the announcement by the Government of Sudan on 16 February 2005 that it would take immediate steps, including withdrawal of its forces from Labado, Qarifa, and Marla in Dar Fur, and the withdrawal of its Antonov aircraft from Dar Fur,

Commending the efforts of the African Union, in particular its Chairman, acknowledging the progress made by the African Union in the deployment of an international protection force, police, and military observers, and calling on all member states to contribute generously and urgently to the African Union Mission in Dar Fur,

Reaffirming its resolutions 1325 (2000) on women, peace, and security, 1379 (2001) and 1460 (2003) on children in armed conflicts, as well as resolutions1265 (1999) and 1296 (2000) on the protection of civilians in armed conflicts and resolution 1502 (2003) on the protection of humanitarian and UN personnel,

Taking note of the Secretary-General's reports of 31 January 2005 (S/2005/57 and Add.1), 3 December 2004 (S/2004/947), 4 February 2005 (S/2005/68), and 4 March 2005 (S/2005/140), as well as the report of 25 January 2005 of the International Commission of Inquiry (S/2005/60),

Determining that the situation in Sudan continues to constitute a threat to international peace and security, *Acting* under Chapter VII of the Charter of the United Nations, 1. *Deplores strongly* that the Government of Sudan and rebel forces and all other armed groups in Dar Fur have failed to comply fully with their commitments and the demands of the Council referred to in resolutions 1556 (2004), 1564 (2004), and 1574 (2004), condemns the continued violations of the 8 April 2004 N'djamena Ceasefire Agreement and the 9 November 2004 Abuja Protocols, including air strikes by the Government of Sudan in December 2004 and January 2005 and rebel attacks on Dar Fur villages in January 2005, and the failure of the Government of Sudan to disarm Janjaweed militiamen and apprehend and bring to justice Janajaweed leaders and their associates who have carried out human rights and international humanitarian law violations and other atrocities, and demands that all parties take immediate steps to fulfil all their commitments to respect the N'djamena Ceasefire Agreement and the Abuja Protocols, including notification of forcepositions, to facilitate humanitarian assistance, and to cooperate fully with the African Union Mission;

2. *Emphasizes* that there can be no military solution to the conflict in Dar Fur, and calls upon the Government of Sudan and the rebel groups, particularly the Justice and Equality Movement and the Sudanese Liberation Movement/Army to resume the Abuja talks rapidly without preconditions and negotiate in good faith to speedily reach agreement, and urges the parties to the Comprehensive Peace Agreement to play an active and constructive role in support of the Abuja talks and take immediate steps to support a peaceful settlement to the conflict in Dar Fur;

3. *Decides*, in light of the failure of all parties to the conflict in Dar Fur to fulfil their commitments,
(a) to establish, in accordance with rule 28 of its provisional rules of procedure, a Committee of the Security Council consisting of all the members of the Council (herein "the Committee"), to undertake to following tasks:
i. to monitor implementation of the measures referred to in subparagraphs (d) and
(e) of this paragraph and paragraphs 7 and 8 of resolution 1556 (2004), and paragraph 7 below;

ii. to designate those individuals subject to the measures imposed by subparagraphs (d) and (e) of this paragraph and to consider requests forexemptions in accordance with subparagraphs (f) and (g);

iii. to establish such guidelines as may be necessary to facilitate the implementation of the measures imposed by subparagraphs (d) and (e);

iv. to report at least every 90 days to the Security Council on its work;

v. to consider requests from and, as appropriate, provide prior approval to the Government of Sudan for the movement of military equipment and supplies into the Dar Fur region in accordance with paragraph 7 below;

vi. to assess reports from the Panel of Experts established under subparagraph (b) of this paragraph, and Member States, in particular those in the region, on specific steps they are taking to implement the measures imposed by subparagraphs (d) and (e) and paragraph 7 below;

vii. to encourage a dialogue between the Committee and interested Member States, in particular those in the region, including by inviting representatives of such States to meet with the Committee to discuss implementation of the measures;

(b) to request the Secretary-General, in consultation with the Committee, to appoint for a period of six months, within 30 days of adoption of this resolution, aPanel of Experts comprised of four members and based in Addis Ababa, Ethiopia, to travel regularly to El-Fasher, Sudan and other locations in Sudan, and to operate under the direction of the Committee to undertake the following tasks:

i. to assist the Committee in monitoring implementation of the measures in subparagraphs (d) and (e), paragraphs 7 and 8 of resolution 1556 (2004), and paragraph 7 of this resolution, and to make recommendations to the Committee on actions the Council may want to consider;

ii. to provide a mid-term briefing on its work to the Committee, and an interim report no later than 90 days after adoption of this resolution, and a final report no later than 30 days prior to termination of its mandate to the Council through the Committee with its findings and recommendations; and

iii. to coordinate its activities as appropriate with ongoing operations of the African Union Mission in Sudan (AMIS);

(c) that those individuals, as designated by the Committee established by subparagraph (a) above, based on the information provided by Member States, the Secretary-General, the High Commissioner for Human Rights or the Panel of Experts established under subparagraph (b) of this paragraph above, and other relevant sources, who impede the peace process, constitute a threat to stability in Dar Fur and the region, commit violations of international humanitarian or human rights law or other atrocities, violate the measures implemented by Member States in accordance with paragraphs 7 and 8 of resolution 1556 (2004) and paragraph 7 of this resolution as implemented by a state, or are responsible for offensive military overflights described in paragraph 6 of this resolution, shall be subject to the measures identified in subparagraphs (d) and (e) below;

(d) that all States shall take the necessary measures to prevent entry into or transit through their territories of all persons as designated by the Committee pursuant to subparagraph (c) above, provided that nothing in this paragraph shall obligate a State to refuse entry into its territory to its own nationals;

(e) that all States shall freeze all funds, financial assets and economic resources that are on their territories on the date of adoption of this resolution or at any time thereafter, that are owned or controlled, directly or indirectly, by the persons designated by the Committee pursuant to subparagraph (c) above, or that are held by entities owned or controlled, directly or indirectly, by such persons or by persons acting on their behalf or at their direction, and decides further that all States shall ensure that no funds, financial assets or economic resources are made available by their nationals or by any persons within their territories to or for the benefit of such persons or entities;

(f) that the measures imposed by subparagraph (d) above shall not apply where the Committee established by subparagraph (a) above determines on a case by case basis that such travel is justified on the ground of humanitarian need, including religious obligation, or where the Committee concludes that an exemption would otherwise further the objectives of the Council's resolutions for the creation of peace and stability in Sudan and the region;

(g) that the measures imposed by subparagraph (e) of this resolution do not apply to funds, other financial assets and economic resources that:

i. have been determined by relevant States to be necessary for basic expenses, including payment for foodstuffs, rent or mortgage, medicines and medical treatment, taxes, insurance premiums, and public utility charges or for payment of reasonable professional fees and reimbursement of incurred expenses associated with the provision of legal services, or fees or service charges, in accordance with national laws, for routine holding or maintenance of frozen funds, other financial assets and economic resources, after notification by the relevant States to the Committee of the intention to authorize, where appropriate, access to such funds, other financial assets and economic resources and in the absence of a negative decision by the Committee within two working days of such notification;

ii. have been determined by relevant States to be necessary for extraordinary expenses, provided that such determination has been notified by the relevant States to the Committee and has been approved by the Committee, or

iii. have been determined by relevant States to be the subject of a judicial, administrative or arbitral lien or judgment, in which case the funds, or other financial assets and economic resources may be used to satisfy that lien or judgment provided that the lien or judgment was entered prior to the date of the present resolution, is not for the benefit of a person or entity designated by the Committee, and has been notified by the relevant States to the Committee;

4. *Decides* that the measures referred to in subparagraphs 3 (d) and (e) shall enter into force 30 days from the date of adoption of this resolution, unless the Security Council determines before then that the parties to the conflict in Dar Fur have complied with all the commitments and demands referred to in paragraph 1 above and paragraph 6 below;

5. *Expresses* its readiness to consider the modification or termination of the measures under paragraph 3, on the recommendation of the Committee or at the end of a period of 12 months from the date of adoption of this resolution, or earlier if the Security Council determines before then that the parties to the conflict in Dar Fur have complied with all the commitments and demands referred to in paragraph 1 above and paragraph 6 below;

6. *Demands* that the Government of Sudan, in accordance with its commitments under the 8 April 2004 N'djamena Ceasefire Agreement and the 9 November 2004 Abuja Security Protocol, immediately cease conducting offensive military flights in and over the Dar Fur region, and invites the African UnionCeasefire Commission to share pertinent information as appropriate in this regardwith the Secretary-General, the Committee, or the Panel of Experts established under paragraph 3 (b);

7. *Reaffirms* the measures imposed by paragraphs 7 and 8 of resolution 1556 (2004), and decides that these measures shall immediately upon adoption of this resolution, also apply to all the parties to the N'djamena Ceasefire Agreement and any other belligerents in the states of North Dar Fur, South Dar Fur and West Dar Fur; decides that these measures shall not apply to the supplies and related technical training and assistance listed in paragraph 9 of resolution 1556 (2004); decides that these measures shall not apply with respect to assistance and supplies provided in support of implementation of the Comprehensive Peace Agreement; further decides that these measures shall not apply to movements of military equipment and supplies into the Dar Fur region that are approved in advance by theCommittee established under paragraph 3 (a) upon a request by the Government of Sudan; and invites the African Union Ceasefire Commission to share pertinentinformation as appropriate in this regard with the Secretary-General, the Committee, or the Panel of Experts established under paragraph 3 (b);

8. *Reiterates* that, in the event the parties fail to fulfil their commitments and demands as outlined in paragraphs 1 and 6, and the situation in Dar Fur continues to deteriorate, the Council will consider further measures as provided for in Article 41 of the Charter of the United Nations;

9. *Decides* to remain seized of the matter.

United Nations S/RES/1593 (2005)
Security Council Distr.: General
31 March 2005
05-29273 (E)
0529273
Resolution 1593 (2005)
Adopted by the Security Council at its 5158th meeting,
on 31 March 2005
The Security Council,
Taking note of the report of the International Commission of Inquiry on vio-
lations of international humanitarian law and human rights law in Dar Fur
(S/2005/60),

Recalling article 16 of the Rome Statute under which no investigation or prosecution may be commenced or proceeded with by the International Criminal Court
for a period of 12 months after a Security Council request to that effect,

Also recalling articles 75 and 79 of the Rome Statute and encouraging States to
contribute to the ICC Trust Fund for Victims,

Taking note of the existence of agreements referred to in Article 98-2 of the Rome
Statute,

Determining that the situation in Sudan continues to constitute a threat to international peace and security,

Acting under Chapter VII of the Charter of the United Nations,
1. *Decides* to refer the situation in Dar Fur since 1 July 2002 to the Prosecutor of
the International Criminal Court;

2. *Decides* that the Government of Sudan and all other parties to the conflict in
Dar Fur, shall cooperate fully with and provide any necessary assistance to the
Court and the Prosecutor pursuant to this resolution and, while recognizing that
States not party to the Rome Statute have no obligation under the Statute, urges
all States and concerned regional and other international organizations to cooper-
ate fully;

3. *Invites* the Court and the African Union to discuss practical arrangements that
will facilitate the work of the Prosecutor and of the Court, including the possibil-

ity of conducting proceedings in the region, which would contribute to regional efforts in the fight against impunity;

4. *Also encourages* the Court, as appropriate and in accordance with the Rome Statute, to support international cooperation with domestic efforts to promote the rule of law, protect human rights and combat impunity in Dar Fur;

5. *Also emphasizes* the need to promote healing and reconciliation and encourages in this respect the creation of institutions, involving all sectors of Sudanese society, such as truth and/or reconciliation commissions, in order to complement judicial processes and thereby reinforce the efforts to restore longlasting peace, with African Union and international support as necessary;

6. *Decides* that nationals, current or former officials or personnel from a contributing State outside Sudan which is not a party to the Rome Statute of the International Criminal Court shall be subject to the exclusive jurisdiction of that contributing State for all alleged acts or omissions arising out of or related to operations in Sudan established or authorized by the Council or the African Union, unless such exclusive jurisdiction has been expressly waived by that contributing State;

7. *Recognizes* that none of the expenses incurred in connection with the referral including expenses related to investigations or prosecutions in connection with that referral, shall be borne by the United Nations and that such costs shall be borne by the parties to the Rome Statute and those States that wish to contribute voluntarily;

8. *Invites* the Prosecutor to address the Council within three months of the date of adoption of this resolution and every six months thereafter on actions taken pursuant to this resolution;

9. *Decides* to remain seized of the matter.

United Nations S/RES/1627 (2005)
Security Council Distr.: General
23 September 2005
05-52157 (E)
0552157
Resolution 1627 (2005)
Adopted by the Security Council at its 5269th meeting, on
23 September 2005
The Security Council,
Recalling its previous resolutions, in particular resolution 1590 of 24 March 2005, and statements of its President concerning the Sudan,

Reaffirming its commitment to the sovereignty, unity, independence and territorial integrity of the Sudan,

Reiterating its expression of sympathy and condolences on the death of First Vice President Dr. John Garang de Mabior on 30 July 2005; *commending* the Government of the Sudan and First Vice President Salva Kiir Mayardit for continued efforts for consolidation of peace in the Sudan,

Welcoming implementation by the Government of the Sudan and the Sudan People's Liberation Movement/Army of the Comprehensive Peace Agreement (CPA) of 9 January 2005, and in particular welcoming the formation of the Government of National Unity as a significant and historic step towards lasting peace in the Sudan,

Urging the parties to meet their outstanding commitments to the CPA, including, as a priority, the establishment of the Assessment and Evaluation Commission,

Determining that the situation in the Sudan continues to constitute a threat to international peace and security,

Acknowledging the commitments by troop-contributing countries in support of the United Nations Mission in the Sudan (UNMIS) and *encouraging* deployment inorder for UNMIS to support timely implementation of the CPA,

1. *Decides* to extend the mandate of UNMIS until 24 March 2006, with the intention to renew it for further periods;

2. *Requests* the Secretary-General to report to the Council every three months on the implementation of the mandate of UNMIS, including its work to reinforce the efforts of the African Union Mission in the Sudan to foster peace in Dar Fur;

3. *Urges* troop-contributing countries carefully to review the Secretary General's letter of 24 March 2005 (A/59/710) and to take appropriate action to prevent sexual exploitation and abuse by their personnel in UNMIS, including predeployment awareness training, and to take disciplinary action and other action to ensure full accountability in cases of such misconduct involving their personnel;

4. *Decides* to remain actively seized of the matter.

United Nations S/RES/1651 (2005)
Security Council Distr.: General
21 December 2005
05-65872 (E)
0565872
Resolution 1651 (2005)
Adopted by the Security Council at its 5342nd meeting,
on 21 December 2005
The Security Council,
Recalling its previous resolutions concerning the situation in Sudan, in particular
resolutions 1591 (2005) of 29 March 2005 and 1556 (2004) of 30 July2004, and
statements of its President concerning Sudan,

Stressing its firm commitment to the cause of peace throughout Sudan, including
through the African Union (AU)-led inter-Sudanese peace talks in Abuja("Abuja
Talks"), full implementation of the Comprehensive Peace Agreement, and an end
to the violence and atrocities in Dar Fur,

Urging all parties at the Abuja Talks to reach without further delay an agreement
that will establish a basis for peace, reconciliation, stability and justice in Sudan,

Recalling the 7 October 2005 midterm briefing of the Panel of Experts appointed
by the Secretary-General, further to paragraph 3 (b) of resolution 1591 (2005),
and *anticipating* the receipt of its final report,

Emphasizing the need to respect the provisions of the Charter concerning privileges and immunities, and the Convention on the Privileges and Immunities
of the United Nations, as applicable to United Nations operations and persons
engaged in such operations,

Reaffirming its commitment to the sovereignty, unity, independence and territorial integrity of Sudan, and recalling the importance of the principles of good-
neighbourliness, non-interference and cooperation in the relations among States
in the region,

Determining that the situation in Sudan continues to constitute a threat to international peace and security in the region,

Acting under Chapter VII of the Charter of the United Nations,

1. *Decides* to extend the mandate of the Panel of Experts appointed pursuant to resolution 1591 (2005) until 29 March 2006, and *requests* the Secretary General to take the necessary administrative measures;

2. *Requests* the Panel of Experts to report and make recommendations to the Council, through the Committee established by paragraph 3 (a) of resolution 1591 (2005), prior to the termination of its mandate, on the implementation of the measures imposed by paragraphs 3, 6 and 7 of resolution 1591 (2005) and paragraphs 7 and 8 of resolution 1556 (2004);

3. *Decides* to remain actively seized of the matter.

United Nations S/RES/1663 (2006)
Security Council Distr.: General
24 March 2006
06-28361 (E)
0628361
Resolution 1663 (2006)
Adopted by the Security Council at its 5396th meeting,
on 24 March 2006
The Security Council,
Recalling its previous resolutions, in particular resolution 1627 (2005) and 1653 (2006), and statements of its President, in particular that of 3 February 2006 (S/PRST/2006/5), concerning the situation in the Sudan,

Reaffirming its commitment to the sovereignty, unity, independence and territorial integrity of the Sudan,

Welcoming implementation by the parties of the Comprehensive Peace Agreement of 9 January 2005, and *urging* them to meet their commitments,

Acknowledging the commitments by troop-contributing countries in support of the United Nations Mission in the Sudan (UNMIS), and *encouraging* deployment in order for UNMIS to support timely implementation of the Comprehensive Peace Agreement,
Reiterating in the strongest terms the need for all parties to the conflict in Dar Fur to put an end to the violence and atrocities,

Stressing the importance of urgently reaching a successful conclusion of the Abuja Talks and *calling on* the parties to conclude a peace agreement as soon as possible,

Welcoming the Communiqué of the 46th meeting of the African Union Peace and Security Council of 10 March 2006, and its decision to support in principle the transition of the African Union Mission in the Sudan (AMIS) to a United Nations operation within the framework of partnership between the African Union and the United Nations in the promotion of peace, security and stability in Africa, to pursue the conclusion of a peace agreement on Dar Fur by the end of April 2006, and to extend the mandate of AMIS until 30 September 2006,

Expressing its deep concern at the movement of arms and armed groups across borders such as the long running and brutal insurgency by the Lord's Resistance

Army (LRA) which has caused the death, abduction and displacement of many innocent civilians in the Sudan,

Determining that the situation in the Sudan continues to constitute a threat to international peace and security,

1. *Decides* to extend the mandate of UNMIS until 24 September 2006, with the intention to renew it for further periods;

2. *Requests* the Secretary-General to report to the Council every three months on the implementation of the mandate of UNMIS;

3. *Reiterates* its request in paragraph 2 of resolution 1590 (2005) that UNMIS closely and continuously liaise and coordinate at all levels with AMIS, and *urges* it to intensify its efforts in this regard;

4. *Requests* that the Secretary-General, jointly with the African Union, in close and continuing consultation with the Security Council, and in cooperation and close consultation with the parties to the Abuja Peace Talks, including the Government of National Unity, expedite the necessary preparatory planning for transition of AMIS to a United Nations operation, including options for how UNMIS can reinforce the effort for peace in Dar Fur through additional appropriate transitional assistance to AMIS, including assistance in logistics, mobility and communications, and that the Secretary-General present to the Council by 24 April 2006 for its consideration a range of options for a United Nations operation in Dar Fur;

5. *Encourages* the Secretary-General to continue to provide maximum possible assistance to AMIS;

6. *Requests* the Secretary-General and the African Union to consult with international and regional organizations and member States to identify resources to support AMIS during transition to a United Nations operation;

7. *Strongly condemns* the activities of militias and armed groups such as the Lord's Resistance Army (LRA), which continue to attack civilians and commit human rights abuses in the Sudan; and *urges* in this regard UNMIS to make full use of its current mandate and capabilities;

8. *Recalls* resolution 1653 (2006) and its request that the Secretary-Generalmake recommendations to the Council; and *looks forward* to receiving by 24 April 2006 these recommendations which would include proposals on how United Nations

agencies and missions, in particular UNMIS, could more effectively address the problem of the LRA;

9. *Encourages* the Sudanese parties to finalize the establishment of national institutions for disarmament, demobilization and reintegration of ex-combatants (DDR), as stipulated in the Comprehensive Peace Agreement, and to expedite the development of a comprehensive DDR programme, with the assistance of UNMIS as provided in resolution 1590 (2005);

10. *Decides* to remain actively seized of the matter.

United Nations S/RES/1665 (2006)
Security Council Distr.: General
29 March 2006
06-29022 (E)
0629022
Resolution 1665 (2006)
Adopted by the Security Council at its 5402nd meeting,
on 29 March 2006
The Security Council,
Recalling its previous resolutions concerning the situation in Sudan, in particular resolutions 1651 (2005) of 21 December 2005, 1591 (2005) of 29 March 2005, and 1556 (2004) of 30 July 2004 and statements of its President concerning Sudan,

Stressing again its firm commitment to the cause of peace throughout Sudan, including through the African Union-led inter-Sudanese peace talks in Abuja, Nigeria ("Abuja Talks"), full implementation of the Comprehensive Peace Agreement of 9 January 2005, and an end to the violence and atrocities in Dar Fur,

Urging all parties at the Abuja Talks to reach without further delay an agreement that will establish a basis for peace, reconciliation, stability and justice in Sudan,

Commending the efforts of, and reiterating its full support for, the African Union, the Secretary-General, and the leaders of the region to promote peace and stability in Dar Fur,

Taking note of the observations and recommendations contained in the 9 December 2005 report (S/2006/65) of the Panel of Experts appointed by the Secretary-General pursuant to paragraph 3 (b) of resolution 1591 (2005) and extended by paragraph 1 of resolution 1651 (2005), anticipating the receipt of the Panel's second report currently under consideration by the Committee established pursuant to paragraph 3 (a) of resolution 1591 (2005), and expressing its intent to study the Panel's recommendations further and to consider appropriate next steps,

Emphasizing the need to respect the provisions of the Charter concerning privileges and immunities, and the Convention on the Privileges and Immunities of the United Nations, as applicable to United Nations operations and persons engaged in such operations,
Reaffirming its commitment to the sovereignty, unity, independence and territorial integrity of Sudan, and recalling the importance of the principles of good

neighbourliness, non-interference and cooperation in the relations among States in the region,

Determining that the situation in Sudan continues to constitute a threat to international peace and security in the region,

Acting under Chapter VII of the Charter of the United Nations,
1. *Decides* to extend until 29 September 2006 the mandate of the Panel of Experts originally appointed pursuant to resolution 1591 (2005) and extended by resolution 1651 (2005), and *requests* the Secretary-General to take the necessary administrative measures;

2. *Requests* the Panel of Experts to provide no later than 90 days after adoption of this resolution a midterm briefing on its work to the Committee established pursuant to paragraph 3 (a) of resolution 1591 (2005), and a final report no later than 30 days prior to termination of its mandate to the Council with its findings and recommendations;

3. *Urges* all States, relevant United Nations bodies, the African Union and other interested parties, to cooperate fully with the Committee and the Panel of Experts, in particular by supplying any information at their disposal on implementation of the measures imposed by resolution 1591 (2005) and resolution 1556 (2004);

4. *Decides* to remain actively seized of the matter.

United Nations S/RES/1672 (2006)
Security Council Distr.: General
25 April 2006
06-32677 (E)
0632677
Resolution 1672 (2006)
Adopted by the Security Council at its 5423rd meeting, on
25 April 2006
The Security Council,
Recalling its previous resolutions concerning the situation in Sudan, in particular
resolutions 1665 (2006) of 29 March 2006, 1651 (2005) of 21 December 2005,
1591 (2005) of 29 March 2005 and 1556 (2004) of 30 July 2004 and statements
of its President concerning Sudan,

Stressing again its firm commitment to the cause of peace throughout Sudan, includ-
ing through the African Union-led inter-Sudanese peace talks in Abuja, Nigeria
("Abuja Talks"), full implementation of the Comprehensive Peace Agreement of 9
January 2005 and an end to the violence and atrocities in Dar Fur,

Determining that the situation in Sudan continues to constitute a threat to international peace and security in the region,

Acting under Chapter VII of the Charter of the United Nations,
1. *Decides* that all States shall implement the measures specified in paragraph 3 of
resolution 1591 (2005) with respect to the following individuals:
– Major General Gaffar Mohamed Elhassan (Commander of the Western Military
Region for the Sudanese Armed Forces)
– Sheikh Musa Hilal (Paramount Chief of the Jalul Tribe in North Dar Fur)
– Adam Yacub Shant (Sudanese Liberation Army Commander)
– Gabril Abdul Kareem Badri (National Movement for Reform and Development
Field Commander)
2. *Decides* to remain actively seized of the matter.

United Nations S/RES/1679 (2006)
Security Council Distr.: General
16 May 2006
06-35024 (E)
0635024
Resolution 1679 (2006)
Adopted by the Security Council at its 5439th meeting, on 16 May 2006
The Security Council,
Recalling its previous resolutions concerning the situation in the Sudan, in particular resolutions 1665 (2006), 1663 (2006), 1593 (2005), 1591 (2005),
1590 (2005), 1574 (2004), 1564 (2004), 1556 (2004) and the statements of
its President concerning the Sudan, in particular S/PRST/2006/5 of 3 February
2006 and S/PRST/2006/21 of 9 May 2006,

Recalling also its resolutions 1612 (2005) on children and armed conflict, 1325
(2000) on women, peace and security, and 1674 (2006) on the protection of civilians in armed conflict, and 1502 (2003) on the protection of humanitarian and
United Nations personnel,

Reaffirming its strong commitment to the sovereignty, unity, independence, and
territorial integrity of the Sudan, which would be unaffected by transition to a
United Nations operation, as well as of all States in the region, and to the cause of
peace, security and reconciliation throughout the Sudan,

Expressing its utmost concern over the dire consequences of the prolonged conflict
in Dar Fur for the civilian population and *reiterating* in the strongest terms the
need for all parties to the conflict in Dar Fur to put an immediate end to violence
and atrocities,

Welcoming the success of the African Union-led Inter-Sudanese Peace Talks on the
Conflict in Dar Fur in Abuja, Nigeria, in particular the framework agreed between the
parties for a resolution of the conflict in Dar Fur (the Dar Fur Peace Agreement),

Commending the efforts of President Olusegun Obasanjo of Nigeria, host of the
Inter-Sudanese Peace Talks in Abuja; President Denis Sassou-Nguesso of the
Republic of Congo, Chair of the African Union (AU); Dr. Salim Ahmed Salim,
the African Union Special Envoy for the Dar Fur Talks and Chief Mediator, the
respective delegations to the Dar Fur Talks; and the signatories to the Dar Fur
Peace Agreement,

Stressing the importance of full and rapid implementation of the Dar Fur Peace Agreement to restore a sustainable peace in Dar Fur, and *welcoming* the statement of 9 May 2006 by the representative of the Sudan at the United Nations Security Council Special Session on Dar Fur of the Government of National Unity's full commitment to implementing the Dar Fur Peace Agreement,

Reaffirming its concern that the persisting violence in Dar Fur might further negatively affect the rest of the Sudan, as well as the region, including the security of Chad, *Noting* with deep concern the recent deterioration of relations between the Sudan and Chad, and *urging* the Governments of both countries to abide by their obligations under the 8 February 2006 Tripoli Agreement and to implement the confidence-building measures which have been voluntarily agreed upon,

Commending the efforts of the African Union for successful deployment of the African Union Mission in the Sudan (AMIS), despite exceptionally difficult circumstances, and AMIS's role in reducing large-scale organized violence in Dar Fur, and *commending* further the efforts of Member States and regional and international organizations that have assisted AMIS in its deployment,

Taking note of the communiqués of 12 January, 10 March and 15 May 2006 of the Peace and Security Council of the African Union regarding transition of AMIS to a United Nations operation,

Stressing that a United Nations operation would have, to the extent possible, a strong African participation and character,

Welcoming the efforts of Member States and regional and international organizations to maintain and strengthen their support to AMIS and potentially to a follow-on United Nations operation on Dar Fur, *looking forward to, in particular*, the convening of a pledging conference in June, and *appealing to* African Union partners to provide the necessary support to AMIS to allow it to continue to perform its mandate during the transition,

Determining that the situation in the Sudan continues to constitute a threat to international peace and security,

Acting under Chapter VII of the Charter of the United Nations,
1. *Calls upon* the parties to the Dar Fur Peace Agreement to respect their commitments and implement the agreement without delay, *urges* those parties that have not signed the agreement to do so without delay and not to act in any way that

would impede implementation of the agreement, and *expresses its intention* to consider taking, including in response to a request by the African Union, strong and effective measures, such as a travel ban and assets freeze, against any individual orgroup that violates or attempts to block the implementation of the Dar Fur Peace Agreement;

2. *Calls upon* the African Union to agree with the United Nations, regional and international organizations, and Member States on requirements now necessary, in addition to those identified by the joint assessment mission of December 2005, to strengthen AMIS's capacity to enforce the security arrangements of the Dar Fur Peace Agreement, with a view to a follow-on United Nations operation in Dar Fur;

3. *Endorses* the decision of the African Union Peace and Security Council in its communiqué of 15 May 2006 that, in view of the signing of the Dar Fur Peace Agreement, concrete steps should be taken to effect the transition from AMIS to a United Nations operation, *calls upon* the parties to the Dar Fur Peace Agreement to facilitate and work with the African Union, the United Nations, regional and international organizations and Member States to accelerate transition to a United Nations operation, and, to this end, reiterating the requests of the Secretary-General and the Security Council, *calls for* the deployment of a joint African Union and United Nations technical assessment mission within one week of the adoption of this resolution;

4. *Stresses* that the Secretary-General should consult jointly with theAfrican Union, in close and continuing consultation with the Security Council, and in cooperation and close consultation with the parties to the Dar Fur Peace Agreement, including the Government of National Unity, on decisions concerning the transition to a United Nations operation;

5. *Requests* the Secretary-General to submit recommendations to the Council within one week of the return of the joint African Union and United Nations assessment mission on all relevant aspects of the mandate of the United Nations operation in Dar Fur, including force structure, additional force requirements, potential troop-contributing countries and a detailed financial evaluation of future costs;

6. *Decides* to remain actively seized of the matter.

United Nations S/RES/1713 (2006)
Security Council
Distr.: General
29 September 2006
06-54513 (E)
0654513
Resolution 1713 (2006)
Adopted by the Security Council at its 5543rd meeting, on
29 September 2006
The Security Council,
Recalling its previous resolutions concerning the situation in Sudan, in particular resolutions 1665 (2006) of 29 March 2006, 1651 (2005) of 21 December 2005, 1591 (2005) of 29 March 2005, and 1556 (2004) of 30 July 2004 and statements of its President concerning Sudan,

Stressing again its firm commitment to the cause of peace throughout Sudan, full implementation of the Comprehensive Peace Agreement of 9 January 2005, full implementation of the framework agreed between the parties for a resolution of the conflict in Dar Fur (the Dar Fur Peace Agreement), and an end to the violence and atrocities in Dar Fur,

Urging those parties that have not signed the Dar Fur Peace Agreement to do so without delay and not act in any way that would impede the implementation of the Agreement, and *further urging* that those that have signed that Agreement implement their obligations without delay,

Deploring the ongoing violence, impunity, and consequent deterioration of the humanitarian situation, and *reiterating* its deep concern about the security of civilians and humanitarian aid workers and about humanitarian access to populations in need, and *calling* upon all parties in Dar Fur to cease offensive actions immediately and to refrain from further violent attacks,

Commending the efforts of, and reiterating its full support for, the African Union, the Secretary-General, and the leaders of the region to promote peace and stability in Dar Fur,

Recalling the 25 July 2006 midterm briefing by the Panel of Experts appointed by the Secretary-General pursuant to paragraph 3 (b) of resolution 1591 (2005) and extended by resolutions 1651 (2005) and 1665 (2006), *anticipating* the receipt of the Panel's final report presented on August 31, 2006 to the Committee established pursuant to resolution 1591 (2005) and currently under consideration, and *expressing* its intent to study the Panel's recommendations further and to consider appropriate next steps,

Emphasizing the need to respect the provisions of the Charter concerning privileges and immunities, and the Convention on the Privileges and Immunities of the United Nations, as applicable to United Nations operations and persons engaged in such operations,

Reaffirming its commitment to the sovereignty, unity, independence and territorial integrity of Sudan, and recalling the importance of the principles of good neighbourliness, non-interference and cooperation in the relations among States in the region,

Determining that the situation in Sudan continues to constitute a threat to international peace and security in the region,

Acting under Chapter VII of the Charter of the United Nations,

1. *Decides* to extend until 29 September 2007 the mandate of the Panel of Experts originally appointed pursuant to resolution 1591 (2005) and previously extended by resolutions 1651 (2005) and 1665 (2006), and requests the Secretary General to appoint a fifth member to enable the Panel to better carry out its mission, and to take the necessary administrative measures;

2. *Requests* the Panel of Experts to provide no later than 29 March 2007 a midterm briefing on its work and no later than 90 days after adoption of this resolution an interim report to the Committee established pursuant to paragraph 3 (a) of resolution 1591 (2005), and a final report no later than 30 days prior to termination of its mandate to the Council with its findings and recommendations;

3. *Urges* all States, relevant United Nations bodies, the African Union and other interested parties, to cooperate fully with the Committee and the Panel ofExperts, in particular by supplying any information at their disposal onimplementation of the measures imposed by resolution 1591 (2005) and resolution 1556 (2004);

4. *Decides* to remain actively seized of the matter.

978-0-595-42979-0
0-595-42979-3